REGULATORY REALITIES

REGULATORY REALITIES

THE IMPLEMENTATION AND IMPACT OF INDUSTRIAL ENVIRONMENTAL REGULATION

Andrew Gouldson
and
Joseph Murphy

Earthscan Publications Ltd, London

First published in the UK in 1998 by
Earthscan Publications Limited

A catalogue record for this book is available from the British Library

ISBN: 1 85383 458 0 paperback
        1 85383 457 2 hardback

Typesetting and page design by PCS Mapping & DTP, Newcastle upon Tyne
Printed and bound by Biddles Ltd, Guildford and Kings Lynn
Cover design by Andrew Corbett

For a full list of publications please contact:

Earthscan Publications Limited
120 Pentonville Road
London N1 9JN
Tel: (0171) 278 0433
Fax: (0171) 278 1142
Email: earthinfo@earthscan.co.uk
http://www.earthscan.co.uk

Earthscan is an editorially independent subsidiary of Kogan Page Limited and publishes in
association with WWF-UK and the International Institute for Environment and Development.

CONTENTS

Boxes, Tables and Figures

ACRONYMS AND ABBREVIATIONS

ALARA   as low as is reasonably achievable
BAT   best available techniques
BATNEEC   best available techniques not entailing excessive cost
BPEO   best practicable environmental option
CBI   Confederation of British Industry
CCvD   Central Committee of Experts (Netherlands)
CEN   European Committee for Standardization
CEP   Company Environmental Plan
DETR   Department of Environment, Transport and the Regions
DoE   Department of the Environment
EA   Environment Agency
ELV   Emission Limit Value
EMA   Environmental Management Act
EMAS   Eco-Management and Audit Scheme
EMS   Environmental Management System
EQS   Environmental Quality Standard
EU   European Union
HMIP   Her Majesty's Inspectorate of Pollution
IETP   Integrated Environmental Target Plan
IPC   Integrated Pollution Control
IPPC   Integrated Pollution Prevention and Control
ISO   International Standards Organization
LSE   London School of Economics
NACCB   National Accreditation Council for Certification Bodies
NEPP   National Environmental Policy Plan
NRA   National Rivers Authority
OPRA   Operator Pollution Risk Appraisal
PSWA   Pollution of Surface Waters Act
QMS   quality management systems
RIVM   National Institute of Public Health and Environmental
           Protection (Netherlands)
RvA   Dutch Council for Accreditation
SCCM   Foundation for Environmental Certification (Netherlands)
SCEEMAS   Small Companies Energy and Environmental Management
           Assistance Scheme
UKAS   UK Accreditation Service
VNCI   Association of the Dutch Chemical Industry
VROM   Ministry of Housing, Spatial Planning and the Environment
           (Netherlands)

PREFACE

This book analyses the nature of industrial environmental regulation. It does not assess the generic merits of the various environmental policy instruments as this has been done extensively elsewhere. Instead it focuses on the implementation and impact of existing approaches to industrial environmental regulation. It suggests that the nature of industrial environmental regulation can be examined through an analysis of the frameworks, structures and styles that are associated with its implementation. Similarly, it argues that the impact of industrial environmental regulation can be assessed by considering the influence that regulation has on the technological, organizational and strategic behaviour of regulated companies.

Based on a conceptual and an empirical analysis of the implementation and impact of industrial environmental regulation, this book combines descriptive policy analysis with prescriptive policy advocacy. Thus, as well as analysing the nature of what is, it seeks to influence the character of what might be. In this respect it seeks to establish whether the performance of industrial environmental regulation, judged in terms of its environmental efficacy and economic efficiency, can be enhanced.

Initially, the examination is pursued conceptually with an assessment of the relationship between macro-economic development and environmental protection and of the role that policy might play in changing this relationship (Chapter 1). This conceptual analysis continues with an assessment of the nature of the innovation process and of the impact that different forms of innovation might have on the relationship between micro-economic development and environmental protection (Chapter 2). From this analysis, it is contended that the performance of policy could be enhanced if particular approaches to implementation are adopted that stimulate the wider development and application of particular forms of innovation. This contention is then examined empirically through an assessment of the design and delivery of two interacting forms of industrial environmental regulation. Firstly, the nature of mandatory environmental regulation is examined with reference to the European Union's Integrated Pollution Prevention and Control Directive (Chapter 3). Secondly, the nature of voluntary environmental regulation is assessed with reference to the European Union's Eco-Management and Audit Scheme (Chapter 4). In each case, the influence that different regulatory structures and styles have on the nature of policy as practice is considered. The implementation and impact of these different forms of regulation are then assessed in two countries with contrasting approaches to environmental regulation, namely the UK (Chapter 5) and the Netherlands (Chapter 6). The discussion of the implementation and impact of, and interaction between, mandatory and voluntary forms of environmental regulation draws particularly on extensive interviews with government, regulatory agencies and industry conducted in 1995 and 1996 in each of the countries studied. From this empirical analysis, a number of proposals are put forward which, it is suggested, would improve both the economic and the environmental performance of environmental regulation if adopted (Chapter 7).

Andy Gouldson and Joseph Murphy
February 1998

Acknowledgements

This book is based on the results of a two-year research project, funded by the UK's Economic and Social Research Council through the Science Policy Support Group's European Context of UK Science Policy programme. Inevitably we owe a debt of gratitude to all those who contributed to that programme. The arguments presented in this book have been drawn from the results of numerous interviews. However, all of those interviewed during the course of this project were promised anonymity. As a result, while we would like to thank all of the people who gave up their time to inform our research, we cannot identify them individually. However, a number of organizations can be acknowledged in a broad sense. In the UK we were helped enormously by representatives of organizations that have now been incorporated into the Department of Environment, Transport and Regions and the Environment Agency as well as by the British Standards Institute and other organizations associated with EMAS and ISO14001 and by the environmental managers of numerous companies. In The Netherlands we were assisted greatly by representatives of The Ministry of Housing, Spatial Planning and the Environment, various provincial regulators, the Foundation for Environmental Certification (SCCM), the Association of the Dutch Chemical Industry (VNCI), other organizations associated with EMAS and ISO14001 and by the environmental managers from a range of companies. Finally, the European perspective was informed particularly by representatives of DGXI (Environment) of the European Commission. Our discussions with all of the individuals interviewed within these organizations were frank and open. Without their input this work would not have been possible.

Beyond those who participated in the interviews upon which this research is based, we would also like to thank a number of other people. We are particularly grateful to Judith Rees and to Sonja Boehmer-Christiansen who, despite busy schedules, have regularly spared time for informative discussions. They have also endured the various drafts of this book and have generally offered encouragement and support. We would particularly like to thank John Lovering for his contribution to the early stages of this project. We would also like to thank (in no particular order) David Fleming, Richard Starkey, Peter Roberts, Richard Welford, Ben Vivian, Alan Irwin, Steve Yearley, Henry Rothstein, Elaine Macarthy, Helen Lawton-Smith, Michael Barzelay, Michael Jacobs, Marius Aalders, Adrian Smith and Stephen Fineman for helping us to bring the ideas presented in this book into focus. The staff and students associated with the MSc in Environmental Assessment and Evaluation at the London School of Economics (LSE) and the MSc in Environmental Policy and Management at the University of Hull also contributed, perhaps unwittingly, to the arguments that are presented. The administrative staff in the Geography

Departments of the London School of Economics and the University of Hull also made an important contribution, particularly by transcribing interviews and by helping to prepare the final text. Our thanks must also go to the staff at Earthscan for their patience, understanding and flexibility.

The discussion presented in this book does not necessarily reflect the views of any of the individuals or organizations that have been associated with the research upon which it is based. Naturally, responsibility for any errors that are included in the text is our own.

Chapter 1

ENVIRONMENT, ECONOMY AND POLICY REFORM

INTRODUCTION

Historically, a mutually antagonistic relationship has prevailed between economic development and environmental protection. Those who have been primarily interested in the performance of the economy have generally perceived environmental protection to be a brake on growth. Conversely, those who have been principally concerned with the quality of the environment have tended to see economic development as the cause of environmental decline. This mutual antagonism has led to a conflict between industrialists and environmentalists that has defined the climate of environmental politics to such a degree that it has severely constrained both the level and the nature of environmental policy-making.

While this conflict is clearly sustained in many instances, theories of ecological modernization propose that policies for economic development and environmental protection can be combined to synergistic effect. Rather than perceiving environmental protection to be a brake on growth, ecological modernization promotes the application of stringent environmental policy as a positive influence on economic efficiency and technological innovation. Similarly, rather than perceiving economic development to be the cause of environmental decline, ecological modernization seeks to harness the forces of entrepreneurship for environmental gain. Thus, ecological modernization seeks to provide an alternative to the mutually antagonistic relationship between economic development and environmental protection that continues to predominate in developed economies.

Whether or under what conditions it is indeed possible to generate a synergistic or mutually reinforcing relationship between economic development and environmental protection is as yet unclear, as the policies that a programme of ecological modernization would demand have yet to be adopted. However, those differences in the relationship between economic development and environmental performance that are displayed at both the macro- and micro-economic levels indicate that this relationship is not fixed. Thus, while it is not yet clear whether a synergistic relationship can be established between economic development and environmental protection, it is apparent that there are opportunities to make the relationship at least less negative than it commonly is at present. The framework of economic incentives and disincentives could also be adjusted through a programme of fiscal reform to extend the areas within which synergies might be found.

This book focuses on one relatively small component of the broader ecological modernization debate. Rather than exploring the scope for a widespread programme of environmental policy reform, it examines whether the economic and the environmental performance of existing modes of environmental policy can be enhanced. The discussion does not assess the generic nature of the various environmental policy instruments as this has been done extensively elsewhere. Rather, it examines the impact of different approaches to policy implementation, and of different forms of policy response, on the relationship between economic development and environmental protection. Throughout the book, the focus of the analysis is on the implementation and impact of industrial environmental regulation in developed economies.

This chapter provides a foundation for the subsequent discussion by analysing the nature of the relationship between economic development and environmental protection. It suggests that this relationship is not fixed and can be improved through certain forms of government intervention. However, to date policy has been restricted in its ability to influence this relationship by a range of factors which preclude policy reform. Consequently, it considers the significance of capacities for environmental policy reform. It argues that as these capacities are commonly under-developed, medium to long term programmes of capacity building are required if policy reform is to be secured. However, it acknowledges that in the absence of the appropriate capacities the prospects for short term change are not entirely absent as new approaches to the implementation of existing policies can also improve the relationship between economic development and environmental protection.

Before moving on to assess the nature of policy and the scope for policy reform, the specific analysis of the influence that policy might have on the relationship between economic development and environmental protection is placed in a broader context by examining the nature of ecological modernization.

THE NATURE OF ECOLOGICAL MODERNIZATION

Broadly, ecological modernization suggests that economic and environmental goals can be integrated within a framework of industrial modernity (see for example Simonis, 1989; Jänicke, 1992; Mol and Spaargaren, 1993; Mol, 1995; Hajer, 1996; Christoff, 1996; Gouldson and Murphy, 1996, 1997). While it cannot yet be suggested that ecological modernization is a coherent doctrine, two elements are at its core.

Firstly, ecological modernization seeks to establish a policy framework that promotes structural change at the macro-economic level. In a search for structures which combine higher levels of economic development with lower levels of environmental impact, ecological modernization seeks to shift the emphasis of the macro-economy away from energy and resource-intensive industries towards value and knowledge-intensive industries. Thus, through a combination of sectoral and technological change, it proposes that the structure of the macro-economy should be reoriented to establish a more environmentally benign development path which consumes less resources and generates less waste while also creating employment and economic welfare.

Secondly, ecological modernization assigns a central role to the invention, innovation and diffusion of new technologies and techniques at the micro-economic level. It seeks to facilitate a move away from existing approaches which tend to favour the application of control technologies towards new approaches based on the development and application of clean technologies and techniques. Control technologies, such as an effluent treatment plant, are end-of-pipe additions to products or processes which capture and/or treat a waste emission in order to limit its ultimate impact on the environment. By contrast, clean technologies, such as an energy efficient light bulb, or clean techniques, such as an environmental management system, integrate environmental considerations into the design and/or application of a product or process in order to anticipate and avoid or reduce its impact on the environment.

By harnessing the forces of entrepreneurship for environmental gain, ecological modernization seeks to encourage structural change in the macro-economy and technological and organizational change in the micro-economy. Despite the inherent faith that ecological modernization places in the role of entrepreneurship and the market mechanism, it also recognizes that market failures are a central determinant of environmental decline. Thus, it is accepted that without intervention the market will allow the over-exploitation of common property resources and lead to the under-provision of public goods. Consequently, ecological modernization emphasises the role that government intervention must play in regulating the operations of the market. However, it also suggests that those forms of government intervention that have been put forward as a response to environmental decline in the past have been both ineffective and inefficient. Continued environmental decline is thus seen to be a consequence of both market and government failures. In response, new forms of policy intervention are proposed to better integrate economic development and environmental protection.

THE MERITS OF ECOLOGICAL MODERNIZATION

Hajer (1996a) contends that ecological modernization can be interpreted in at least two ways: optimistically it represents 'institutional learning'; pessimistically it is a 'technocratic project'. The central belief of the interpretation of ecological modernization as institutional learning is that rational institutions can adapt and that this adaptation can produce meaningful change compatible with the goals of ecological modernization. Alternatively, its interpretation as a 'technocratic project' sees it as modern society continuing to do what has always been done and protecting established institutions and centres of power against the green threat by absorbing it. To bring this about, the natural and social sciences are conscripted to work towards preconceived policy goals (eg to define critical loads for pollution). Under this interpretation a considerable victory is simply won in splitting the radical green lobby from the moderate greens by adopting the latter.

Of course it is probable that some combination of these two interpretations would be encountered should a programme of ecological modernization be followed. However, as Spaargaren and Mol (1991) point out, it is the industrial and not the capitalist nature of modernity that is the concern of ecological modernization. In this respect ecological modernization can be viewed as very selective in just where it apportions blame for environmental degradation. Also, given its implicit acceptance of capitalism, it is essentially silent on issues of social justice, the distribution of wealth and society-nature relations. The absence of an explicit consideration of these issues suggests that as a holistic framework for social change the concept of ecological modernization is flawed and it may thus be seen as a further attempt to legitimize and sustain the structures and systems that form the foundations of environmental decline.

However, while it may be argued that policy-makers in the developed world do not have time to engage themselves further in the modernist experiment, it is suggested here that ecological modernization can offer useful guidance on policy reform in the short to medium term. Despite its limitations, ecological modernization succeeds in setting out an agenda for policy reform which, within a framework of capitalistic industrial modernity, would promote a more rational, proactive and integrated approach to environmental protection than that which is currently in place throughout the developed world.

INTEGRATING ENVIRONMENT AND THE MACRO-ECONOMY

In an empirical study on the relationship between economic development and environmental impact in 31 countries, Jänicke et al (1989) found that over several decades many countries had experienced a change in both the technological and sectoral composition of their economies. This structural change had been accompanied by improvements in their macro-economic environmental performance so that the environmental intensity of production in certain key sectors had fallen, whether measured in terms of resources consumed or emissions generated. However, despite the presence of a general trend, Jänicke et al also found that the nature and extent of the decoupling of economic development from environmental impact differed from country to country. Some countries, such as Denmark, France, Germany and the UK, had experienced an absolute decoupling. In these cases economic output had increased and environmental impact had decreased in absolute terms in certain key sectors. Others, such as Austria, Finland, Norway and Japan, had experienced a relative decoupling of economic output and environmental impact. In these instances, although each unit of output had been associated with a lower environmental impact, these relative improvements had been more than off-set by additional impacts arising from an expansion of output in the key sectors studied. Finally, a minority of countries, mostly the former command and control economies of Central and Eastern Europe, had experienced an increase in the environmental impact of each unit of economic output.

Jänicke et al noted that for those countries that had realized an absolute or relative improvement in the relationship between economic development and environmental impact, there had been a general shift away from structures emphasising the volume of production towards those emphasising the value of production. This shift away from volume to value produced a decline in the absolute or relative importance of energy and resource-intensive industries in favour of an increase in the relative or absolute importance of the service and knowledge-intensive industries. This structural change led to what Jänicke et al termed 'an environmental gratis effect' reflecting the fact that the benefits of an absolute or relative decoupling of economic development from environmental impact had been achieved unintentionally or as if the gratis effect was exogenous to the influence of policy.

Jänicke et al's findings indicate that many countries have, to varying degrees, realized improvements in the environmental performance of their macro-economies. Three critical issues follow from this observation. Firstly, it is at least possible that the improvements in the relationship between the macro-economy and the environment observed in some countries have only been realized at the expense of deteriorations in this relationship in other countries. Thus, it is not clear whether the gratis effect can only offer benefits to a select number of post-industrial economies or whether all countries can simultaneously secure an improved relationship between macro-economic development and the environment. It may be that some industrial sectors have merely relocated over time, that development has been spatially uneven or that patterns of trade have changed. In such instances it is possible to gain the impression that some countries have improved their environmental performance when in fact, intentionally or unintentionally, they have merely externalized their impacts by importing rather than manufacturing certain goods. Secondly, it is important to ask whether the benefits offered by the gratis effect have been sufficient. It may be that any relative improvements in macro-economic environmental performance, reflected in terms of falling environmental impact per unit of output, have been more than off-set by increases in the overall level of output. Furthermore, it may be that any absolute improvements in macro-economic environmental performance have still fallen short of the improvements that are required if irreparable damage to the environment is to be avoided. Thirdly, if the gratis effect is desirable, it is as yet unclear whether government intervention can actually promote it. This lack of practical experience stems from the fact that to date the environmental benefits of macro-economic structural change have in general been secured by accident. Thus, if the gratis effect can be endogenous rather than exogenous to the influence of policy, it is not yet clear how government intervention can best be applied in order to secure its benefits.

Despite these criticisms, Jänicke et al's findings indicate that at least some improvements in the relationship between macro-economic development and environmental protection have been achieved. Furthermore, although the improvements to date have generally been secured unintentionally, forecasts suggest that policies are available with which to improve the relationship between economic development and environmental protection further. For example, a study by DRI (1994) examined the potential benefits of integrating environmental and economic policies by modelling European Union (EU) economic performance under various environmental policy scenarios. The first scenario examined the economic and environmental implications of a continuation of recent economic trends and existing environmental policies. Under this scenario there was a significant deterioration in environmental quality to 2010. The second scenario examined the relationship that would be realized if policies currently under consideration at the EU level, including a carbon/energy tax, were applied, and demonstrated that notable environmental benefits were realized in some areas but these benefits were secured only with a significant negative impact on economic development. The third scenario assessed the implications of integrating environmental objectives into economic and sectoral policies. These measures included the widespread application of fiscal instruments addressing energy and resource use and the establishment of support mechanisms for the research, development and rapid diffusion of clean technologies. Under this scenario, significant environmental benefits were achieved without restricting economic development.

THE EVOLUTION OF ENVIRONMENTAL POLICY

It is therefore apparent that the relationship between macro-economic development and environmental protection could be improved at least to some extent. However, despite this potential, the progress that has been made to date has either been largely unintentional or has been restricted to a relatively small number of countries or issues. Before moving on to consider the factors which influence the development of environmental policy, the evolution of policy should be examined.

Environmental policy has evolved in a process based not on strategic thinking but on short term reaction to crisis or failure (see Jänicke and Weidner, 1995). A popular typology sees environmental policy evolving through a number of stages to incorporate additional measures as the limits of existing responses are realized (Weale, 1992; Andersen, 1994; Verbruggen, 1995). In the primary stage, policy seeks to address the impacts of pollution by moving either the source or the receptor so that the cause and effect are separated. In the secondary stage, policy seeks to promote the dilution and dispersal of emissions so that the effects of pollution become less apparent or are made external to the region surrounding the source. In the tertiary stage, which characterizes many contemporary responses to industrial environmental regulation in developed economies, policy seeks to encourage the application of measures that allow emissions to be contained and possibly treated at source.

Over time, this phased evolution has allowed policy to gradually shift its emphasis from the effect to the cause of pollution. However, while these changing approaches have had an impact on the rate of environmental decline relative to that which would have been realized without any intervention, policy continues to be largely reactive rather than proactive in nature. As Jänicke (1997, p 2) notes:

> success [in environmental policy] is more or less restricted to problems that can be handled (mainly by 'additive' technical standard solutions) without restricting markets or relevant societal routines. As regards the big environmental problems … government failure and capacity overload can be frequently observed.

In essence then, environmental policy continues to respond to the negative impacts of the economic development that virtually every other area of policy seeks to promote. As such, although the evolution of environmental policy has perhaps reduced the degree of its reactivity, at the macro-economic level it continues to be largely reactive in nature as it is generally a secondary consideration when compared with economic development. However, the continued reliance of environmental policy on reactive measures is seen by many to be fundamentally flawed as a consequence of the increasingly complex nature of modern industrial society, of the pervasive social and ecological risks that are commonly associated with technological progress and of the actual or perceived inability of science to recognize and control these risks (see for example Beck, 1992). Thus, it is increasingly accepted that more proactive forms of environmental policy are needed if further reductions in the level of environmental quality are to be avoided.

Ultimately, proactive environmental protection can only be achieved with a realignment of broader policy goals so that environmental objectives are integrated into non-environmental policy areas related to issues such as industry, energy, transport and trade. This integration would help to ensure that the impacts of policies concerned with economic development reinforce rather than undermine the efforts of policies associated with environmental protection. As is apparent from the continued reliance on reactive approaches to environmental protection, such reforms have yet to take place on any significant scale. Given the widespread acknowledgment of the need for more proactive approaches to environmental protection, and the increasingly common contention that more efficient and effective approaches to environmental regulation are available, it is appropriate to examine the barriers which preclude change.

THE BARRIERS TO ENVIRONMENTAL POLICY REFORM

The theory of state failure argues that blame for the lack of progress toward proactive approaches to environmental policy should be attributed to those alliances between government and industry that direct the formulation of policy (Jänicke, 1990). State failure suggests that both government and industry tend to favour reactive approaches to environmental protection as they fail to challenge the nature of those structures, strategies and systems that make up the status quo. Reactive approaches are therefore more readily accommodated within a governmental and industrial framework that has evolved while assigning a higher priority to economic development than to environmental protection.

However, it is not only systemic inertia which precludes a change in the emphasis of environmental policy. An exclusive focus on the long term, societal advantages of proactive approaches to environmental protection ignores the fact that the costs and benefits associated with such a change will be unevenly distributed between actors and over time. A shift from reactive to proactive approaches to environmental protection would impose definite transition costs on a concentrated group of actors in the short to medium term. These actors are likely to be established, organized and exerting influence within current structures. However, the adoption of proactive approaches which may be untried and untested can only promise uncertain benefits which would be dispersed throughout a wider range of actors in the medium to long term who are less likely to be established, organized and exerting influence within current decision making structures. Proactive approaches which may be both more efficient and more effective for society as a whole in the longer term are there-fore at a political and an economic disadvantage in the short to medium term when compared with those reactive approaches that are already established.

As a consequence of these factors, existing interests within both govern-ment and industry may attempt to resist calls for changes in the nature of environmental policy. The extent to which they are able to do so depends upon their ability to influence the policy process. If it is accepted, as it is by the theory of state failure, that alliances between government and industry exert a defin-ing influence on the agenda for policy making, then the policy process can be constrained in a number of ways. At a basic level, government and industry may attempt to alter the climate of opinion that surrounds the policy process to ensure that particular issues do not come to be perceived as problems that need to be addressed by policy-makers (Lukes, 1974). Where the need for action is recognized, they may attempt to ensure that decisions which have uncom-fortable consequences do not find their way on to or up the policy making agenda (Bachrach and Baratz, 1970). Finally, and perhaps most tangibly, they may seek to change the nature of the decisions that are taken so that they reflect or at least fail to challenge their own interests. In these ways influential govern-mental and industrial interest groups can limit the extent to which the policy process considers and adopts proactive approaches to environmental protec-tion. Such views of decision-making and the influence of power clearly run counter to pluralist notions of the policy process where competing interests are seen to have equal opportunity to influence.

Within this constrained agenda for environmental policy reform it is unlikely that the decisions that are taken will lead to the optimal outcome. It is readily apparent that the policy process does not generally conform with the rational ideal which identifies problems, establishes goals, evaluates alternative approaches and then selects and implements the optimum response based on its functional merit. Instead, the rationality of the policy process is likely to be restricted in a number of ways. Critically, the ability of modern society to antic-ipate potential environmental problems, or even to recognize actual environmental problems, is far from complete. As Christoff (1996) points out, scientific and technical systems are always one step away from the understand-ing which would control their impacts and are always on their way to creating new problems. Where problems are recognized, the objectives that policy-makers are asked to realize are often vague and ambiguous. Even where an objective is clearly established, the time, resources and capacities needed to identify and evaluate all of the impacts of all of the possible alternative responses to a problem are rarely if ever available (Simon, 1957). Finally, as different groups are likely to have different rationalities, there are commonly multiple and competing objectives for policy so that fragmentation or conflict exists both within and between policy areas.

Thus, under conditions of bounded rationality, the outcomes of decisions cannot be accurately predicted, the functional merits of alternative approaches cannot be compared and an overall optimum cannot be identified. Consequently, administrative decision-making processes are likely to seek a satisfactory rather than an optimum solution (Simon, 1957). Furthermore, decisions will be influ-enced not only by the results of any analysis that does take place but also by the values, experiences, attitudes, aptitudes, goals and conventions of the individuals who make decisions and of the organizations and professional groups that they represent (see Simon, 1957; Downs, 1967; Perlman, 1976; Dunleavy, 1980). The outputs of the policy process are therefore the result of a complex interplay between the results of formal analysis and the impact of the values and goals of decision-makers within the policy process.

Numerous techniques have been proposed which could enhance the ratio-nality of the policy process. Through the application of these techniques, it is argued that policy-makers can better search for an optimum rather than a satis-factory solution. However, Lindblom (1959) terms this search for rationality a 'futile attempt at superhuman comprehensiveness'. He distinguishes between 'root' decision-making which seeks to select the optimum approach based on a comprehensive and rational appraisal of all policy options and 'branch' decision making where policy evolves in small steps through successive limited compar-isons with the status quo. Lindblom argues that under conditions of bounded rationality the branch approach is not only a more accurate description of how the policy process does operate but also a more realistic prescription for how it should operate. Thus, Lindblom argues that policy does and should evolve in an incremental process that he terms 'the science of muddling through' (Lindblom, 1959, 1979).

The incremental approach to decision-making in the policy process that is supported by Lindblom is based on a restricted evaluation of policy options. Consequently, when compared with the root approach to decision-making, it reduces the costs of policy analysis and the risks associated with policy reform. Incremental approaches to policy analysis and decision-making may therefore be desirable in stable situations where the basic approach is broadly satisfactory but needs to be refined or updated. However, where more radical change is necessary, a reliance on incremental analysis and decision-making is likely to reinforce pro-inertia and anti-innovation forces within the policy process (Dror, 1964; Etzioni, 1967). However, Lindblom (1979, p 520) argues that incremental change need not be restricted in its ultimate impact:

> ... *incrementalism in politics is not, in principle, slow moving. It is not necessarily, therefore, a tactic of conservatism. A fast-moving sequence of small changes can more speedily accomplish a drastic alteration of the status quo than can only infrequent major policy change... Incremental steps can be made quickly because they are only incremental. They do not rock the boat, do not stir up the great antagonisms and paralyzing schisms as do proposals for more drastic change.*

Thus incrementalists such as Lindblom do not subscribe to the normative ideal of those rationalists who argue that the policy process should seek to analyse every policy alternative and select the optimum approach even if this involves a radical departure from the approaches of the past.

Despite the different prescriptions that flow from the rationalist and incrementalist views of the policy process, Rees (1990) argues that in their description of the realities of policy-making both approaches share some common ground. They both recognize that decision-makers operate under conditions of bounded rationality and that the goals of the policy process are set with some degree of subjectivity. They both accept that only a narrow range of policy options are evaluated and therefore that a satisfactory rather than an optimum solution is commonly adopted. Finally, they both accept that under conditions of uncertainty decision-makers tend to be risk averse and therefore resort to conventional modes of operation where possible.

THE CAPACITIES FOR ENVIRONMENTAL POLICY REFORM

We have seen that the scope for change within the environmental policy process is restricted in a number of ways. The prospects for environmental policy reform therefore depend upon the ability of any society to recognize environmental problems and opportunities, to acknowledge the limits of existing approaches to environmental protection and to search for, develop and implement effective if not optimum solutions. It is clear that the presence of this capacity for environmental protection within any society does not depend upon a single isolated factor but on a wide range of factors which interact in a complex way within a dynamic setting.

Jänicke (1997) identifies five particular factors which together constitute a country's capacity for environmental protection. These are the character of the various actors that influence the policy process, the strategies that they adopt, the structural conditions within which they operate, the situative contexts within which they find themselves at a particular time and the character of the problem that they are seeking to address. In relation to the actors that surround the policy process, Jänicke argues that particular coalitions of proponents and opponents are likely to emerge around a particular issue. The capacity for action of a particular coalition depends not only on the structural conditions that characterize the policy process but also on the strength, competence and constellation of the actors that seek to influence policy. Concerning the strategies that the various actors and coalitions adopt, Jänicke suggests that their ability to achieve long term goals depends not only on the structural conditions and the situative opportunities that they encounter but also on their ability to build their own capacity for strategic action.

In each of these instances Jänicke suggests that actors are able to exert some degree of influence, as individuals or as coalitions of interests, but that they are also constrained by the structural conditions within which they operate. In this respect, Jänicke distinguishes between three sets of structural framework conditions. The first relates to the conditions under which knowledge is produced, distributed, interpreted and applied (cognitive-informational framework conditions). The second refers to the constitutional, institutional and legal structures, rules and norms that make up the framework for interaction between actors (political-institutional framework conditions). The third includes factors such as the performance, sectoral composition and technological standard of the economy (economic-technological conditions). However, Jänicke recognizes that the situative context, or the short term conditions for action, faced by actors operating within these underlying structures is variable. In essence then opportunities arise and to an extent can be created by actors and alliances operating within these structures depending upon their situation, strength and strategy.

Finally, Jänicke acknowledges that the ability of all of the actors within a society to solve a problem depends very much on the character of the problem. Thus, it is recognized that some problems are easily solved and others, particularly those of a systemic or structural nature, are not. It is acknowledged that the economic and political influence either of the actors that are affected by a problem, or of those that might be affected by a response to that problem, are significant. Similarly, it is accepted that the imperative for action depends on whether a problem is urgent and affects the current generation or whether it is latent and affects future generations.

Jänicke subsequently differentiates between capacity, which is seen as a relatively stable condition of action, and its utilization which generates particular outcomes. The preceding factors are then reformulated in the model presented in Box 1.1.

BOX 1.1 THE CAPACITY FOR ENVIRONMENTAL PROTECTION

The capacities for the environment are constituted by:

- The strength, competence and configuration of organized governmental and non-governmental proponents of environmental protection;
- the cognitive-information, political-institutional and economic-technological framework conditions.

The utilization of the existing capacity depends on:

- The strategy, will and skill of proponents;
- their situative opportunities.

This has to be related to:

- The kind of the problem: its urgency as well as the power, resources and options of the target group.

Source: Jänicke (1997)

According to this model, the capacity for environmental protection can be developed in a number of ways. Enhancing the strength and ability of both governmental and non-governmental proponents of environmental protection is an important first step. However, whatever their strategic capacity, these proponents require a favourable structural framework within which to operate if they are to influence the policy process. This is likely to demand access to information and understanding, involvement in decision-making and access to influence and the provision of suitable resources and expertise.

Over time, the development of these capacities for environmental protection could help many societies to overcome the barriers to policy reform that are outlined above. At the macro-economic level the presence of such capacities could help to establish the conditions for policy integration that would allow environmental objectives to be integrated into non-environmental policy areas such as industry, energy, transport and trade. As stated above, this integration would help to ensure that the impacts of policies concerned with economic development reinforce rather than undermine the efforts of policies associated with environmental protection. Such policy integration would also help to secure the macro-economic structural change that is a key component of ecological modernization.

While initiatives for capacity building may be prerequisites for environmental policy reform in the medium to long term, in the short to medium term these capacities commonly remain underdeveloped. Where the capacity of a country to develop new forms of policy is underdeveloped, it may be assumed that its ability to promote an improved relationship between economic development and environmental protection is fundamentally limited. While this may be the case in some instances, an improved relationship between economic development and environmental protection can be pursued by redesigning the implementation of existing policies as well as through the formulation of new policies. It is to issues of implementation that the discussion now turns.

WHAT ROLE FOR IMPLEMENTATION?

Although a number of studies have recognized the importance of the implementation phase in defining the performance of environmental policy (see Levitt, 1980; Mazmanian and Sabatier, 1981; Mann, 1982; Richardson et al, 1982; Blowers, 1984; Vogel, 1986; Rees, 1990; Jordan, 1993; van Muijen, 1995; Wallace, 1995), in practice the environmental policy process continues to underemphasise the significance of implementation. As Collins and Earnshaw (1993, p 213) note:

> *[Environmental] policy implementation, like policy formulation, is a fundamentally political process on which the success or failure of individual policies depends. Nevertheless, decision-makers and public authorities in general tend to neglect policy delivery as they inevitably become involved in the legislative process itself.*

While the basic scope and format of policy is defined by decisions taken during the process of policy formulation, the implementation phase is a central determinant of the performance of policy in practice. Implementation transforms formal policy outputs such as legislative documents into actual policy outcomes. In essence, therefore, although policy is designed during the formulation stage, it is made in the implementation stage. An examination of the nature of implementation is therefore central to a wider analysis of the impact that policy might have on the relationship between economic development and environmental protection.

Views of implementation are generally based on a perceived divide between the political process of policy formulation and the bureaucratic process of policy implementation. If it is assumed that such a divide between formulation and implementation does exist, and that the bureaucrats who implement policy are completely under the control of the politicians who formulate policy, then Hogwood and Gunn (1984), following authors such as Pressman and Wildavsky (1973) and Hood (1976), argue that it is possible to establish a number of theoretical preconditions for 'perfect implementation'. These are outlined in Box 1.2.

It is acknowledged by Hogwood and Gunn (1984) that perfect implementation based on total obedience or complete control is politically and morally unacceptable as well as practically unattainable. Thus, they do not put forward prescriptions to promote perfect implementation. Instead, by presenting such a list of preconditions for perfect implementation, they seek to illuminate the

BOX 1.2 THE CONDITIONS FOR PERFECT IMPLEMENTATION

1   Circumstances external to the implementing agency do not impose crippling constraints; *a policy may be rendered ineffective if it is unacceptable to any interest that has the power to veto it.*

2   Adequate time and sufficient resources are made available for implementation; *unfeasible deadlines or a failure to provide sufficient resources may undermine the ability of the implementing agency to meet the stated objectives of a policy.*

3   The required combination of resources is available at the appropriate time; *temporary shortages of finance or of appropriately skilled staff may delay or disrupt implementation.*

4   The policy to be implemented is based upon a valid theory of cause and effect; *a policy may not realize its stated objective if it is based on an inadequate understanding of the problem to be solved.*

5   The relationship between cause and effect is direct and there are few if any intervening links; *a policy may not realize its stated objective if there are too many links in the chain of causality between the measures adopted and the objectives sought.*

6   Dependency relationships in the implementation phase are minimal both in number and importance; *implementation is more likely to fail if an agency or actor relies on another for their agreement on, or participation in, a necessary action.*

7   There is a common understanding and acceptance of the objectives to be realized; *different interpretations of the objectives of a policy may divert implementation from its intended objective.*

8   The tasks required to meet the desired objective are fully specified in the correct sequence; *if the required steps in the implementation phase are not taken or if they are taken in the wrong order then a policy may not realize its objective.*

9   There is perfect coordination of, and communication between, the different parties involved in the implementation phase; *imperfect coordination and communication may reduce the potential for the performance of a policy to be monitored and managed.*

10 Those in authority can demand and obtain perfect obedience from those associated with implementation; *imperfections in the implementation phase cannot be resolved without a fully effective hierachy of control.*

Source: Adapted from Hogwood and Gunn (1984)

many areas of the policy process where the values, goals and behaviour of those agencies and actors involved in implementation can influence the outcomes of the policy process in a potentially fundamental and often unpredictable way.

In the absence of perfect implementation, the freedom of agencies and actors to whom responsibility for implementation has been delegated to exercize discretion determines the nature of policy as practice. Any actor in the implementation phase is able to exercize discretion when the effective limits on their power leave them free to make a choice among possible courses of action or inaction (Davis, 1969). Discretion can be exercized both by the implementing agency as a corporate body and by the 'street-level bureaucrats' within the agency who enact policy on a day-to-day basis (Lipsky, 1980). It can be exercized in the way that the key principles and objectives of a policy are interpreted, prioritized and delivered. It can also influence the provision of assistance or support and the level of sanction that is applied in cases of non-compliance. It can allow actors to change the substance of policy or the style of its delivery. In each instance the values and behaviour of the organizations and individuals involved in implementation shape the nature of policy in practice. Given the potential for the real nature of policy to be defined only during its delivery, it may be that a clear divide does not exist between policy formulation and implementation. The exercize of discretion ensures that policy continues to be made throughout the entire policy process.

Discretionary elements can be deliberately incorporated into legislation to allow implementing agencies to take decisions at a level and with a degree of specificity that is not available during policy formulation. As Hill (1993) notes, it may be that those top-level decision-makers involved in policy formulation do not want to, or are not able to, set clear policy goals but would rather leave responsibility for defining the true nature of policy to those who are expected to implement it. However, as has been discussed, discretion can also arise unintentionally if any of the conditions for perfect implementation break down so that implementing agencies or the individuals within them are required to select priorities and to explore different approaches to the delivery of policy.

The exercize of discretion in the implementation phase can have both positive and negative impacts. As has been mentioned, discretionary aspects may enable regulators to fine-tune the delivery of policy to reflect the specific circumstances of its application. Allowing implementing agencies and individuals to exercize discretion can thus allow policy to recognize the complexity and heterogeneity of the organizations and individuals that it seeks to influence (Richardson et al, 1982). Furthermore, given the commonly unpredictable nature of change, the exercize of discretion in the implementation phase allows policy to be refined over time to reflect those temporal and spatial contingencies that cannot be addressed in a general sense at the design stage. However, the benefits of this process of fine-tuning may only be available where regulators have the necessary expertize and sufficient resources to apply discretion in a suitable way. In such instances the appropriate exercize of discretion in policy implementation under variable and specific conditions at the micro-level can

15

increase the efficiency and effectiveness of policy in a way that is not possible by issuing generic guidance at the macro-level.

However, while the exercize of discretion in the implementation phase may allow the performance of policy to be enhanced through flexibility and fine-tuning, it is also likely to be based on negotiation between the implementing agency and the organization or individual that it seeks to influence. As Barrett and Fudge (1981, p 25) note:

> *It is appropriate to consider implementation as a policy/action continuum in which an interactive and negotiative process is taking place over time, between those seeking to put policy into effect and those upon whom action depends.*

It may mean, therefore, that public interest decisions are taken by non-elected civil servants in a process of negotiation with the parties that they regulate. This process of negotiation may not be open to external scrutiny or legal challenge, particularly where negotiations are based upon complex, heterogeneous and dynamic criteria that are not readily monitored or communicated. Furthermore, negotiations are likely to be based on unequal access to information between the regulator and the regulated (Weale, 1992; Ogus, 1994). This commonly means that the implementing agency or individual has to choose between alternative courses of action on the basis of the potentially incomplete or inaccurate information that has been supplied by the party that they are regulating. The rationality of negotiated decision-making during implementation may therefore be far from comprehensive, particularly if an adversarial relationship between the regulator and the regulated encourages the latter to withhold information or only to present information that leads towards what the regulated would perceive to be a favourable outcome.

Aside from concerns related to rationality, transparency and accountability, by its very nature the exercize of discretion within such negotiations will generate uncertainty and may allow arbitrary discrimination based on improper criteria (Richardson et al, 1982). In cases where discretion may be exercized in an arbitrary way, the prospect of regulatory capture is raised. In such instances, rather than working towards public interest goals, a regulatory agency comes to reflect the interests of those parties that it was originally charged with regulating. As Ogus (1994, p 58) notes, regulatory capture may occur in a number of ways:

> *There are various hypothesized methods of influencing agency policy: the information required by the [implementing] agency may only be obtainable from the regulated industries; lack of expertise in the subject-matter may mean that the agency has to recruit its officials from those industries; and the industries may threaten the agency with costly, or even trivial, time wasting appeals should it fail to be 'cooperative'.*

It has also been suggested that, intentionally or otherwise, implementing agencies and the individuals within them may be more lenient in their interpretation of the requirements of policy if they aspire to eventual employment with the bodies they regulate, if such a style of enforcement is more pleasant as it incurs the least resistance or if they are reluctant to impose sanctions on offenders with high social status (Richardson et al, 1982). Regulated organizations may also be able to influence or resist the demands of regulatory agencies as a consequence of the political leverage that they derive from their economic power (see Blowers, 1984).

Thus, as well as allowing the performance of policy to be enhanced, the exercize of discretion can also generate uncertainty, allow arbitrary decision-making and increase the prospect of regulatory capture. Discretion can therefore lead to uneven and unintended policy outcomes and may in some instances allow the original goals of policy to be subverted. Consequently, as Richardson et al (1982, p 23) suggest, a compromise must be reached between policies which are based on precisely defined legislation and those that allow the exercize of uncontrolled discretion:

> *If discretion is located along a continuum it is possible to think of broad standards and wide discretion at one end, while precise rules and restricted discretion provide the opposite pole. In practice the problem is to discover the appropriate compromise between legalism and uncontrolled discretion.*

It is clear from the above that the exercize of discretion during the implementation phase is a critical factor influencing the nature of policy as practice. As such, an examination of the ways in which different approaches to implementation can influence the efficacy and efficiency of policy is central to a wider analysis of the impact that policy can have on the relationship between economic development and environmental protection.

CONCLUSIONS

It is apparent that policy has a key role to play in changing the relationship between economic development and environmental protection. To date, however, policy has had a limited influence on this critical relationship. Despite the apparent potential, the progress that has been made to date has either been largely unintentional or has been constrained to a relatively small number of countries or issues. In general, environmental policy continues to respond to the negative impacts of the economic development that virtually every other area of policy seeks to promote.

Various factors conspire to limit the potential for environmental policy reform. The scope for reform is constrained by the influence of vested interests; the nature of reform is restricted by factors which bound the rationality of decision-making. The prospects for environmental policy reform may therefore appear limited. However, new approaches to implementation could improve the performance of existing policies in the short to medium term, while building capacities for environmental protection could enhance the potential in the medium to long term. Change that is compatible with the goals of ecological modernization is therefore a possibility. Whether this change should be seen as institutional learning or as a technocratic project is debatable. However, if policy can only evolve incrementally, it may be that modern industrial society must explore the potential for ecological modernization as a step towards a more radical reconceptualization of the relationship between economic development and environmental protection.

Chapter 2

ENVIRONMENT, INNOVATION AND TECHNICAL CHANGE

The need for regulation to protect the environment gets widespread but grudging acceptance: widespread because everyone wants a livable planet, grudging because of the lingering belief that environmental regulations erode competitiveness. The prevailing view is that there is an inherent and fixed trade-off: ecology vs. economy.

Porter and van der Linde (1995, p120)

INTRODUCTION

At the centre of the debate on the future of industrial environmental regulation is the question of whether regulation enhances or erodes economic competitiveness. Some argue that under certain conditions regulation can enhance competitiveness by promoting efficiency, stimulating innovation and creating new market opportunities (see for example Porter, 1991; Gore, 1992; Porter and van der Linde, 1995). According to this view, regulation can either facilitate or force organizations to overcome those barriers which prevent them from exploiting economically attractive opportunities for environmental improvement. Consequently, new approaches to environmental regulation should be explored because, if designed and delivered appropriately, regulation can lead to combined economic and environmental benefit. This view is compatible with a central proposition of ecological modernization, namely that with the aid of particular forms of government intervention a synergistic or mutually reinforcing relationship can be established between economic development and environmental protection.

Counter to this argument, others contend that despite its obvious and widespread appeal such a win-win view of the relationship between environmental regulation and economic competitiveness is unlikely to be realized other than in limited instances and for limited periods (see for example Walley and Whitehead, 1994; Palmer et al, 1995; Cairncross, 1995). This argument is based on the belief that the market normally ensures that any economically attractive opportunities for environmental improvement are exploited without the incentive or imperative that is provided by government intervention. Thus, in general regulation is only needed if environmental improvements are required which are not associated with an economic benefit. Accordingly, regulation normally imposes extra costs on the market. While those who hold such a view still assign a role to regulation as a response to market failure, they suggest that as win-win outcomes are the exception rather than the rule there is an inherent trade-off between the social environmental benefits and private economic costs of regulation. However, it is recognized that the extent of this trade-off is not fixed as different forms of regulation are seen to have different economic and environmental implications. Therefore the challenge is to design and deliver environmentally effective and economically efficient regulations that minimize the costs of environmental improvement.

The dispute about whether environmental regulation enhances or erodes economic competitiveness is important in principle as it is based on differing beliefs about the efficiency of markets and the rationality of organizations. However, in practice it is apparent that both sides of the debate accept a role for some amount of regulation and acknowledge that the relationship between environmental regulation and economic competitiveness is not fixed. Thus, rather than debating whether environmental regulations enhance or erode competitiveness in an absolute sense, it may be more appropriate to consider how, relative to existing approaches, the performance of regulation can be improved so that at the least a less negative and possibly a positive relationship can be established between environmental regulation and economic competitiveness.

The preceding chapter examined the relationship between economic development and environmental protection. It recognized that as this relationship is not fixed there is potential for policy to promote particular forms of economic development that generate lower environmental impacts. However, it suggested that existing approaches to policy are limited in their ability to influence the relationship between economic development and environmental protection and that a variety of factors restrict the potential for environmental policy reform. While recognizing that programmes of capacity building could increase the potential for environmental policy reform in the medium to long term, it argued that new approaches to the implementation of existing policies could improve the relationship between economic development and environmental protection in the short to medium term. In this respect, it proposed that both the economic and the environmental performance of regulations could be enhanced through fine-tuning in the implementation phase.

This chapter moves beyond an analysis of the role of implementation to consider the impact that regulation might have on the relationship between economic development and environmental protection at the level of the firm. It assesses the relationship between business and the environment and examines the various factors that shape the response of industry to environmental regulation. It suggests that the impact of environmental regulation is determined both by the level and by the nature of the technologies and techniques that are developed and applied in response to it. The chapter examines the nature of this innovation process, which is taken to include the research, development and diffusion of new technologies and techniques, and the economic and environmental performance of different forms of innovation. The potential for various forms of innovation to improve the relationship between economic development and environmental protection at the level of the firm is highlighted. However, it is recognized that various barriers to innovation are commonly encountered and, where these barriers are overcome, each phase of incremental innovation will eventually encounter diminishing marginal returns before encountering subsequent barriers to radical innovation. In each instance it is argued that, in the absence of continuous innovation, the costs of further environmental improvement will gradually escalate.

Thus, it is contended that the presence of these barriers to innovation and the prospect of diminishing marginal returns establishes a clear rationale for regulation which promotes the establishment of particular conditions for innovation and the development and application of particular technologies and techniques. Finally, in order to sustain continuous environmental improvement in the absence of escalating costs, an evolutionary framework is proposed through which the response to regulation should emerge as diminishing marginal returns are encountered in each phase.

THE EVOLUTION OF INDUSTRIAL ENVIRONMENTAL MANAGEMENT

Various authors have highlighted changes in the way that industry has responded to environmental pressures in recent decades (see for example Groenewegen and Vergragt, 1991; Schot and Fischer, 1993; Welford and Gouldson, 1993). Groenewegen and Vergragt (1991) identify three overlapping phases which they suggest characterize the evolving nature of the industrial response to environmental issues. In the first phase that they identify, which lasted through the 1970s and into the early 1980s, they suggest that environmental issues were primarily addressed by industry as a reaction to regulatory demands. Schot and Fischer (1993) similarly suggest that during this period firms lacked interest in and commitment to environmental improvement and resisted adaptation to growing regulatory and public pressures.

In the second phase, which lasted throughout the 1980s and into the early 1990s, Groenewegen and Vergragt contend that companies began to respond to environmental issues more positively by developing technologies and techniques which sought to control their operational impacts. Schot and Fischer (1993) argue that during this period firms began to accept responsibility for their environmental performance and to move beyond the defensive and reactive stance that was previously common. However, they also argue that the responses that were developed during this period continued to focus on regulatory compliance and lacked an innovative dimension.

In the third phase, which began in the early 1990s and is on-going, Groenewegen and Vergragt argue that companies began to recognize the environment as a core rather than a peripheral concern and to shift the emphasis of their activities away from reactive or curative responses toward proactive or anticipatory approaches. Schot and Fischer suggest that this period has seen, and will continue to see, some companies adopting innovative strategies that attempt to take their environmental performance beyond the baseline of compliance with regulatory demands. They suggest that as regulatory and public pressures for environmental improvement become stronger and more powerful, an increasing number of firms will search for, develop and apply initiatives that seek to avoid environmental impacts and anticipate regulatory and market pressures.

While there is general evidence to support these three broad phases of industrial environmental management, it is important to note that the take up of environmental management initiatives in industry has been influenced by a number of spatial, sectoral and scale-related variables. The application of environmental management initiatives is highest in developed economies with stringent regulatory and market pressures. Within those countries uptake is highest in those industrial sectors that are heavily regulated or highly scrutinized. Within those sectors larger companies are more likely to adopt environmental management initiatives than smaller companies. Nonetheless, the general principles that relate to the design, application and impact of industrial environmental management initiatives remain valid.

Aside from the wider external or social costs and benefits of environmental improvement, there are a range of internal or private costs and benefits that fall directly onto companies that develop and apply environmental management initiatives. The level of these private costs and benefits, and the balance between them, influences the demands of regulators and the decisions of companies. While the private costs associated with the application of environmental management initiatives can be significant, it is increasingly apparent that over time these costs can be off-set at least to some extent by a range of benefits. For companies that develop and apply environmental management initiatives, the private costs of environmental improvement include the financial and the managerial resources that must be committed to the research, development and application of new technologies and techniques. As these resources must be drawn away from other possibly more profitable or productive uses, there are also associated opportunity costs. The benefits include both the direct economic returns from environmental improvement and the catalytic impacts that environmental initiatives can have on broader economic performance. These benefits include both tangible improvements in price competitiveness, resulting for instance from improved process efficiency, and less tangible improvements in non-price competitiveness, arising for example as a consequence of improved product quality or stakeholder relations. The range of private benefits associated with the application of industrial environmental management initiatives is illustrated in Figure 2.1 below.

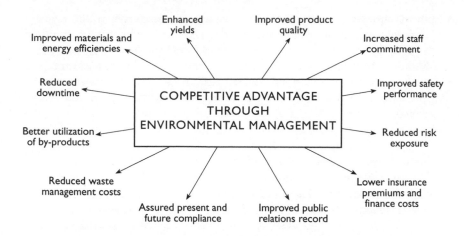

Figure 2.1 *The Benefits of Industrial Environmental Management*

The costs and benefits accruing to companies who adopt environmental management initiatives have been examined by a number of empirical studies. For example, the Dutch PRISMA project sought to establish the costs and benefits associated with various environmental management options (Dieleman and de Hoo, 1993). These options included both minor changes in the technologies and organizational practices of companies and major innovations in their products and processes. For the ten participating companies, the study identified 164 environmental management options, of which 45 were immediately implemented, 66 were implemented in the medium term and the remainder were explored through on-going research and development. Of the 45 options implemented, 20 generated cost savings and 19 were cost neutral. A range of indirect benefits, relating for instance to improvements in product quality, were also realized. The common finding of this and other similar studies (see for example Ashford, 1993; CEST, 1994; Porter and van der Linde, 1995) has been that there is often a considerable amount of potential to improve environmental performance at the micro-economic level and that the costs associated with the exploitation of this potential can often be offset, to some extent at least, by a range of economic benefits.

THE BARRIERS TO CHANGE

Hypothetically, profit maximizing companies that are free to take decisions on purely economic grounds will only pursue environmental management initiatives if the associated private costs are more than offset by the related private benefits. However, for profit maximising companies that are constrained by the demands of regulation, the challenge is to achieve compliance in the most efficient way. Although it is of broader significance, for the individual company it does not matter whether environmental improvement enhances or erodes competitiveness as in theory at least improvement can be an absolute requirement of regulation. In such instances, profits will be increased if the regulated company minimizes the costs and maximizes the benefits of regulatory compliance.

While economic theory normally assumes that companies are profit maximizers, it is important to recognize that there are a range of barriers which may prevent companies from responding to regulatory imperatives and economic incentives in the optimum way. As Porter and van der Linde (1995, p 127) note:

> *The belief that companies will pick up on profitable opportunities ... makes a false assumption about competitive reality – namely that all profitable opportunities for innovation have already been discovered, that all managers have perfect information about them and that organizational incentives are aligned with innovating. In fact, in the real world, managers often have highly incomplete information and limited time and attention. Barriers to change are numerous.*

These barriers may be both organizational and technical. Ashford (1993) suggests four essentially organizational barriers to innovation which may explain a lack of micro-economic commitment to improving environmental performance even where it may lead to economic benefit:

1 Lack of information on the costs and benefits of environmental management;
2 Lack of confidence in the performance of new technologies and techniques;
3 Lack of managerial capacity and financial capital to deal with the transition costs of reorganizing the production process; and
4 Lack of awareness of the long run benefits of environmental management resulting in low priority being assigned to environmental issues.

As implied by the preceding points, a central factor preventing the development and application of environmental management initiatives is the distribution over time of the associated private costs and benefits. It is likely that for companies seeking to improve their environmental performance the costs of action will be concentrated in the short term while the benefits will be diffused through the longer term. Consequently, lack of access to information and shortages of managerial capacity and financial capital in the short term commonly prevent environmental management initiatives from being adopted whatever their longer term potential. These barriers are compounded where decision-makers are confident about the costs but uncertain about the benefits of environmental improvement. Thus, the issue is not only about whether environmental improvement enhances or erodes competitiveness, it is also about the distribution and the predictability of the costs and benefits and the capacities of companies to respond in the short term to threats and opportunities that exist in the longer term.

Aside from these organizational barriers, there is also a range of technical barriers which limit the potential of environmental management initiatives over time. Ashford (1993) suggests that the main emphasis of those environmental management initiatives that have been applied in industry to date has been on process management. In this respect, the majority of environmental management initiatives have sought to improve the performance of existing production systems incrementally. Thus, rather than changing what they do, companies have been gradually adapting the way that they do it. However, as Freeman (1992) notes, no amount of experience, learning and technical improvement can overcome the basic limits of incremental innovation. Ultimately discontinuous or more radical change is needed if environmental improvement is to continue without encountering technical barriers and escalating costs. Environmental management initiatives therefore need to expand their influence beyond process management to consider the more fundamental issues of product formulation and process design if the technical and economic limits of environmental improvement are to be avoided.

In essence, therefore, in a dynamic setting the relationship between economic development and environmental protection at the level of the firm depends upon the conditions for and the nature of innovation. Before examining these issues with specific reference to the links between economic development and environmental protection, it is first necessary to explore the general nature of innovation in more detail.

THE NATURE OF INNOVATION

Innovation is normally taken to include all stages of new economic activity from initial invention through product development and introduction to the market. Dosi (1988, p 222) defines innovation as a process involving:

> *the search for and discovery, experimentation, development, imitation and adoption of new products, new processes and new organizational set-ups.*

Innovations may be either radical innovations which involve discontinuous change and the introduction of new technologies and techniques or incremental innovations which involve continuous improvement to existing technologies and techniques. While historically greater emphasis has been placed on radical innovations as they are seen to open new areas of economic opportunity and allow quantum leaps in economic performance, the importance of incremental innovation should not be understated. As Freeman (1992, p 77) suggests, the incremental innovation associated with the diffusion of a new technology or technique is itself a critical component in the innovation process:

> *Most of the productivity gains associated with the diffusion of a new technology do not come about as an immediate consequence of the first radical innovation. On the contrary, they are usually achieved as a result of a fairly prolonged process of learning, improving, scaling up and altering new products and processes.*

While radical innovations often rely on incremental improvement for their success, it is apparent that incremental innovation must eventually encounter diminishing marginal returns as it encounters both economic and technical limits. These limits are maintained by those elements of the existing system that remain fixed. The periodic introduction of radical or discontinuous change is thus a prerequisite for subsequent phases of incremental innovation.

THE PROCESS OF INNOVATION

A typology of the innovation process which highlights the stages of invention, development and diffusion may be taken to imply that innovation is a linear process that flows sequentially through each stage. However, it is commonly acknowledged that this linear view of the innovation process is inappropriate. Rothwell (1992) suggests that the dominant perception of the innovation process has evolved through a number of phases during the past 30 years. He suggests that initially the innovation process was based on a technology-push model which emphasized the role of the supply-side as the source of the innovation process. Under this model, the discovery of new technologies and techniques was the first step in a linear process which moved from invention through development and finally to diffusion. However, the dominance of this technology-push model was later challenged by a second generation market-pull model which placed greater emphasis on the influence of the demand-side. Under this model innovations were perceived to be generated in a linear way as a response to perceived or articulated needs and wants in the market place. The third generation model recognized the combined importance of both the supply-side and the demand-side in the innovation process. As such it suggested that the innovation process was not purely linear but involved 'some interaction and coordination between the different functional stages in the process' (Rothwell, 1992). This third generation model continued to see innovation as an essentially linear process but acknowledged the importance of coordination and communication between its stages. The fourth generation or integrated model recognized the importance of parallel interaction between the various stages in the innovation process. This involved an amount of functional integration between the stages of innovation both within and between those organizations involved in the innovation process and as such began to move away from the linear view of innovation. Finally, the fifth generation or systems model, which Rothwell accepts is a somewhat idealized development from the fourth generation integrated model, emphasises a parallel innovation process with full functional integration between all actors and stages in the innovation process.

The concepts underlying the fourth or fifth generation models put forward by Rothwell are supported by authors such as the OECD (1992) and Soete and Arundel (1995) who characterize a systems approach to innovation. This systems approach emphasises the importance of multidirectional linkages in the innovation process which facilitate the transfer of information, formal knowledge and tacit understanding between the actors at various stages of the

innovation process. Depending on the ability of the relevant actors to understand, filter and accumulate appropriate information (their assimilative capacity)
and to apply that information in a productive way (their absorptive capacity),
these flows then encourage interactive learning between the various actors in
the system. This interactive learning in turn facilitates a cumulative and self-
reinforcing process of innovation so that systems that have been innovative in
the past are more likely to be innovative in the future. This is particularly the
case where a threshold of information, knowledge and understanding is
required to facilitate innovation.

THE SUPPLY AND DEMAND FOR INNOVATION

As has been stated, although the interactive nature of the innovation process
may render a distinction between the supply-side and the demand-side of the
innovation process inappropriate, it is still possible to identify a number of
determinants affecting the supply of and demand for innovations. Dosi (1988)
suggests that the supply of innovation is dependent upon the technological
opportunities, market structure and the ability of the innovator to appropriate
a proportion of the benefits associated with the innovation. Similarly, Kemp
and Soete (1992) suggest that the demand for innovation is dependent upon
the price and quality (and therefore the costs and benefits) of the innovation,
the transfer of knowledge and information relating to an innovation and the
perceptions of economic risk and uncertainty associated with the application
of that innovation.

However, the ultimate success of an innovation depends upon what Nelson
and Winter (1977) term the selection environment. The concept of the selection environment recognizes that innovations are not adopted and applied on
the basis of their isolated characteristics but also on the extent of their compatibility with existing components of the system. Consequently, the selection
environment has a direct influence on the demand for different innovations
and thereby an indirect influence on the supply of different innovations. Kemp
(1993, p 85) describes the selection environment as:

> *A techno-economic system or network of supplier-user linkages involving activities
> such as production of materials, machinery, intermediate and final goods and
> transport, marketing, finance, insurance, repair and waste disposal. Within this
> network, economic activities are coordinated and have in the past been optimized.
> A new technology, whether a new material, production technique or product must
> be integrated into this techno-economic system and may require changes in several
> components of the system.*

Thus, innovations depend upon a system or network of relations without which
their adoption would be impossible. As a consequence, new technologies and
techniques must be introduced into systems which have often been developed
for and adapted to older technologies and techniques. The introduction of an

innovation into one part of an existing system may require far-reaching changes to other parts of the system to ensure compatibility with the system as a whole. Considerable resistance and inertia may be apparent in this respect. For example, firms which have successfully mastered the operation of old technologies and techniques commonly face difficulties in overcoming the limits of existing skills and knowledge and in acquiring the new skills and knowledge needed to successfully apply new technologies and techniques (OECD, 1992). Depending on the ability of an innovation to influence existing systems, an innovation which requires only incremental change to existing systems is more likely to be adopted than one which requires more radical change. Consequently, the dynamic nature of innovation tends to favour incremental rather than radical innovation and as a consequence change normally takes place within particular trajectories in an evolutionary form.

The ability of a new technology or technique to influence existing trajectories is not static but varies over time. Soete and Arundel (1995) and Kemp (1993) suggest that the inability of new technologies and techniques to influence existing systems is compounded over time by the dynamic and self-reinforcing impacts of scale and learning effects. On the supply-side the diffusion of innovations is normally associated with improvements in the quality of the innovation as a consequence of accumulating experience with its production and feedback from the demand-side on its use. This supply-side learning effect which improves the quality of the innovation is complemented by a scale effect which potentially reduces the price of the innovation as economies of scale are realized in its production. On the demand side, as the innovation is adopted users learn to apply it more efficiently and effectively and establish or adapt an appropriate system to surround the innovation. As well as these internal benefits, the diffusion of the innovation also generates positive externalities. For instance, information and knowledge gathered by actual users are often transferred to potential users so that the uncertainty associated with the application of an innovation is decreased. Further, the increased community of users facilitates joint problem solving and cumulative learning while also encouraging factors such as the availability of an appropriately skilled labour force or the provision of training and maintenance services. All of these factors increase the efficacy and efficiency of the innovation as it is diffused so that rather than encountering diminishing returns, innovations commonly experience a period of increasing returns to adoption (OECD, 1992).

While the scale and learning effects may appear to be beneficial, as their impacts increase, for a period both the supply-side and the demand-side become increasingly locked into the particular trajectory of the selected innovation. By comparison, whatever their apparent potential, innovations which have not benefited from the dynamic scale and learning effects often are, or are perceived to be, expensive, inadequate, incompatible, unproven, unknown and without the necessary support mechanisms. In essence, therefore, potentially beneficial innovations may not be selected due to their initial inefficiency, although paradoxically the only way that they can become efficient is by being selected (OECD, 1992). The rationality of actors choosing whether to develop or use an innovation is thus bounded by the nature of the existing system.

Ultimately, however, the scale and learning effects and the technical and economic benefits of incremental innovation must encounter diminishing marginal returns. As Freeman (1992, p 74) notes:

> *Although slower productivity gains may continue for a long time and even receive further stimulus from the competition of new radical innovations, in the end the focus shifts to radically new types of production which offer once more the potential scope for more substantial gains.*

Thus, in the longer term economic dynamism may allow the competitive potential of a radical innovation to challenge the apparent logic of existing systems. The scale of this challenge may increase as pioneers or first movers adopt the radical innovation and begin to secure the benefits of the scale and learning effects. However, as stated above, the initial adoption and subsequent diffusion of a radical innovation depend not only on its inherent characteristics but also on the nature of the selection environment. Thus, innovations which display some complementarity with existing systems are more likely to be adopted than those which do not. In this respect, even radical innovations are likely to reflect some of the path-dependencies discussed above.

PERSPECTIVES ON INNOVATION AND ENVIRONMENT

The following analysis synthesizes the different elements of the preceding discussion to present three inter-related perspectives on the relationship between economic development, innovation and environmental performance at the level of the firm. Firstly, the transition from reactive to anticipatory approaches to the environment will be examined from a technological perspective. Secondly, the shift of the environment from a peripheral to a central position in business decision making will be assessed from a managerial perspective. Finally, the importance of radical as well as incremental change will be explored from a strategic perspective.

The Technological Perspective

All technologies, including both materials and equipment, have actual and potential environmental impacts. Nonetheless, it is still possible to identify a range of technologies that may be categorized as 'environmental technologies'. In this respect, environmental technologies are taken to include any technology that reduces the absolute or relative impact of a process or product on the environment. Broadly, environmental technologies can be categorized as either control technologies or clean technologies, each of which is associated with different economic and environmental characteristics (see Irwin and Hooper, 1992; ECOTEC, 1992; Kemp, 1993).

Control technologies are end-of-pipe additions to production processes which capture and/or treat a waste emission in order to limit its ultimate impact on the environment. Thus, control technologies are distinct or stand-alone additions to existing products or processes which react to environmental impacts and commonly involve limited change to the process or product to which they are added. By contrast, clean technologies are general processes or products which fulfil a non-environmental objective as their primary purpose but which integrate environmental considerations into their design and/or application in order to anticipate and avoid or reduce their impact on the environment.

As control technologies do not require the redesign of the process or product to which they are added, then at least in relation to clean technologies, they are relatively inexpensive to purchase and install. This is particularly the case where technologies must be added to existing processes, a process which can be characterized as the lowest level of incremental change. Furthermore, as technologies that perform an explicitly environmental purpose, there is a distinct market for control technologies. Consequently, suppliers are easily identified and the analysis of their economic and environmental performance is relatively straightforward. This ease of analysis is of benefit both to purchasing companies and to regulators. Collectively, these factors tend to support the development and application of control technologies. This support for control technologies allows the realization of the benefits associated with the scale and learning effects which in turn generates some of the path-dependencies discussed above.

In contrast, and as a consequence of their integrated nature, the compatibility of clean technologies with existing processes must be secured either by adapting the technology itself or by changing the process with which it is to be integrated. This need for adaption means that it is often expensive to retro-fit clean technologies into existing processes. Thus, while the integration of clean technologies into existing processes still represents incremental change, it is a higher level of change than that which is needed if control technologies are to be added to existing systems. As general processes and products which fulfil their primarily non-environmental objectives with a lower environmental impact, the market for clean technologies is not distinct from the market for general processes and products. Consequently, suppliers of clean technologies are difficult to identify and due to their integrated nature the analysis of their economic and environmental performance is relatively complicated for both companies and regulators. Together these factors conspire against the development and application of clean technologies. Consequently, the benefits of the scale and learning effects that can only be generated through adoption are not realized and the bias in favour of control technologies is exacerbated.

It is therefore apparent that control and clean technologies display different economic and environmental characteristics both in isolation and in relation to their compatibility with existing systems. While these differences may mean that control technologies are more expedient in the short term to medium term, in the longer term clean technologies are generally held to be more economically efficient and environmentally effective (OECD, 1987; CEC, 1993;

DTI/DoE, 1994). The longer term desirability of clean technologies is derived from their integrated and anticipatory approach which offers the potential to address environmental impacts at source. Thus, although in the short term the costs of clean technologies may be more significant, in the medium to long term their economic and environmental benefits are generally higher than control technologies as they open new areas of opportunity and allow quantum leaps in both economic and environmental efficiency. By contrast, control technologies can only offer limited improvements in the efficiency with which emissions streams are managed as they are restricted to capturing and concentrating emissions so that they can be treated in an appropriate way.

While clean technologies may be more economically efficient and environmentally effective in the medium to long term, a continuing role for control technologies may still exist. Control technologies may be an appropriate response in the short to medium term while appropriate clean technologies are being developed or where the limited life of an existing process would make the retro-fitting of clean technologies inappropriate. Similarly, although they may display absolute or relative improvements in economic and environmental efficiency, it is unlikely that all emissions will be avoided through the application of clean technologies. In these instances a second phase of control technologies may be applied to limit the unavoidable impacts of clean technologies.

The Managerial Perspective

The transition from control to clean technologies commonly requires the integration of environmental issues into existing processes. This transition, which begins to integrate environmental considerations into the mainstream of business decision making, is associated with both technological and organizational change. Combining technological and organizational change may be associated with a range of direct and indirect benefits. For example, relatively simple managerial or organizational changes may negate the need for potentially costly investments in technology. Where technological investments are necessary, the application of associated managerial or organizational systems will help to secure the direct and indirect benefits associated with the new technology by facilitating incremental improvement and by helping to ensure that the learning effect is exploited.

Management systems are designed to pull a potentially disparate system into an integrated and organized one. They seek to assign responsibilities, to coordinate activities and to facilitate flows of resources and information throughout an organization. In so doing they attempt to develop coherency and to address and manage the interdependencies of the various activities that take place within an organization. The structured coordination that an effective management system can offer enables organizations to translate corporate objectives into departmental and individual working practices. By monitoring performance under different conditions, management systems also allow organizations to pursue continuous improvement.

Management systems can play an essential role in the transition from control to clean technologies. As stated above, the introduction of clean technologies often demands changes both to the technology itself and to the production process that surrounds it. Thus, rather than responsibility for environmental issues resting with an isolated environment department or manager, for clean technologies to fulfil their potential, environmental issues must be integrated into the activities of the organization as a whole. This may demand changes in organizational structures and in working practices. Such a transition, which can be readily restricted by inertia and resistance, relies on corporate commitment and coordination, on appropriate flows of resources and information and on organizational learning. These conditions are more likely to be realized where an effective management system is in place.

However, it is apparent that the efficacy of the management system relies upon factors such as management structure and style. Burns and Stalker (1994) note that different management structures and styles may be appropriate at different stages. In this respect they distinguish between mechanistic and organic forms of management. They suggest that mechanistic management promotes specialized differentiation of functional tasks within the firm. It demands the precise definition of the rights and responsibilities attached to each functional role. It also requires a hierarchy of control, authority and communication, with instructions and information cascading from each level of the hierarchy. In contrast, organic management is characterized by flexibility and the continual redefinition of individual tasks through interaction between the various activities within the organization. Under such structures, communication typically takes place as consultation, not command, and with bottom-up as well as top-down flows of information.

Burns and Stalker (1994, p 11) suggest that neither organic nor mechanistic management is preferable in all cases but that each style becomes appropriate under different conditions. The organic approach is required under conditions of change and heterogeneity with the mechanistic approach being more appropriate under conditions of stability and homogeneity. Organic management is better under conditions of change because:

> ...it comprehends more eventualities than [those] necessary in concerns under stable conditions. More information and considerations enter into decisions, the limits of feasible action are set more widely.

The implications of this analysis are significant. Where firms face the uncertainties commonly associated with the introduction of clean technologies, the 'limits to feasible action' must be addressed throughout the organization. Organic management styles and an effective management system are likely to be enabling factors which allow the shift from control to clean technologies and the integration of environmental considerations into mainstream business activity. In essence the presence of these factors helps to create a selection environment which is sympathetic to the successful introduction and application of clean technologies and techniques.

The Strategic Perspective

While certain approaches may better facilitate the integration of environmental considerations into existing technological and organizational systems, it is apparent that the nature of change will be limited by those aspects of the existing production process that remain fixed. Consequently, the incremental improvement of the environmental performance of existing production processes must eventually encounter diminishing marginal returns although these may be delayed if more components of the existing system are made flexible. Therefore, as well as focusing on incremental change there is a need to assess the potential for radical change. In seeking to explore the nature of radical and incremental change a distinction can be drawn between operational decision-making which focuses on the continual improvement of existing processes (as under the technological and managerial perspectives above) and strategic decision-making which focuses on the overall direction of business development and therefore on the research and development of prospective processes and products.

By its very nature, innovation is associated with the search for new modes of activity. As stated above, Ashford (1993) highlights the importance of information, confidence, managerial capacity and financial capital in explaining why companies may or may not explore potentially profitable areas of opportunity associated with the environment. In the case of radical change, there may be little information available on the economic or environmental performance of an innovation and significant amounts of managerial capacity and financial capital may be required if the potential of an innovation is to be explored. Thus, there are risks associated with both the search for and the application of radical innovations. Consequently, the attitude of strategic decision-makers to risk and uncertainty is of critical importance in assessing the potential for radical change.

Sharp and Pavitt (1993) suggest that the senior management of an organization may approach strategic decisions in either a myopic or a dynamic way. Myopic approaches to decision-making consider the variety of opportunities through traditional cost-benefit analyses which focus on the direct and tangible economic impacts of an investment. Consequently, myopic forms of decision-making are less likely to explore the potential for radical change where unquantifiable risk and uncertainty are critical factors. By contrast, dynamic approaches to strategic decision-making recognize the indirect and intangible impacts of an investment, related for example to technological, organizational and market learning. Such approaches are particularly appropriate where decisions include an environmental dimension, as integrating environmental considerations into economic investment criteria naturally introduces a greater element of uncertainty. Consequently, dynamic approaches to strategic decision-making may be required if the risks and uncertainties associated with radical innovation or a switch of trajectory are not to preclude change.

THE CONCEPTUAL FRAMEWORK

The following discussion draws together the issues and perspectives discussed above to propose a conceptual framework which characterizes the evolutionary nature of industrial environmental management initiatives. The framework is illustrated by Table 2.1, which shows the various phases through which a hypothetical firm might evolve as it increases the extent to which environmental considerations are integrated into its business activities.

While such a generic framework is useful for illustrative purposes, it makes a number of assumptions that should be acknowledged. For example, the framework introduces discrete phases into the evolution of industrial environmental management initiatives. Instead, it is probable that different phases will

Table 2.1 *The Evolution of Industrial Environmental Management Initiatives*

Phase	Approach	Response	Example
1a	Operational	Reactive	Technological	Installation of emissions filter for total waste stream
1b			Organizational	Establishing external market for total waste stream
2	Operational	Anticipatory	Technological	Installation of energy efficient motors
			Organizational	Installation of environmental management system
3	Strategic	Anticipatory	Organizational	Incorporation of environment into R&D activities
			Technological	Re-engineering of production process
4a	Strategic	Reactive	Organizational	Establishing external market for residual waste stream
4b			Technological	Installation of emissions filter for residual waste stream

Key terms
Operational   The incremental improvement of existing activities.
Strategic   The search for and selection of future activities.
Reactive   Ex-post responses which are added to a process or product.
Anticipatory   Ex-ante responses which are integrated into the design and/or application of a process or product.
Technological Changes to the design and/or application of materials and/or equipment.
Organizational Changes to the design and/or application of managerial activities and/or working practices.

be explored simultaneously and that interaction between the stages will influence the nature of each stage. Similarly, the framework infers that responses to the environment can be characterized by a sequential or linear progression from one phase to the next. Instead, it may be that the progression is restricted if barriers to change are encountered, if change is discontinuous or if the conditions for progression from one phase to another only occur at particular times. Indeed, at the extreme, it may be that these barriers to change preclude evolution within firms so that change occurs primarily through the 'winds of creative destruction' (Abernathy and Clarke, 1985) as new firms with new conditions, operations and strategies challenge the restricted behaviour of existing firms. Nonetheless, despite its simplified and generic nature, such a framework affords insights into the various stages that may be experienced as environmental issues permeate the operations and strategies of the firm through both incremental and radical change.

The Operational-Reactive Phase

During the operational phase, companies respond to the environmental impacts of their existing activities through incremental change. In the first instance, incremental change within the Operational-Reactive phase involves the installation of reactive control technologies. Technological responses are initially preferred to organizational change as they are readily available, cause mimimal disruption and do not present significant demands on under-developed managerial capacity. However, as managerial capacity relating to environmental issues develops, reactive organizational changes are sought which seek to avoid the demand on financial capital associated with technological responses. However, as a consequence of existing technological responses and the fact that some emissions streams cannot be addressed by organizational change alone, a combination of reactive responses based on both technological and organizational change will eventually be realized in this phase.

Although some economic benefits may be secured through the application of reactive responses, throughout their lifetime technological responses tend to draw on the financial capital and organizational responses on the managerial capacity of the firm. Similarly, although some environmental benefits may be realized, the main environmental benefit of reactive responses is to ensure the capture and appropriate treatment of emissions streams. Furthermore, as reactive changes only respond to and do not anticipate emissions, their ability to avoid environmental impacts is fundamentally restricted.

The Operational-Anticipatory Phase

As further environmental improvement is sought, firms begin to realize the limits of the Operational-Reactive phase and begin to examine anticipatory options. These anticipatory options may involve the incremental integration of either clean technologies into the materials or equipment of the production process or clean techniques into the management systems or working practices of the organization. It is likely that technological and organizational changes will be required simultaneously and that the options for addressing waste streams at source will be explored incrementally. Consequently, initial emphasis will be on relatively simple or low cost technological change or on relatively minor changes to organizational practices. Once the most readily exploitable options have been addressed, more fundamental change will be sought, although this change will be limited by the extent to which the elements of existing technological and managerial systems remain fixed. Incremental change must therefore become increasingly searching in its objectives if it is to secure continued environmental improvement without encountering escalating costs.

Anticipatory changes will demand an initial investment of either financial capital or managerial capacity. However, this initial investment is likely to be associated with short pay-back periods, particularly in the early stages of activity where low-cost changes can result in significant and on-going economic returns. Once the low-cost options have been exploited and diminishing marginal returns set in, more significant investments will be required which generate lower returns and have more extended pay-back periods. Similarly, although in the early stages significant environmental benefits may be secured rapidly, once the easy options have been exploited the rate of improvement will decrease. Diminishing marginal returns are therefore encountered but may be postponed by making more elements of the system variable.

The Strategic-Anticipatory Phase

The economic and environmental benefits associated with change under the Operational-Anticipatory phase are limited by those elements within the firm that are not flexible or are not amenable to incremental change. Consequently, if further changes are sought, fundamental alterations to the design and operation of technological and managerial systems are required. These changes, which involve simultaneous organizational and technological innovation, seek to anticipate and avoid potential environmental impacts at the design stage. Such an approach may entail input substitution, process redesign and/or product reformulation. Given the interdependencies between these factors, a systems approach to change is required. In relation to organizational change, this demands effective communication between the various actors and departments at different stages of the process. In relation to technological change, experimentation and iteration in the design stage will be required throughout the system.

Strategic change requires significant investments of financial capital and managerial capacity at the design stage. It also requires increases in the level of investment associated with the construction of the process and may lead to delays or inefficiencies at the early stages of its operation. However, where environmental impacts have been designed-out of the process, no further investments of financial capital or managerial capacity are required throughout the lifetime of the new process. Furthermore, if the new process incorporates the best available technologies and techniques, quantum leaps in resource efficiency will be secured in the short term which will be associated with on-going economic benefits relative to those that would have been secured without radical change. The environmental benefits of this phase are similar to the economic benefits in that many emissions can be avoided at source during the design stage while others will experience dramatic reductions as a consequence of the application of the best available technologies and techniques. The impacts of the Strategic-Anticipatory phase are consolidated by the continued search for incremental change pursued under the Operational-Anticipatory phase which can now exploit the renewed potential for incremental improvement established by the phase of radical change.

The Strategic-Reactive Phase

Despite the economic and environmental benefits that may eventually be secured through the Strategic-Anticipatory phase, it is unlikely that radical change and the redesign of the technological and managerial systems will allow all emissions to be addressed at source. Consequently, even when all emissions have been minimized, a role for a second phase of reactive technologies and techniques will remain. However, unlike the Operational-Reactive phase, the Strategic-Reactive phase will seek to instigate organizational changes that utilize the managerial capacity that has developed within the firm in order to avoid more costly technological change. However, as with the Operational-Reactive phase, as some emissions streams cannot be addressed by organizational change alone, a combination of technological and organizational change will be required.

Although in general the economic and environmental costs and benefits of the Strategic-Reactive phase are similar to those of the Operational-Reactive phase, there are important differences. The need for responses put forward under the Strategic-Reactive phase will have been anticipated at the design stage so that a proportion of the additional economic costs of retrofitting reactive responses to existing processes will be avoided. Furthermore, as these reactive responses follow the Strategic-Anticipatory phase, the volumes of emissions to be controlled and/or treated are significantly lower than those experienced under the Operational-Reactive phase.

CONCLUSIONS

This chapter began by introducing the nature of the dispute about the relationship between environmental regulation and economic competitiveness. It suggested that while this dispute is important in principle, in practice it may be more appropriate to consider how, relative to existing approaches, the performance of regulation can be improved so that at least a less negative and possibly a positive relationship can be established between environmental regulation and economic competitiveness.

The chapter proposed that the impact of environmental regulation is determined by the level and by the nature of the technologies and techniques that are developed in response to it. Consequently, it examined the nature of the innovation process and the economic and environmental performance of different forms of innovation. It highlighted the potential for different forms of innovation to improve the relationship between economic development and environmental protection at the level of the firm. However, it also acknowledged the presence of various barriers to innovation and the prospect of the costs of continued environmental improvement escalating in the absence of innovation. These factors establish a clear rationale for regulation which promotes the establishment of particular conditions for innovation and the development and application of particular technologies and techniques.

The discussion then considered the relationship between economic development, innovation and environmental performance at the level of the firm from three interrelated perspectives. Firstly, the technological perspective was examined and the importance of a shift from reactive control technologies to anticipatory clean technologies was highlighted. Secondly, the organizational perspective was considered and the significance of a shift in the position of the environment from the periphery to the core of business decision-making was stressed. Thirdly, the strategic perspective was assessed and the need for radical as well as incremental change was established. Based on this analysis, it suggested that over time regulation should seek to facilitate an evolution of the industrial response to the environment if continuous environmental improvement is to be sustained in the absence of escalating costs.

Chapter 3

MANDATORY REGULATION AND THE EUROPEAN UNION'S INTEGRATED POLLUTION PREVENTION AND CONTROL DIRECTIVE

INTRODUCTION

Within advanced industrial societies, government is commonly relied upon to deliver those public interest goals that are not delivered by the market. Command and control or mandatory regulation have historically been at the centre of government attempts to fetter the operations of the market. Mandatory regulation is formulated and implemented by government and its agencies and represents control by a superior authority over the operations of private organizations (Ogus, 1994). Given the apparent reluctance of many governments to explore new approaches to environmental policy, mandatory regulation continues to be the primary instrument applied by government in this field. Consequently, any examination of the design, delivery and impact of mandatory environmental regulation remains of widespread significance.

The following chapter examines the design and implementation of mandatory environmental regulation both in theory and in practice. The discussion is divided into three sections. Firstly, with reference to the broader policy context, mandatory environmental regulation is defined and its function is assessed. Secondly, a more practical and empirical examination of mandatory environmental regulation is put forward through a case study of the European Union's Integrated Pollution Prevention and Control Directive. The design of this directive is outlined to provide the background for subsequent chapters which consider the implementation and impact of similar legislation in the UK and The Netherlands. Finally, the chapter establishes a range of variables which can be used to examine the design and implementation of mandatory environmental regulation. It is proposed that for the purposes of analysis the numerous dimensions of regulatory design and implementation can usefully be simplified to consider the frameworks, structures and styles of regulation. These variables are used to guide the analysis of environmental policy as practice that follows in subsequent chapters.

THE NATURE OF MANDATORY REGULATION

The broad context for regulation is established by the wider policy framework. Policies establish strategy and the general approach to be taken on a given issue. Major policy decisions, such as those that surround the interface between environment and industry, have traditionally been taken by national governments although supra-national and sub-national policy strategies are increasingly common. The policy documents that result can include statements of ideology and intent as well as more concrete proposals for action with explicit targets and goals. As a result policy documents can range from being almost meaningless in practical terms to highly influential statements which provide clear direction and strategic vision.

It is because of the distinct but foundational nature of policy that Ball and Bell (1995, p 90) state that:

> *The process of establishing general policies is not really part of the regulatory system, but a necessary precondition for any system of environmental control.*

Thus, policy provides the context for mandatory regulation by defining the general climate of government and governance and by establishing the specific operating framework within which regulatory agencies must operate. This indicates that any discussion of mandatory regulation would not be complete without also considering the broader policy context within which it is embedded.

Having established that there is a difference between policy and regulation it is now possible to examine the nature of mandatory regulation in more detail. Selznick (1985), Jacobs (1991) and Ball and Bell (1995) have all provided definitions of mandatory regulation which together provide a clear idea of its nature. Selznick (1985, p 363) for example states that regulation is 'sustained and focused control exercized by a public agency over activities that are valued by a community.' Thus, mandatory regulation is exercized by government or its representatives to control activities which are seen to be legitimate and of value but which are associated with undesirable side-effects. Mandatory regulation establishes controls either in the form of an imperative 'you must' or a prohibitive 'you must not'. Therefore, in the first instance it is not about persuasion, although negotiation and persuasion are commonly characteristics of the implementation phase.

Jacobs (1991, p 136) adds a further dimension to the nature of mandatory regulation, describing it as 'any administrative measure taken by government which has the backing of law, but does not involve either a direct financial incentive or direct government expenditure.' Thus, mandatory regulation is founded upon a legislative basis which assigns government some degree of control over the target activity. It does not establish direct financial incentives or disincentives although some economic costs and benefits are normally associated with the measures that are needed to ensure compliance and fines can follow non-compliance. However, contrary to Jacobs' statement, mandatory regulation frequently does entail direct government expenditure as a result of the need to establish and run implementing agencies. In some instances, however, these agencies may recover their costs from regulated parties.

Finally, Ball and Bell (1995, p 88) consider that mandatory regulation is 'the application of rules and procedures by public bodies so as to achieve a measure of control over activities carried on by individuals and firms.' Thus, mandatory regulation is not simply defined by the written form of legislation as it also establishes the procedures which shape the implementation of that legislation. This expands the domain of a discussion of mandatory regulation considerably.

By reviewing the components and definitions proposed by other authors a number of the key components mandatory regulation have been established. Consequently, drawing on the points raised above, it is possible to define mandatory regulation as:

A system of direct control over market organizations and activities, operated by government and its representatives, which has a legal basis and is operationalised through a range of implementing structures and procedures.

This definition of mandatory environmental regulation can be clarified further by contrasting mandatory regulation with the other instruments that are available to government as it attempts to influence the relationship between economic development and environmental protection. Aside from mandatory regulation, Jacobs (1991) identifies three main categories of instrument. It should be noted that this list is not exhaustive and that a clear distinction cannot always be drawn between the different categories.

The first category proposed by Jacobs (1991, p 134) is that of voluntary initiatives which include 'all those actions unforced by law and unpersuaded by financial incentives, which individuals, groups and firms take to protect the environment.' The principle difference between mandatory regulation and voluntary action is that the latter is not forced by law. Although government may seek to persuade companies to undertake voluntary action in a number of ways, for instance by providing information or various forms of business support, they are not necessarily involved in providing direct financial incentives to encourage the development and diffusion of voluntary initiatives.

The second category identified by Jacobs (1991, p 137) is that of government expenditure which involves 'actions taken directly by government or state-owned bodies, ... [or] subsidies or grants provided by government to private organizations and households.' In this case government pays directly for environmental improvement or provides grants to private organizations so that they better support environmental goals.

The third and final category identified by Jacobs (1991, p 138) is that of financial incentives. Financial incentives aim to reward good practice and penalize bad practice through the market as they 'make environmentally damaging activities less attractive by making them more expensive. They thus use the price system to achieve environmental targets.' Although mandatory regulation may also have financial impacts in the form of regulatory charges and fines, financial incentives explicitly use taxes and subsidies to influence the behaviour of organizations and individuals operating within the market.

This chapter has established that policy frameworks establish the context within which mandatory regulations operate. It has also distinguished mandatory regulation from a range of other instruments that can be used to manage the environmental impacts of industrial activity. However, the discussion has not yet examined the realities of regulation. To do this it is necessary to move beyond broad definitions to consider mandatory regulation in practice.

THE PRACTICE OF MANDATORY REGULATION

Formally, there are a number of different stages associated with the design and implementation of mandatory regulation. In the case of industrial environmental regulation these stages include those where principles are established and standards are set, where licenses and permits are issued, where performance is monitored and where compliance is enforced (see Rees, 1990; O'Riordan, 1985; Ogus, 1994; Macrory, 1990). However, it is important to note that a range of less formal factors define the nature of policy in practice. O'Riordan (1985) suggests that to a greater or lesser extent all frameworks of mandatory regulation are influenced by the nature and the level of the consultation, expertize, self-regulation and political compromise that surrounds them. Thus, the implementation of regulation must be seen as an inherently political process that is fundamentally influenced by the behaviour of the organizations and individuals that work within the formal structures that are typically established by government. Whilst acknowledging that the nature of policy in practice cannot be assessed without an examination of the associated political processes, it is useful to examine the different stages that are commonly associated with the design and implementation of mandatory regulation.

The process of using mandatory regulation to control or manage the environmental impacts of industry is begun by establishing principles and setting standards which govern the operations of regulated companies. Standards include quantitative measures such as emission limit values (ELVs) and environmental quality standards (EQSs) whilst principles are qualitative and involve the application of measures such as 'best practicable means' or 'as low as is reasonably achievable (ALARA)'. These standards and principles form the basic guidelines within which regulated activities must take place. While these standards and principles can take many forms, on the whole those systems that impose standards are more rigid than those that apply principles as quantitative standards are less open to interpretation than qualitative principles.

Similarly, by their nature regulations based on the application of standards are more able to specify relatively simple emissions limits than highly complex operating conditions. Conversely, regulations based on the application of principles are more able to stipulate specific operating conditions that often depend on a wide range of interacting and heterogeneous factors that are not easily defined or monitored. Consequently, as within regulated companies it is the operating conditions which generate emissions, regulations that are based on qualitative principles may be better suited to anticipatory approaches than those that rely on quantitative standards alone.

This process of establishing principles and setting standards is commonly followed by a permitting stage where licenses are issued which embody these principles and standards. At this point the regulatory authorities issue a specific permit which confirms that a plant has the right to operate whilst also outlining the limits or conditions within which operation must take place. The permit itself may be an extensive document outlining requirements for operating, monitoring, upgrading and so on. The threat of refusal or withdrawal of the licence is one of the main sanctions available to the regulatory agency and therefore one of the main ways of encouraging compliance. However, related to previous decisions on the nature of the standards and principles that are applied, a variety of approaches can be taken to the licensing process. The licence may demand that a relatively hands-on and intensive relationship is established between the regulator and the regulated company that involves the regulator in regular site visits and direct and detailed intervention in the site's operation. Conversely, the licence may demand that an arms-length and extensive relationship is adopted to ensure that intervention is less prescriptive or intrusive. In such instances regulated companies are set broad conditions or targets and left to achieve them with minimal direct intervention from the regulator as long as compliance is demonstrated.

Between successive permits being issued most regulatory regimes stipulate that some amount of monitoring should take place. This monitoring function ensures that there is an ongoing relationship between the regulator and the regulated company. Although this is likely to entail a less intensive degree of interaction than that which is required at the permitting stage, it may still be conducted in a relatively hands-on or arms-length way. For example, any particular industrial site may be left to monitor and report its own compliance, or the regulator may continue to play an active role in monitoring compliance. An alternative to both of these is that an independent inspectorate which is organizationally distinct from the regulator can assume responsibility for monitoring compliance with permits. In practice a combination of these options is possible.

Finally, the enforcement stage becomes important when monitoring reveals cases of non-compliance with the requirements of a permit. Again it is possible to identify different approaches to regulation at this stage. For example, regulatory agencies may pursue a conciliative or a litigious approach to enforcement or in the terms of Ball and Bell (1995) a 'compliance strategy' or a 'sanctioning strategy'. Under the conciliative approach a breach in compliance rarely leads to an immediate appeal to the rule of law. Instead, the regulator may draw on a range of enforcement options ranging from persuasion and warning through to the imposition of detailed schedules of compliance. In such instances prosecution is only sought in the last resort. For those regulators that have a more litigious approach, legal action to punish non-compliance will be enacted more quickly and more forcefully. This is likely to generate an adversarial relationship between the regulator and the regulated rather than the more consensual relationship that is likely to follow a conciliative or compliance based approach.

This review of the principle steps involved in establishing and implementing mandatory regulation suggests that it is possible for a considerable amount of variety to exist in each stage of the regulatory process. Collectively, the variations that characterize each stage of the regulatory process play a fundamental role in determining the nature, and therefore the impact, of different regulatory frameworks. Before moving on to present a conceptual framework which can be used to guide further investigation into the various approaches to regulation, it is useful to supplement the discussion so far with the consideration of a practical example, namely the European Union's Integrated Pollution Prevention and Control (IPPC) Directive. This Directive is an example of mandatory regulation that embodies the principles of integrated pollution control.

THE CASE FOR INTEGRATED POLLUTION CONTROL

The application of integrated approaches to pollution control is a relatively recent development in industrial environmental regulation. Haigh and Irwin (1990) provide an account of the pressures that have led to integrated pollution control initiatives in recent years. They argue that through the 1980s at least three specific problems became apparent which compromised the ability of mandatory regulation to address the environmental impacts of industry. The growing recognition of these problems encouraged the search for alternative approaches to industrial environmental regulation.

Firstly, Haigh and Irwin (1990) suggest that pollution control legislation, and its associated institutional structures, had developed in an additive way to address different environmental media (that is air, water and land) separately. This resulted in a fragmented approach to pollution control that did not solve problems but merely transferred them from one medium to another. Perhaps naturally, the tendency was for pollution to be diverted toward the medium that was covered by the least stringent legislation or was regulated by the least demanding regulator at any given time. It also allowed regulated companies to channel their resources toward the diversion rather than the reduction of their emissions.

Secondly, they argue that because the legal and institutional framework of environmental protection had developed over time in an ad-hoc way, opportunities to improve the efficiency of mandatory regulation remained unaddressed. Typically a wide variety of regulators had developed, each with the resources and support services they required to fulfil their responsibilities. In many cases opportunities to rationalize these structures were apparent both through the integration of the different media specific regulators and through the amalgamation of the legislation that they were supposed to implement.

Thirdly, and linked to the previous point, Haigh and Irwin (1990) suggest that there was an increasing recognition of the need to simplify administrative and regulatory systems. Due to the complexity of regulation and the structures that surrounded it, industry commonly claimed to be confused about its responsibilities and uncertain about the required response. Complex legislation and institutional structures often required industry to report the same information to different authorities but in different formats. It also resulted in requirements for action from one regulator which were clearly in conflict with the demands of another.

In many instances the problems outlined above led to calls for the amalgamation and integration of legislative and regulatory structures. The goal was thus to establish an integrated permitting or authorization system to be administered and delivered by an integrated agency. It was recognized that as well as dealing with many of the concerns outlined above, such integration would increase the ability of industry and government to set coherent priorities with respect to the many problems faced and to enhance the level of complementarity between environmental policy and other policy areas. In reality the impact of some of these arguments can be seen in the EU's IPPC Directive.

THE EU'S INTEGRATED POLLUTION PREVENTION AND CONTROL DIRECTIVE

The IPPC Directive will transform a significant proportion of industrial environmental regulation in the European Union in the next decade. Consequently an understanding of it, and its potential impacts, is of the greatest importance. In the section that follows, the IPPC Directive's objectives, key principles, implied institutional frameworks, scope of application and timetable of implementation will be outlined. This will be accompanied by a broader discussion on the nature of the Directive drawing on interviews with members of DGXI (Environment) of the European Commission, the body that was initially responsible for drafting, and that will ultimately be responsible for administering, the legislation.

The objective of IPPC is to achieve integrated prevention and control of pollution arising from a range of industrial processes. Broadly it aims to prevent, or, where that is not practicable, to reduce emissions to air, water and land from these activities. Being informed by previous experience with integrated pollution control, notably in the UK, the Directive calls for emissions to all media to be considered simultaneously during permitting and it establishes a waste hierarchy that promotes prevention in the first instance and reduction if prevention is not possible.

The Directive's objectives are to be realized through the application of two key principles. Firstly, permits must 'achieve a high level of protection for the environment taken as a whole'. This statement enshrines the integrated pollution control principle within the Directive. Secondly, limits for releases to all media are to be established based on the 'best available techniques' (BAT). This term represents the bedrock of the Directive and is defined as follows:

- 'techniques' shall include both the technology used and the way in which the installation is designed, built, maintained, operated and decommissioned;
- 'available' techniques shall mean those developed on a scale which allows implementation… under economically and technically viable conditions, taking into consideration the costs and advantages;
- 'best' shall mean most effective in achieving a high general level of protection of the environment as a whole.

In other words BAT implies the application of both technologies and techniques that are economically and technically viable.

The Directive has relatively little to say about the institutional framework within which it must be applied as under the terms of subsidiarity such detailed intervention at the member state level falls outside the competence of an EU Directive. However, as with all EU Directives it must pass into the legal framework of member states. At this point a competent body (or bodies) will be assigned the responsibility of implementation. In recognition of the fact that all member states have differing legal and institutional frameworks a degree of flexibility is allowed in this process. Most importantly, member states have the option of issuing an integrated permit from an agency responsible for all media, or, where such an organization does not exist, offering a coordinated permit where more than one competent authority is involved. Thus, the IPPC Directive does not necessarily demand the creation of a unified or integrated regulatory agency in each member state.

Finally, concerning the Directive's scope of application and timetable of implementation, the scope of the Directive is defined to include a range of industrial activities above a certain size. While the size thresholds vary from industry to industry, the industrial sectors covered include the energy sector, the metals production and processing sector, the minerals extraction and processing sector, the chemicals sector, the waste management sector and certain activities within the agricultural and food processing sector. New or significantly altered installations in the sectors covered by the Directive should be regulated by October 1999 and existing installations by October 2007.

It can be seen then, that the IPPC Directive is based on the application of key principles and procedures and is flexible in many respects. It outlines permitting procedures and stipulates what should be included in permits, who has to apply for a permit and the level of access to information that must be available to the public. It does not establish quantitative standards or explicit targets in any generic sense. Its flexibility derives from this lack of targets and from the fact that it is based on a number of critical principles and terms that must be interpreted and applied in individual situations, as described by a member of the European Commission:

The Directive isn't that flexible in terms of its delivery in member states and the procedures involved. It is more flexible with respect to targets, these will not be generic. What it provides is the authority for each member state to tailor and push control requirements for individual installations. Of course, the interpretation of BAT can result in emissions limits and targets for plants, and these can be linked to a system of national environmental targets but these are not established in the Directive.

This kind of flexibility necessarily means that beyond providing broadly similar permitting systems in member states, the Directive in isolation cannot be relied upon to create a level playing field of environmental standards, although a coordinated exchange of information to establish BAT for regulated processes may emerge in time. Even so, such flexibility may be useful, as a representative of DGXI stated:

Due to the flexibility [that is inherent in the Directive] we do not anticipate a level playing field as such. All countries will be under the same regime but sectors and countries may have different targets. This means there is potential for variation depending on the environment, age of plant, economic viability of the plant and so on. This is essential.

Flexibility and fine-tuning during implementation are thus integral to the Directive. Such flexibility and fine-tuning allows differences in the institutional structures of the member states to be accommodated. They also allow regulators to take into account the dynamic and heterogeneous conditions they are likely to encounter within regulated companies as they apply the Directive.

Finally, regarding the nature of national permitting systems and the coordinated permit option. In allowing a co-ordinated permit to be provided in situations where no single agency with responsibility for all media exists, the Directive will allow structures which in the past have been widely criticised to continue to operate. However, it is possible that despite the arguments given above this situation may have some advantages. These advantages were also outlined by DGXI:

IPPC does not need a single body to deliver it. It can be delivered by many co-ordinated institutions and this may not be a bad thing. In the arguments between regulators you may get a perfectly reasonable trade-off, even a more demanding and searching form of regulation. I don't think this will lead to poor policy necessarily.

It can therefore be seen that while the IPPC Directive will redefine the form and function of a considerable proportion of the industrial environmental regulation that exists throughout the EU, the way that the Directive is implemented will reflect the different and sometimes widely divergent conditions that exist both in the various member states and in the range of sectors and companies that it regulates. The ultimate impact of the Directive will therefore depend upon the specific conditions in which it is applied. Before moving on to consider the implementation and impact of the IPPC Directive in subsequent chapters, this chapter concludes by establishing a range of variables which can be drawn upon to channel an analysis of this nature.

THE DESIGN AND IMPLEMENTATION OF MANDATORY ENVIRONMENTAL REGULATION: ANALYTICAL VARIABLES FOR THE CASE OF IPPC

This chapter has reviewed the nature of mandatory environmental regulation both in theory and in practice. In each instance it has suggested that a range of design and implementation variables play a fundamental role in defining the character, and therefore the impact, of mandatory environmental regulation. The following discussion will analyse these variables further with reference to three dimensions of mandatory regulation, namely the frameworks, structures and styles of regulation. The different dimensions and the variables that characterize them are summarized in Table 3.1.

The Regulatory Framework

Policy Framework
As has been discussed, specific regulations are situated within a broader policy context. The nature of the policy context can therefore be considered as a variable which is likely to have a significant influence on the performance of a regulatory regime. However, to some extent all mandatory regulation is associated with a wider policy framework. As a result it is important to differentiate between those frameworks that are strategic in their nature and those that are merely symbolic. The difference between strategic and symbolic policy frameworks revolves around the presence of firm commitments rather than vague promises. Strategic policy frameworks establish explicit goals, identify particular mechanisms to be applied and commit definite resources to the realization of its goals. Symbolic policy frameworks do none of these things. Consequently, while symbolism can sometimes be of broader significance, in terms of the specific context for regulation strategic policy frameworks are more likely to enable effective regulation than symbolic policy frameworks.

Implementation Structures

Any framework of mandatory regulation will have a series of implementation structures associated with it. In a dynamic setting these structures can be changed but at any point in time they are reasonably stable.

Legal Structures
Systems of integrated pollution control seek to establish a cohesive legal framework which can be used to address all of the environmental impacts of industrial activity. The goal is to develop an amalgamated legal framework that

Table 3.1 *The Design and Implementation of Mandatory Environmental Regulation: Analytical Variables for the Case of IPPC*

REGULATORY FRAMEWORK

Issue	Framework	Feature	Example
Policy Frameworks	Strategic	Establishes objectives	Clear commitments which include explicit targets
	Symbolic	Creates uncertainty	Vague promises with support for existing approaches

IMPLEMENTATION FRAMEWORK

Issue	Framework	Feature	Example
Legal Structures	Amalgamated	Comprehensively restructured	All industrial emissions considered under one piece of legislation
	Additive	Established incrementally	Emissions to different media considered under separate legislation
Institutional Structures	Integrated	Comprehensively restructured	Emissions to different media considered by one agency
	Fragmented	Established incrementally	Emissions to different media considered by separate agencies
Resource Structures	Strong	Appropriate capacities	Sufficient resources and staff with appropriate expertise
	Weak	Inappropriate capacities	Insufficient resources and staff lacking appropriate expertise

IMPLEMENTATION STYLES

Issue	Framework	Feature	Example
Design Styles	Anticipatory	Process focused	Emphasis is placed on principles like 'best available techniques'
	Reactive	Emissions focused	Emphasis is placed on standards like Emission Limit Values
Delivery Styles	Hands-on	Intensive relationship	Regulator frequently on site and advises on industrial processes
	Arms-length	Extensive relationship	Regulator rarely on site and does not advise on industrial processes
Enforcement Styles	Conciliative	Consensual relationship	Regulator adopts a 'compliance based' strategy
	Litigious	Adversarial relationship	Regulator adopts a 'sanction based' strategy

allows all emissions to be considered simultaneously during the licensing, monitoring and enforcement stages so that the most appropriate destination for any emission can be selected. However, in most advanced industrial countries the legal structures associated with industrial environmental management have not been amalgamated but have developed in an additive and incremental way. In such cases emissions to different environmental media are likely to be addressed separately under different pieces of legislation. However, without a comprehensive reformulation of legal structures it is difficult to achieve a truly integrated assessment of industrial emissions. Consequently the nature of those legal structures associated with regulation will have an important influence on the ultimate nature of mandatory environmental regulation.

Institutional Structures

Establishing a system of integrated pollution control, as outlined above, is likely to involve a reorganization of the legal structures associated with industrial environmental regulation. However, if it is to be effective it is important to consider not only legislative reorganization but also institutional restructuring. As Majone (1976, p 589) states:

> *The performance of policy instruments depends more on the institutional framework within which they are used than on their technical characteristics.*

In a similar way to the legislative structures discussed above, institutional structures may be fragmented, having developed in an additive and incremental way over time, or they may be integrated. In practical terms fragmented institutional structures result in a range of regulatory agencies with a patchwork of responsibilities. In such cases emissions to different media are considered separately by different regulatory agencies. In contrast, integrated institutional structures result in one agency being responsible for emissions to all media.

Resource Structures

A crucial aspect of the effectiveness of implementation is likely to be the degree to which adequate resources are committed to the task. Mandatory regulation is essentially useless without offices, infrastructure, finance, staff and so on to administer its implementation. Resources are therefore required and, although in some cases regulators may be able to recover their costs from the regulated companies, there is no guarantee this will be successful. The extent to which resources are made available will have an important bearing on the impact of any regulatory regime. As Baram (1985, p 61) notes:

> *Too often, government promises in the form of laws have not been supported by legislative provision of funds and manpower levels which are crucial to implementation.*

As a result it is possible to speculate that weak and strong resource structures are possible, the presence of which will influence the regulator's capacity to undertake its task.

Implementation Styles

The ultimate character of mandatory regulation is also influenced by a range of more ambiguous and indeterminate implementation styles. These implementation styles are likely to be just as influential as the structures discussed above although to a large extent they are established in an ad-hoc way during the process of interaction between the regulator and the regulated.

Design Styles

Any system of mandatory regulation, including one which is associated with integrated pollution control, is influenced by the principles and standards that are designed into it during formulation. Mandatory regulation can incorporate both qualitative principles and quantitative standards although most regulations are likely to emphasise one more than the other. Those regulations that emphasise the application of qualitative principles such as 'best available techniques' tend to focus on the operating conditions that give rise to emissions. As they attempt to regulate pollution before it is created they may be termed anticipatory. In contrast, those systems that emphasise the application of quantitative standards such as Emissions Limits Values (ELVs) may be termed reactive as they are more likely to focus on emissions once they have been created.

Delivery Styles

The delivery style of an agency relates to the day-to-day nature of the relationship between the regulator and the regulated. Broadly the regulator has the option of adopting either a hands-on or an arms-length approach, with the former being more intensive than the latter. However, the style of delivery adopted by the regulator can be determined to some extent by the degree of discretion that they are afforded and by the scope for expert judgement that is built into mandatory regulation at the design stage. Qualitative principles allow discussion between interested parties whilst quantitative standards allow little flexibility, particularly if they are statutory obligations. Hands-on approaches may be more prevalent if the regulator assumes an advisory as well as a policing role so that the regulator and the regulated search for responses to regulation in a cooperative and interactive way.

Enforcement Styles

Finally, the implementation style is defined by the approach taken to enforcement by the regulatory agency. In this case the regulator has the option of treating breaches of compliance in a relatively conciliative or litigious way, one promoting consensus and negotiation and the other being adversarial and promoting conflict. In the former the regulator is likely to make much greater use of warnings and detailed schedules of compliance rather than legal prosecutions. In the latter there will be a much swifter move to legal action. These are respectively compliance based or sanction based strategies. However, the approach to enforcement is again likely to be at least partially determined by many of the previous variables. For example, mandatory regulation that is based on easily measurable quantitative standards and is delivered in an arms-length way lends itself to legal action much more readily than regulation that is based on qualitative principles that are often difficult to define precisely and involve a close working relationship between the regulator and the regulated.

When considering the categories and variables presented in Table 3.1 and in the discussion above, it should be noted that there are numerous potential problems associated with such an evaluation. As Rees (1990) notes, once the idea of a rationally staged management process is discarded, analysis of regulation becomes more complex. Thus, the regulatory process may not follow the logical sequence that is implied in Table 3.1. Furthermore, the selection of the criteria for analysis is inevitably subjective to a degree as any regulation could be assessed against an almost endless range of criteria. Finally, most if not all of the variables outlined above are not susceptible to objective measurement. As Baram (1985, p 72) notes:

> *Implementation usually eludes numerical or objective measurement. As a result, most approaches to evaluating implementation are highly dependent on the criteria, values and goals deemed important by the particular evaluator.*

Thus, it is important to acknowledge that the list of variables presented in Table 3.1 and in the associated discussion is not exhaustive, that the boundaries between the variables are not necessarily distinct and that such a list could not be established and cannot be measured on purely objective grounds. Nonetheless, the categories and variables presented above serve to simplify an otherwise complex area of debate and thereby provide some clear guidance for the subsequent analysis.

CONCLUSIONS

The review of mandatory regulation provided above has established that the goal of perfectly designed and delivered mandatory environmental regulation is probably unattainable. As O'Riordan (1985, p 24) has said:

> *Regulators aim to define the degree of danger that results from an activity, to ensure it is commensurable with benefits arising from the activity, and to try to achieve an equitable distribution of costs and benefits in as efficient a manner as possible. In practice, there are many obstacles that make this challenge almost impossible to achieve fully. The whole regulatory process is characterized by uncertainty and by being subjected to diverse, and often contradictory, social, technical, political and economic pressures.*

Indeed mandatory regulation may be doomed to imperfection as it may not be possible for individuals or organizations to command the required amounts of knowledge from which to construct a desirable social order (Ogus, 1994).

However, it will always be possible to enhance the performance of mandatory regulation. With this goal in mind, a range of critical issues in the design and implementation of mandatory regulation have been established with particular reference to systems of integrated pollution control. These will be examined in more detail in the empirical chapters that follow so that the analysis of implementation can be linked to an examination of the impact that mandatory regulation has on industrial behaviour.

Chapter 4

VOLUNTARY REGULATION AND THE EUROPEAN UNION'S ECO-MANAGEMENT AND AUDIT SCHEME

As governments around the world begin to face up to the challenge of sustainable development, they can no longer afford to be tied to a restricted number of policy instruments...

Jenkins (1995, p 1)

INTRODUCTION

In many instances, mandatory regulation continues to be the primary instrument applied by government as it attempts to influence the relationship between economic development and environmental protection. However, it is increasingly recognized that the performance of mandatory regulation can be enhanced if it is applied as one of a number of different policy instruments. Interest in the potential contribution of alternative policy instruments stems from an acknowledgement that every instrument has a range of strengths and weaknesses. Consequently, it is broadly accepted that the policy framework should not limit itself to the application of one instrument but should instead seek to develop a complementary mix of different instruments.

The contribution that voluntary regulation might make to environmental protection is an important aspect of the debate about alternative policy instruments. From both government and industry perspectives voluntary regulation can have a number of advantages. For government, effective voluntary action might deliver benefits which reduce the need for mandatory regulation and therefore the requirement for costly regulatory agencies. For industry, reductions in the level of government intervention may allow scarce resources to be channelled toward environmental improvement rather than bureaucratic compliance. However, particularly amongst the public and pressure groups, voluntary regulation commonly generates suspicion that voluntary regulation may in fact mean no regulation.

This chapter examines the nature of voluntary environmental regulation in detail. Building on the analysis presented in Chapter 3, the discussion is divided broadly into four sections. Firstly, voluntary regulation is defined in theory and is subsequently characterized in practice through an examination of a contemporary example which exemplifies many of the characteristics of voluntary regulation. Secondly, the contrasting motives and agendas for voluntary action are assessed. Thirdly, a more practical and empirical position is adopted by looking at a case study of voluntary regulation, namely the European Union's Eco-Management and Audit Scheme Regulation. The design of this Regulation is outlined to provide the background for subsequent chapters which consider its implementation and impact in the United Kingdom and The Netherlands. As the Eco-Management and Audit Scheme is indicative of a wider range of environmental management systems standards, this analysis also has broader relevance. Finally, in parallel with the discussion presented in Chapter 3, the discussion establishes a range of variables which can be used to examine the design and implementation of voluntary regulation in the form of environmental management system standards. Again it is proposed that for the purposes of analysis the numerous dimensions of design and implementation can usefully be simplified to consider the frameworks, structures and styles of voluntary regulation. As with those presented in the previous chapter, these variables are used to guide the analysis of environmental policy as practice that follows in subsequent chapters.

DEFINING VOLUNTARY REGULATION

As discussed in the previous chapter, Jacobs (1991, p 134) defines voluntary action as 'all those actions unforced by law and unpersuaded by financial incentives, which individuals, groups and firms take to protect the environment.' Thus, the defining features of voluntary action are that it is unforced by law and unpersuaded by financial incentives. While it is important to acknowledge that any definition is likely to be found wanting in some respect, these features require further examination.

By its very nature voluntary regulation must be unforced by law. However, this does not necessarily mean that government has no influence over the design, implementation and impact of voluntary regulation. Government and its agencies can facilitate and encourage the use of voluntary regulation in a variety of ways. Government can catalyze voluntary action by establishing frameworks or institutions to develop and administer voluntary initiatives or to verify their quality and integrity. It may encourage companies to take voluntary action by providing various forms of business support or by requesting evidence of voluntary action in their purchasing or contracting criteria. It can provide the impetus for voluntary action by negotiating targets for environmental improvement with industrial groups. Government can also establish a legal context that encourages, but does not require, voluntary action. For example, it may threaten to bring forward legislation unless voluntary action is taken. Similarly, if regulators perceive voluntary action to be effective, they might subject companies that are taking such action to less intensive scrutiny than those that are not. Therefore, although voluntary regulation is unforced by law, it can be encouraged by government in a variety of other ways. At the extreme this encouragement could evolve into a *de facto* requirement for voluntary action.

The extent to which voluntary action is unpersuaded by financial incentives is unclear. As discussed above, government may encourage voluntary action by providing various forms of business support or by requesting evidence of voluntary action in their purchasing or contracting criteria. Government may encourage voluntary action by reforming the fiscal system to present various incentives and disincentives for environmental improvement. The framework of mandatory regulation can be used to encourage companies to apply voluntary initiatives to minimise the costs of compliance and the risk of fines for non-compliance. A framework of civil law can encourage voluntary action to minimise exposure to various financial liabilities. Measures that raise awareness and ensure freedom of access to information and the courts can allow different stakeholders to put pressure on companies to improve their environmental performance and thereby encourage voluntary action to protect market share or to maintain public relations. As a result it is not at all clear that voluntary action is undertaken unpersuaded by financial incentives.

Thus it can be seen that the only distinguishing feature of voluntary action is that it is unforced by law. However, while by its nature voluntary action cannot be secured by legal imperative, it may come about in response to the threat of legal action, it may be linked with the demands of mandatory regulation and it may be persuaded by financial incentives and other inducements.

The nature of voluntary regulation can be further clarified by briefly considering a practical example, the Confederation of British Industry's (CBI) Agenda for Voluntary Action. This essentially represents a code of environmental practice which is very similar to the Chemical Industry Association's Responsible Care Programme (Chemical Industry Association, 1992), although it is applicable to all industries. The CBI represents the interests of industry and business in the UK and, according to Cridland (1994, p 234), one dimension of this is that it wishes:

> '...to promote voluntary efforts by business to enhance environmental performance and to ensure that the policy and regulatory framework within which business operates is consistent with the need to gain competitive advantage.'

In line with this the CBI (1994) has proposed that the government should define broad environmental goals and priorities and set minimum standards, but, where possible, should leave industry to achieve these objectives in the most efficient way. According to the CBI (1994) voluntary action '... should always be the first recourse of government when seeking environmental improvement' because in this way the likelihood of securing competitive advantage from environmental action is maximized.

However, the CBI accepts that the success of voluntary regulation depends upon a change in the way that industry perceives and addresses environmental issues. The CBI's Agenda for Voluntary Action is an attempt to promote such a change. The main components of the Agenda are presented in Box 4.1. The Agenda is based on the practices of firms that the CBI claims have successfully dealt with environmental issues. The characteristics of these companies and the structures and approaches that they have developed and applied have been distilled to form five points of action. In all cases the goal is to maximize the potential for securing economic advantage from environmental improvement.

Therefore the CBI's Agenda for Voluntary Action can be seen as an attempt by industry to take the initiative on environmental issues. It proposes that

---

BOX 4.1 THE CBI'S AGENDA FOR VOLUNTARY ACTION

Gaining the Advantage from the Environment, Health and Safety: Agenda for Voluntary Action

- *Designating a Board-level director with responsibility for the environment and safety.*
  Businesses which most successfully integrate environment and safety performance into corporate decision-making have visible leadership and commitment from the top.
- *Publishing a corporate environment and safety policy statement.*
  Business policy statements help to provide the stability necessary to take a longer term view of environment and safety performance.
- *Setting clear targets, measuring current performance and implementing improvement plans.*
  Establishing improvement programmes and setting clear targets can drive a company toward its own goals and help maintain competitive advantage.
- *Communicating company policy to employees and reporting publicly on progress in achieving the objectives.*
  Employee involvement is part of continuous improvement in all aspects of management. Public reporting completes a programme by bringing the results back into the public domain, reinforcing earlier objectives.
- *Establishing partnerships to better manage safety and the environment, particularly with smaller companies.*
  The total environmental impact of business can be reduced by applying pressure to raise performance along the supply chain.

Source: Confederation of British Industry (1994).

---

mandatory regulation should establish a baseline for environmental performance but that, where appropriate and possible, companies should attempt to go beyond this baseline. Clearly such an agenda has the potential to impact on almost all dimensions of industrial activity. However, given that there is no form of external verification associated with the Agenda, there is also the potential for it to be no more than a rhetorical device which has no discernible impact on reality. Before moving on to consider the nature of voluntary regulation in practice, the discussion will first assess the various arguments that can be put forward to support or reject calls for voluntary regulation.

THE CASE FOR VOLUNTARY REGULATION

Jenkins (1995) outlines a number of arguments that may be used to support calls for a move away from mandatory regulation and toward voluntary regulation. Broadly, these arguments suggest that voluntary regulation may be both more efficient and more effective than mandatory regulation in a number of respects.

In relation to efficiency it is suggested that voluntary regulation might impose lower costs on both government and industry than mandatory regulation. From the government perspective, voluntary action may allow a reduction in the public expenditure that is associated with environmental protection or a diversion of that expenditure toward more productive uses. Primarily this may be the case if a shift from mandatory to voluntary regulation reduces the need for an expensive regulatory agency. However, if the agency implementing mandatory regulation is obliged to recover its costs from the companies that it regulates, the cost savings that might follow a shift from mandatory to voluntary regulation may in effect be passed on to industry. Efficiency gains may also be realized if voluntary regulation allows industry to search for, develop and apply environmental initiatives in a more flexible way. A lack of flexibility in mandatory regulation can result in environmental problems being dealt with in an effective but costly way. The increased flexibility that voluntary action might allow may save money by allowing industry to adopt the least cost responses to environmental problems.

In relation to effectiveness it is suggested that voluntary regulation might secure higher or accelerated levels of environmental improvement than those which typically arise from mandatory regulation. Aside from its flexibility, voluntary regulation may be better able to foster commitment to environmental improvement than mandatory regulation precisely because it is voluntary. The benefits of this commitment are particularly apparent when compared to the defensive position that some companies adopt when faced with the demands of mandatory regulation. In such instances companies may spend time and money resisting or trying to avoid the demands of mandatory regulation rather than improving their environmental performance. Finally, voluntary action can often be enacted over a shorter time frame than mandatory regulation as it does not have to go through the same governmental and legislative procedures. Consequently it is possible to speculate that voluntary regulation may secure higher levels of environmental improvement than mandatory regulation and in a shorter time frame.

However, drawing on an analysis of voluntary regulation in practice, Jenkins (1995) argues that practical experience with the application of voluntary regulation commonly contradicts the arguments put forward above. Far from encouraging innovation and accelerated environmental improvement, Jenkins (1995) suggests that a switch to voluntary regulation alone removes what is commonly a major impetus for innovation, namely the imperative to comply with the demands of mandatory regulation. In essence, in the absence of mandatory regulation companies are free to assign a higher priority to the economic pressures of the short term than to the environmental opportunities of the medium to long term.

More broadly, a shift from mandatory to voluntary regulation can mean that government hands over responsibility for significant areas of public policy to the private sector. This generates concern about the credibility of voluntary regulation and the accountability of voluntary regulators. For example, there is a suspicion that because of their voluntary and sometimes commercial nature, the verification structures that are developed to assure the quality and demonstrate the integrity of voluntary regulation may be more susceptible to regulatory capture than those that seek to ensure compliance with mandatory regulation. Finally, the costs that are saved through a reduction in the administration of mandatory regulation may be offset by an increase in the costs that follow a rise in voluntary regulation. Aside from the distributional issues, in aggregate the cost savings associated with a shift from mandatory to voluntary regulation depend upon the relative efficiencies of each.

It is clear from the discussion above that in principle a range of different agendas favour the wider application of voluntary regulation. The critical issue then is whether voluntary regulation can replace mandatory regulation or whether it can merely supplement it. In some instances voluntary action is clearly motivated by the threat of mandatory regulation. In other instances voluntary initiatives are taken either to ensure compliance with the requirements of mandatory regulation or to respond to the financial incentives and disincentives that are established by mandatory regulation. Given the central role that mandatory regulation plays in stimulating the development and application of voluntary regulation it is likely that voluntary regulation will have a greater influence on industrial behaviour where it is applied as a complement to mandatory regulation rather than as a replacement for it.

THE CASE OF THE EU'S ECO-MANAGEMENT AND AUDIT SCHEME

Having considered the general issues associated with voluntary regulation in some detail, this section will assess the nature of the EU's Eco-Management and Audit Scheme (EMAS) as an example of voluntary regulation. EMAS is also an example of a broader category of environmental management systems (EMS) standards. Although there are differences between EMAS and other EMS standards, the similarities are sufficient to allow them to be considered under the same heading. The following discussion briefly considers the history behind the development of EMS standards in general before assessing the nature of EMAS in particular. The analysis draws on the findings of interviews with representatives of DGXI (Environment) of the European Commission, the body that coordinated the development of EMAS and that is ultimately responsible for its administration.

The development of the various EMS standards can be viewed as the result of two relatively recent trends, namely the success of various quality management systems (QMS) standards in the 1980s and the general rise in environmental awareness in the late 1980s and early 1990s. Although lagging behind quality management by at least a decade, the development of systems based approaches to environmental management has undoubtedly benefited from the experience that has accumulated with QMS standards in industry. Following the success of these QMS standards, and reacting in some way to an upsurge in public concern about the environment, industry began to request the development of an EMS standard toward the end of the 1980s.

In the UK, the British Standards Institute developed the first EMS standard (BS7750) which after an earlier pilot scheme was finally launched in 1994. In order to allow the introduction of a common international EMS standard, the British standard was subsequently withdrawn and replaced in 1997 by the International Standards Organization's (ISO) EMS standard (ISO14001). At the EU level a separate EMS based initiative was developed and launched in 1993 as the EMAS Regulation. Together, EMAS and ISO14001 represent the most important EMS standards currently available. Both EMAS and ISO14001 provide an opportunity for industry to establish an EMS which can be certified or verified against the requirements of an external standard by an independent agency. The following discussion will examine the broader nature of EMS standards by focusing on EMAS.

The EMAS Regulation 'allowing voluntary participation by companies in the industrial sector in a Community eco-management and audit scheme' was developed by the European Committee for Standardization (CEN) and became operational in 1995. EMAS is generally regarded as the most demanding EMS standard. The objective of EMAS is to promote 'continuous improvement in environmental performance' on a site-specific basis. For registered sites this is to be achieved by ensuring that these sites:

- Adopt a company environmental policy;
- conduct an environmental review;
- introduce an environmental programme and an environmental management system;
- carry out an environmental audit;
- prepare an environmental statement to be released to the public.

EMAS establishes the principles upon which each of these stages must be based. Theoretically the environmental programme must be based on the adoption of objectives and targets which address a range of the site's environmental impacts, including some of its most significant ones. Once developed, an accredited environmental verifier must check that the approach taken by the site complies with the requirements of the scheme. Once compliance has been assured, a site is able to register its participation in the scheme.

EMAS was established as an EU Regulation and thus does not require enabling legislation at the national level. Instead it demanded that member states establish structures to promote and administer the scheme by early 1995. Thus, member states were obliged to designate a competent body to administer the scheme and to establish a body and a system to accredit independent environmental verifiers who essentially act as regulators by checking the compliance of those sites that choose to register under the scheme. Within each member state, the primary role of the competent body is to hold and maintain a register of registered sites. The competent body may be a government department or agency or an independent organization. The accreditation body is charged with the task of accrediting individuals or organizations as environmental verifiers, indicating that they have the necessary skills and capacities to assess a site against the requirements of EMAS. The accreditation body must supervise the performance of verifiers over time to ensure their continuing compliance with the accreditation criteria. Finally, the role of the verifier is to assess the performance of companies wishing to register under the scheme and therefore to ensure that they comply with the requirements of EMAS. This includes the validation of the environmental statement. If this is completed successfully the site can be registered with the competent body.

Beyond the basic requirements of EMAS outlined above, the nature and purpose of the scheme can be further clarified by drawing on the results of interviews with representatives of DGXI (Environment) of the European Commission. One representative clearly described the aim of EMAS as follows:

> *The objective of the scheme is to bring about continual improvement in the environmental performance of organizations. However, the scheme doesn't have a lot of prescription in it. It gives you an indication of what you should do and provides a structure, it doesn't really tell you what you should do. For example, you could implement it in a simple and elegant way or a bureaucratic and enormous way. It's about dragging some people who would not have gone quite so far, and, for pro-active organizations, it is a differentiating instrument. For that reason it must be voluntary. How can you demonstrate yourself to be environmentally excellent if everybody has to do it?*

Although according to the comment above EMAS must remain a voluntary instrument, it is acknowledged that a link between mandatory regulation and voluntary regulation must exist:

> *EMAS in principle has no effect on command and control policy [mandatory regulation]. For example, command and control could never rely on EMAS because it is voluntary. It does establish a baseline for an EMAS site though and EMAS drives people beyond basic command and control requirements.*

However, although in principle EMAS is distinct from mandatory regulation, it is anticipated that it may interact with it in a variety of ways. The same commentator raised the following point:

> *An interesting thing will be how mandatory regulation responds to EMAS and the way regulators at the member state level actually formulate their policy in the light of EMAS.*

Thus it can be seen that although EMAS is a voluntary scheme, those sites that wish to register for the scheme choose to subject themselves to a considerable degree of external scrutiny from an independent organization. Despite its voluntary nature, EMAS can demand a considerable input from government if it assumes responsibility for establishing and running the institutional structures that are required to administer the scheme. Government can also influence the way that mandatory regulations interact with voluntary schemes such as EMAS. However, despite the involvement and influence of government, EMAS registration is at this point voluntary for all companies.

THE STRENGTHS AND WEAKNESSES OF ENVIRONMENTAL MANAGEMENT SYSTEMS STANDARDS

Having outlined the nature of EMAS as an example of an EMS standard, and more broadly as an example of voluntary regulation, in the following section the strengths and weaknesses of this form of regulation will be discussed (see Welford and Gouldson, 1993; Barnes, 1994; Ball and Bell, 1995; CBI, 1995; DoE, 1995; Webber, 1994; Lovelock, 1993; Stern, 1994; Institute of Environmental Management, 1995; Simmons and Wynne, 1993). The potential strengths that can be associated with the application of an EMS can be outlined as follows:

*   *They can provide a framework for a comprehensive approach to the environment:* A management system can help to reduce the uncertainty and complexity associated with the environment as a business issue. In particular it may increase the amount of meaningful data available to managers, thus helping to improve the level of control that they are able to exert over the environmental performance of their business.
*   *They create the potential for improved economic performance:* A systematic and periodic assessment of the environmental problems of a business may reveal opportunities for a range of waste minimization and energy efficiency gains which previously had not been recognized or exploited.

Where action is taken to exploit these opportunities, economic competitiveness may be enhanced.

- *They can improve public image and reputation:* A well designed management system can aid effective communication by helping to relay information to and from stakeholders both inside and outside the firm. The presence of a management system can also improve a company's image by helping to communicate commitment and responsibility.
- *They can change the relationship between regulators and business:* Management systems can help to ensure compliance with the demands of mandatory regulation. They may also help to improve the relationship between the business and the mandatory regulator, particularly by developing trust and by creating conditions that are conducive to compliance and continual improvement.
- *They can establish a new learning network:* An externally verified management system can help to develop links between the business and other organizations with related experience and expertise. Whilst interacting in this network the opportunity is presented for a company to learn about alternative approaches to environmental management.

Thus, an EMS can offer a number of benefits. These include direct cost savings, enhanced management control and improved relationships with regulators and stakeholders. However, it is important to note that the benefits outlined above do not necessarily follow the application of an EMS as the performance of management systems can vary considerably. It is also apparent that there are a number of potential weaknesses associated with the development and application of an EMS:

- *They do not guarantee any level of environmental performance:* The presence of a management system does not in itself demonstrate any particular standard of environmental performance although registration with an EMS standard normally demands a minimum level of compliance with mandatory regulation. Furthermore, although EMS standards commonly require continuous improvement, the speed of improvement required to retain registration is not specified. Thus, they may lend legitimacy and credibility to environmentally damaging companies that are only improving slowly.
- *They may be costly to develop and apply:* Particularly during their development but also throughout their application, management systems can draw on the managerial capacity and financial capital of a firm. These costs and the associated opportunity costs may not be recouped, particularly in the short term.
- *They may increase the risks associated with legislative non-compliance:* Although management systems can help companies to minimize the risk of non-compliance, the information that a management system collects and presents may enable prosecution or litigation if it is disclosed or discovered. This may also increase the consequences of non-compliance by making it easier to allocate blame and by allowing charges to be pursued

on the basis of negligence rather than ignorance.

- *They may encourage short termism:* In cases where companies communicate their performance and publish targets for environmental improvement they can be held to account more readily by various stakeholders. If these stakeholders demand improvement in the short term, attention and resources may be diverted from longer term opportunities with the potential to realize more significant benefits.
- *They may increase the likelihood that the means are confused with the ends:* Companies may channel their resources toward the development of a management system or registration with an EMS standard. As management systems in themselves do not secure environmental improvement this may reduce or delay the benefits which they are designed to realize.
- *They may engender complacency:* Once a company has installed an EMS, or is registered with an EMS standard, its interest in further initiatives may decline. In such instances the EMS may be passively relied upon to deliver environmental improvement rather than being used as an active mechanism for environmental improvement. Similarly, the management system may limit the emphasis of environmental management initiatives to operational rather than strategic change.

It is clear then that, as with any form of regulation, voluntary regulation in general and EMS standards in particular have a range of potential strengths and weaknesses. Other than in limited instances, the economic and environmental performance of voluntary regulation has yet to be generally established. However, in the case of EMS standards practical experience associated with the application of voluntary regulation is accumulating rapidly. It is clear from this experience that there are potential benefits associated with the application of this form of regulation. Despite this experience it is as yet unclear whether the external verification structures that have been designed to administer and ensure the integrity of EMS standards are sufficiently developed to ensure that the potential weaknesses of voluntary regulation are avoided.

THE DESIGN AND IMPLEMENTATION OF VOLUNTARY ENVIRONMENTAL REGULATION: ANALYTICAL VARIABLES FOR THE CASE OF EMAS

This chapter has reviewed the nature of voluntary environmental regulation both in theory and in practice with reference to EMS standards such as EMAS. In each instance it has suggested that a range of design and implementation variables play a fundamental role in defining the character, and therefore the impact, of voluntary environmental regulation. The following discussion will analyse these variables further with reference to three dimensions of voluntary regulation, namely the frameworks, structures and styles of regulation. The different dimensions and the variables that characterize them are summarized in Table 4.1.

Table 4.1 *The Design and Implementation of Voluntary Environmental Regulation: Analytical Variables for the Case of EMAS*

REGULATORY FRAMEWORK

Issue	Framework	Feature	Example
Policy Frameworks	Active	Strong foundation	Establishes a clear role for voluntary action within the wider policy framework
	Passive	Weak foundation	Does not establish a clear role for voluntary action within the wider policy framework

IMPLEMENTATION STRUCTURES

Issue	Framework	Feature	Example
Legal Structures	Formal	Explicit recognition	Voluntary regulation is given a clear legal basis
	Informal	Implicit recognition	Voluntary regulation is not given a clear legal basis
Institutional Structures	Mechanistic	Explicit requirements	The requirements of the standard are clearly communicated and quality control is assured
	Organic	Implicit requirements	The requirements of the standard are unclear and quality control is not assured
Resource Structures	Adequate	Appropriate capacities	Verifier has access to staff with appropriate expertise and adequate facilities
	Inadequate	Inappropriate capacities	Verifier does not have access to staff with appropriate expertise or adequate facilities

IMPLEMENTATION STYLES

Issue	Framework	Feature	Example
Design Styles	Impacts	Focus on environment	Emphasis placed on realizing 'continuous improvement' as environmental gains
	Systems	Focus on management	Emphasis placed on realizing 'continuous improvement' as systems gains
Delivery Styles	Hands-on	Intensive relationship	The relationship is likely to be open and informal with regular external audits
	Arms-length	Extensive relationship	The relationship is likely to be bureaucratic and formal with relatively infrequent audits
Enforcement Styles	Conciliative	Consensual relationship	Removal/suspension of registration as last option
	Litigious	Adversarial relationship	Removal/suspension of registration occurs immediately

The Regulatory Framework

Policy Frameworks

Voluntary regulations are developed and applied within a broader policy context. The extent to which this policy context favours or supports voluntary action is likely to be a significant influence on the character and performance of any framework of voluntary regulation. Voluntary regulation is likely to be favoured by some policy frameworks more than others. As stated above, government can provide a strong basis for voluntary action by establishing frameworks for voluntary regulation, by negotiating targets for environmental improvement, by providing various forms of business support, by threatening to bring forward legislation unless voluntary action is taken or by acknowledging the role of voluntary standards in the implementation of mandatory regulation. Similarly, it may present various incentives and disincentives for voluntary action either directly through fiscal policy or indirectly through mandatory regulation. Thus, the performance of voluntary regulation depends to some degree on the role that government assigns to voluntary action and the steps that government takes to promote it. Consequently, it is possible to distinguish between those frameworks that actively support voluntary action and those that do not.

Implementation Structures

Any framework of voluntary regulation will have a series of implementation structures associated with it. In a dynamic setting these structures can be changed, but at any point in time they are reasonably stable.

Legal Structures

The legal structures that influence the design, implementation and impact of voluntary regulation are established indirectly by the nature of any interaction that takes places between voluntary regulation and mandatory regulation. Governments can ensure that voluntary regulations are formally recognized by acknowledging a role for them in the design of mandatory regulation. For example, government can adopt voluntary targets for environmental improvement as the basis for mandatory regulation. Regulators can also assign a role to voluntary regulation during both implementation and enforcement. For example, regulators can subject companies that are registered with an EMS standard to less intensive scrutiny than those that are not. Consequently it is possible to contrast legal structures that formally establish a role for voluntary regulation and links between mandatory and voluntary regulation and those that do not.

Institutional Structures

The character and performance of voluntary regulation is determined to a large degree by the institutional structures that are associated with its administration. In the case of EMS standards such as EMAS, institutional responsibilities are divided between the competent body, the accreditation body and the accredited environmental verifiers. Together these organizations oversee registration, accreditation, verification and validation. Broadly, institutional structures can either be mechanistic or organic. Mechanistic structures hand down specific guidance and explicit requirements from one tier of administration to another. In such instances the activities of the implementation process will be formalised to ensure that organizations and individuals who are charged with delivering the standard interpret and apply its requirements in a consistent and rigorous way. Alternatively, institutional structures can be organic where no specific or binding guidance is issued from above and the requirements of the standard are interpreted on a case-by-case basis so that the implementation phase is characterized by flexibility and the exercize of discretion.

Resource Structures
The resource structures associated with the implementation of voluntary regulation can vary considerably. In the case of EMS standards such as EMAS, accredited verifiers are contracted by a company or a site seeking registration to establish whether or not it complies with the requirements of the standard. At this point the capacities and resources of the verifier influence the practical nature of the scheme. Where the resources that are assigned to verification are adequate, an appropriately qualified and suitably resourced team or individual will assess compliance in a rigorous way. However, when the resources that are assigned to verification are inadequate, the team or individual seeking to assess compliance will lack the necessary qualifications and experience or may not have access to the appropriate facilities needed to assure compliance in a rigorous way.

Implementation Styles

The ultimate character of voluntary regulation is also influenced by a range of more ambiguous and indeterminate implementation styles. These implementation styles are likely to be just as influential as the structures discussed above although to a large extent they are established in an ad-hoc way during the process of interaction between the verifier and the company or site seeking registration.

Design Styles
Any system of voluntary regulation is influenced by the principles and standards that are designed into it during formulation. While EMS standards such as EMAS do not demand any particular level of environmental performance other than compliance with mandatory regulation, they do stipulate that registered companies or sites should demonstrate 'continuous improvement'. However, this central principle can be interpreted or emphasised in two ways. Firstly, emphasis can be placed on the performance of the management system itself. Secondly, emphasis can be placed on the environmental performance that the EMS is designed to improve. Consequently, EMS standards can focus either on management systems or on environmental impacts.

Delivery Styles

As with mandatory regulation, the delivery style associated with voluntary regulation relates to the nature of the day-to-day relationship between the regulator or verifier and the company or site seeking registration. However, in the case of voluntary regulation the regulator or verifier lacks the legal authority that defines this relationship in cases of mandatory regulation. Despite this lack of legal authority, the verifier or regulator may still be able to choose whether to adopt a hands-on or an arms-length approach, with the former being more intensive than the latter. The style of delivery adopted by the regulator or verifier can be determined to some extent by the degree of discretion that they are afforded and the scope for expert judgement that is built into voluntary regulation at the design stage. In the case of voluntary EMS standards such as EMAS, the delivery style can also be influenced by the commercial nature of the relationship between the regulator or verifier and the company or site seeking registration.

Enforcement Styles

Finally, the implementation style is defined by the approach taken to enforcement by the various organizations and individuals that administer and apply the framework of voluntary regulation. These actors may choose to treat breaches of compliance in a conciliative or in an adversarial way. For EMS standards such as EMAS, a conciliative style is characterized by a reluctance to suspend a company's registration in cases of non-compliance with the requirements of the standard. Conversely, an adversarial approach is characterized by a willingness to suspend registration as soon as a breach of compliance is identified.

As discussed in the previous chapter, it is important to acknowledge that the list of variables presented in Table 4.1 and in the associated discussion is not exhaustive, that the boundaries between the variables are not necessarily distinct and that such a list could not be established and cannot be measured on purely objective grounds. Nonetheless, the categories and variables presented above serve to simplify an otherwise complex area of debate and thereby provide some clear guidance for the subsequent analysis.

CONCLUSIONS

It is increasingly acknowledged that governments have traditionally relied on a restricted number of policy instruments in their attempts to influence the relationship between economic development and environmental protection. More recently, however, governments have begun to explore the ability of alternative policy instruments to mobilise the problem solving capacities of industry for environmental ends. While various approaches to regulation demonstrate some potential in this respect, as Jänicke and Weidner (1995, p 18) have noted, it is apparent that 'there is no single ideal instrument or type of instrument, we need the full orchestra.'

The review of voluntary regulation provided above has suggested that it has the potential to influence the relationship between economic development and environmental protection. However, it has also been argued that voluntary action is commonly motivated by the direct and indirect impacts of mandatory regulation. Consequently, it is likely that voluntary regulation will have a greater influence on industrial behaviour where it is applied as a complement to mandatory regulation rather than as a replacement for it.

In addition to the nature of its interaction with mandatory regulation, the performance of voluntary regulation depends upon the manner of its application. In parallel with the analysis of mandatory regulation presented in the previous chapter, this chapter has suggested that the performance of voluntary regulations such as EMAS can be analysed with reference to the frameworks, structures and styles that characterize their implementation. These variables will be examined in more detail in the empirical chapters that follow so that the analysis of implementation can be linked to an examination of the impact that voluntary regulation has on industrial behaviour.

Chapter 5

THE IMPLEMENTATION AND IMPACT OF INDUSTRIAL ENVIRONMENTAL REGULATION IN THE UK

INTRODUCTION

In previous chapters it has been argued that the implementation process can be examined through an analysis of the frameworks, structures and styles of regulation. It has also been argued that the impact of regulation can be assessed through an analysis of the influence that regulation has on the technological, organizational and strategic behaviour of the firm. This chapter draws on the categories and variables established in the preceding discussion to analyse the implementation and impact of mandatory and voluntary environmental regulation in the UK. The discussion presents the results of fieldwork conducted in the UK during 1995 and 1996. This work consisted largely of semi-structured interviews with policy-makers, regulators and representatives of industrial installations associated with the mandatory and voluntary regulations in question.

The discussion that follows is broadly divided into three sections. Firstly, the nature of the UK Government's approach to environmental policy at the national level is outlined to establish the nature of the policy framework within which the other more specific instruments operate. Secondly, the implementation and impact of mandatory environmental regulation is examined with particular reference to the Integrated Pollution Control (IPC) regulations introduced in England and Wales as part of the 1990 Environmental Protection Act. This legislation is examined as currently representing a close approximation to the EU's Integrated Pollution Prevention and Control (IPPC) directive. Thirdly, the implementation and impact of voluntary environmental regulation is assessed with particular reference to the European Union's Eco-Management and Audit Scheme (EMAS) regulation and the International Standards Organization's environmental management systems standard (ISO14001).

THE UK CONTEXT FOR ENVIRONMENTAL POLICY

As one of the first countries to experience the industrial revolution, the UK has witnessed the negative impacts of industrial activity for over 200 years. As a result it has one of the longest histories of regulatory action to protect the environment. The overall approach which has now established itself in the UK has a number of important features which characterize the policy context within which the various forms of industrial environmental regulation are developed and applied.

In recent decades the UK has gained a reputation for being an environmental laggard in Europe (Weale, 1992). However, as with all countries, there are complex issues underlying the UK's approach to environmental protection. In the field of industrial environmental policy and regulation an intricate mix of ideology, tradition and experience has established particular cultures and norms that influence the approaches and methods that are selected and applied. A review of a number of existing studies of environmental policy and regulation in the UK clearly shows this to be the case (see particularly Vogel, 1986; Boehmer-Christiansen and Skea, 1993; Weale, 1992; Hajer, 1995; Wintle and Reeve, 1994; Boehmer-Christiansen and Weidner, 1995). The importance of this policy context can be ascertained by considering three established dimensions of the UK's approach to environmental policy and regulation.

Firstly, concerning the role of science in the policy process, it is established that action to protect the environment in the UK has often been taken only on the basis of a sound scientific understanding of the issues involved. An example of a UK representative adopting this position was provided by William Waldegrave whilst commenting as Environment Minister on a draft of the EC's *Fourth Environmental Action Programme*:

> *I have been struck by how often we have been dealing with subjects not really on the basis of an objective assessment of environmental priorities... It is necessary in an area which should be science-based to put up pretty formidable hurdles and tests of a scientific nature if we are to make rational priorities ...*

Weale (1992, p 80).

Weale's (1992, p 81) interpretation of this comment is that:

> *Mr Waldegrave was only expressing an established feature of the British approach to environmental policy, namely that a scientific understanding of cause-and-effect relationships in natural systems is a necessary condition for adequate and rational policy-making.*

One outcome of this is that scientific uncertainty, whether real or perceived, has often been enough in itself to stall the environmental policy process in the UK (see Hajer, 1995). A further consequence is that precautionary action, implying action without scientific certainty, has been discouraged and is rarely pursued.

71

Secondly, the UK's approach to policy and regulation has commonly been determined by an established view of the most desirable policy style. Generally there has been a preference for settlements to be negotiated informally between experts at the local level. As a result, rigid frameworks, for example making wide use of quantitative targets and statutory standards, have been avoided where possible. Thus, according to Weale (1992, p 81):

> *By tradition British policy... is conceived as a series of problems, constituting cases that have to be judged on their merits. General norms are to be avoided if the decision can be left to the exercise of continuous administrative discretion.*

While the application of such discretion may in some instances have allowed regulators to fine-tune regulations to reflect the specific circumstances that are apparent in each regulated company (see Richardson et al, 1982), it has also been associated with a certain degree of administrative secrecy and with suspicions of regulatory capture (see Jordan, 1993; Boehmer-Christiansen and Weidner, 1995; Fineman, 1997; Smith, 1997).

Thirdly, environmental policy-making in the UK in recent years has been influenced by free market doctrine. The commitment to free market thinking began with the Conservative victory in the election of 1979. Its impact on environmental policy has been described by Boehmer-Christiansen and Weidner (1995, p 117) as follows:

> *... spending on the environment should be kept as low as possible and environmental regulation was, in principle, undesirable as it meant interference by the state with market forces. In practice this meant that senior politicians made environmental decisions in the hope that firms would regulate themselves.*

In essence the UK Government of the 1980s and early 1990s put its faith in the role of the market and consequently sought to minimize the level of government intervention. In terms of the relationship between economic development and environmental protection, this ideological stance has favoured voluntary rather than mandatory regulation. One explanation for this emphasis on voluntary regulation has been provided by Weale (1992, p 88), who, after reviewing UK environmental policy through the 1980s, makes the point that:

> *British debates never escaped the belief that there was an inevitable tension between environmental protection and economic development.*

This brief review of some of the features that have characterized the UK's approach to environmental policy is not exhaustive. However, the wider policy context that has been outlined above has had a significant influence on the UK's approach to industrial environmental regulation in recent decades. There has been a general reluctance on the part of government to interfere in the operations of private industry for the benefit of the environment because of the presumption that regulation has a negative impact on competitiveness. If scientific proof establishes the need for intervention, then government has preferred voluntary action to mandatory regulation. Where mandatory regulation is adopted it is applied within a flexible framework which allows the negotiation of solutions between experts at the local level. In the following section, clear evidence of the influence of these ideas will be found in the two most important environmental policy documents to emerge from the UK Government in the 1990s, namely *This Common Inheritance* (HMSO, 1990a,b); and *Sustainable Development: The UK Strategy* (HMSO, 1994).

THE UK ENVIRONMENTAL POLICY FRAMEWORK IN THE 1990s

In the autumn of 1989 Chris Patten, then the UK Environment Secretary, announced that the UK Government was to begin work on the first White Paper on the Environment. The document was developed at the highest level of government with Margaret Thatcher, then the Prime Minister, chairing the cabinet committee that oversaw its preparation. In September 1990 the Government published the result, *This Common Inheritance*, the most important statement by the Government on the environment at that time. The White Paper outlined the principles underlying the UK's approach to environmental issues. It also set out how the Government viewed its role domestically as well as at the European and world scales. It then focused specifically on the issue of the greenhouse effect, reflecting a concern that had recently gained international attention. Town and country planning, pollution control, environmental awareness and organizational/institutional issues were also explored. A brief review of the strengths and weaknesses of this document is informative, especially as it relates directly to the previous discussion on the national policy context.

Two particular strengths can be identified in *This Common Inheritance*. Firstly, the fact that the document was produced at all represented progress in environment policy. That its production involved the direct input of the Prime Minister underlines the importance of this. Secondly, and more practically, it took some significant steps towards greening the machinery of government as it proposed some important institutional and procedural changes. For example, the Government committed itself to an annual White Paper on the Environment to report on the progress made toward the commitments that were established in *This Common Inheritance*.

However, beyond these strengths, it has been suggested that the document has a number of weaknesses. For example, although it listed 350 measures that were already in place to protect the environment, it presented few new measures, activities or ideas for legislation and it did not make any commitment to an exploration of innovative policy mechanisms. Furthermore, there was an almost complete absence of target setting for waste streams and pollution (see McCormick, 1991; Young, 1993; ENDS, 1994).

Largely because of the weaknesses outlined above, *This Common Inheritance* was regarded by commentators such as Young (1993) and McCormick (1991) as a missed opportunity. However, it is important to see it as an example of the output that could be expected to follow the established approach to environmental policy in the UK set out above. A reluctance to set targets, an unwillingness to interfere in the free operation of the market and a disinterest in the potential of alternative policy mechanisms are established aspects of this approach.

An opportunity to respond to these criticisms came shortly after the publication of *This Common Inheritance* in 1990. In 1992 the then Prime Minister John Major made a commitment to publish a national plan to implement Agenda 21 and commitments made at the Earth Summit in Rio de Janeiro. The result was *Sustainable Development: The UK Strategy*, published in January 1994. Again commentators have identified some strengths in the document although these are counterbalanced by a number of weaknesses which bear a striking resemblance to those of *This Common Inheritance*.

Regarding the strengths of *Sustainable Development: The UK Strategy*, it has been acknowledged that simply the task of preparing the document must have involved intense discussion about sustainability issues, thus in itself contributing to the long process of greening the machinery of government. Also, new institutions were established which were external to the civil service to advise the Government on environmental issues. In some cases these institutions had access to government at the highest level and included a panel of 'five wise persons' and a UK Round Table on Sustainable Development (ENDS, 1994).

However, aside from these strengths, *Sustainable Development: The UK Strategy* has been criticised on a number of levels (ENDS, 1994; ENDS, 1995a; OECD, 1994). It is largely devoid of any specific proposals for new policies and with respect to industry the report appears to place its faith in a process of voluntary regulation without any significant level of government involvement (ENDS, 1994). Furthermore, and perhaps most importantly, the OECD (1994, p 117) has suggested that: 'The 1994 UK Strategy for Sustainable Development, like the 1990 White Paper on the Environment, reflects the United Kingdom's long-standing reluctance to set targets.'

In a subsequent year long review of the Strategy, a House of Lords Select Committee on Sustainable Development also highlighted the lack of clear targets and objectives as the document's most significant weakness, stating that:

> *Targets can give a clearer sense of direction; they can add to the pace of policy implementation and development; and they can make explicit those aspects of policy that might otherwise remain opaque.* ENDS (1995a, p 26).

There are a number of conclusions to be drawn from this brief review of environmental policy in the UK. Both *This Common Inheritance* and *Sustainable Development: The UK Strategy* reflect established approaches to environmental policy in the UK. The 1990s presented two clear opportunities for policy-makers to address environmental issues and in both cases the output reflected existing, deep seated, approaches to policy. These documents placed their faith in a voluntary greening of industry and focused on procedural changes internal to government. They contain few specific proposals, objectives or targets. As a result it can be argued that the broad context for environmental policy in the UK has provided little strategic vision or guidance particularly for regulators and industry. Consequently, in relation to the broader policy framework, they can be characterized as being largely descriptive documents which include many symbolic and rhetorical statements. However, it should be noted that recent initiatives have sought to address this shortfall by formulating strategic goals for regulation in specific areas such as air quality or waste management.

MANDATORY ENVIRONMENTAL REGULATION IN THE UK: THE CASE OF INTEGRATED POLLUTION CONTROL

In 1976 the UK's Royal Commission on Environmental Pollution criticised the fragmented nature of industrial environmental regulation in the UK. Their fifth report, *Air Pollution Control: An Integrated Approach* (1976), called for a unified inspectorate with a multi-media approach to industrial environmental regulation. Government action in response to calls for a system of integrated pollution control took a long time to materialize; however, important legislation was passed in 1990 and institutional reorganization occurred in the late 1980s and again in 1996. The implementation structures and styles associated with this reorganization are discussed below.

Implementation Structures

When the Royal Commission called for a system of integrated pollution control they suggested that it should focus on the best practicable environmental option (BPEO) for emissions. In other words the most appropriate media (air, water or land) for a given pollutant should determine its destination. After a long delay the Royal Commission's suggestion was adopted in Part 1 of the 1990 Environmental Protection Act, which introduced Integrated Pollution Control (IPC) to England and Wales with separate systems operating in Scotland and Northern Ireland. The main objective of IPC is to prevent, minimize and, as the last option, render harmless emissions of substances which are actually or potentially harmful (prescribed substances) from larger or more environmentally significant processes (prescribed processes). Essentially this should account for those processes which represent the greatest actual or potential threat to the environment or to health. The operators of these processes have had to apply for IPC authorizations at specific times from 1991, with the final round of authorizations being applied for at the start of 1996. It is illegal to operate without such an authorization which outlines various requirements for the operation of the process concerned and not the management of its emissions.

To achieve its goals, the framework of IPC relies on the application of a second principle, the best available techniques not entailing excessive cost (BATNEEC). In theory BPEO is the primary consideration of IPC and requires that the environmental implications of all the disposal options available for a prescribed substance are evaluated simultaneously. Following this, the disposal option which results in the least environmental damage, consistent with the prevailing regulations, should be identified and adopted as a priority to guide regulatory decision-making. According to the IPC regulations, BATNEEC should be applied once the BPEO assessment has been completed. BATNEEC requires the operator of an industrial plant covered by IPC regulations to apply the most effective technology or technique for achieving BPEO. This is the case unless it can be shown that the associated costs would be excessive compared to the environmental protection achieved.

Therefore IPC legislation in England and Wales has involved the amalgamation of the pre-existing legal structures that related to the different environmental media separately. These have been comprehensively restructured to produce legislation which considers all emissions simultaneously. At the heart of this legislation are two key principles, BPEO and BATNEEC. However, IPC legislation also requires that authorizations issued under this regime respect any statutory environmental quality standards that are currently in force in the UK. These currently apply in the areas of water and air quality and in practice this means that the IPC regime, whilst being based on the principles discussed above, is, to some extent at least, underpinned by statutory standards.

From its inception in 1990, responsibility for the implementation of IPC was delegated to Her Majesty's Inspectorate of Pollution (HMIP). HMIP was established in 1987 as a combination of a number of pre-existing central government pollution inspectorates, namely the Industrial Air Pollution Inspectorate, the Radiochemical Inspectorate and the Hazardous Waste Inspectorate. While this institutional history has certainly had implications for the delivery of IPC, the specific impact is difficult to assess as a result of the many conflicting signals that led to the creation of HMIP. For example, William Waldegrave, Environment Minister at the time that HMIP was created, favoured the creation of such an agency for two reasons. Firstly, he was in favour of a powerful, integrated environmental protection agency. Secondly, he was keen to retrieve the Industrial Air Pollution Inspectorate from the Health and Safety Executive, where it was considered to be a weak and secretive organization (Jordan, 1993). However, contrasting agendas also favoured the establishment of HMIP which had less to do with environmental protection and more to do with a desire to roll back the boundaries of the state and minimize government expenditure on regulation. For example, the then Prime Minister Margaret Thatcher saw the creation of HMIP as an opportunity to improve efficiency through a rationalization of the system of industrial environmental regulation (Owens, 1990). Thus, it is not clear whether HMIP was established in order to secure higher environmental standards or to minimize government expenditure on environmental regulation.

HMIP was responsible for implementing IPC regulations between 1990 and 1996 when it became part of the Environment Agency in a move toward further integration of regulatory structures. This new agency was a combination of HMIP, the Waste Regulation Authorities and the National Rivers Authority. Within this structure the prior activities of HMIP essentially became represented by an Integrated Pollution Prevention and Control division of the Environment Agency, named in anticipation of the EU Directive on IPPC. As with the creation of HMIP, the formation of the Environment Agency was driven by desires both for effective environmental regulation and for the financial savings that such a rationalization affords.

This outline of the institutional structures associated with the implementation of IPC shows that not only has legislation been reorganized but so have the institutions that deliver it. At least on paper there has been a move away from the traditionally fragmented nature of environmental institutions toward integrated institutional structures. In reality the Environment Agency is likely to require a number of years to achieve integration in practice, but the achievement represented by the comprehensive reorganization of these institutional structures should not be underestimated if the benefits associated with systems of integrated pollution control are accepted.

By looking at the resource structures associated with HMIP and the delivery of IPC through the 1990 to 1996 period, there is some evidence to suggest that the rationalization theme identified above has impacted negatively on the effectiveness of the integration of institutional and legal structures. In a submission to the then Environment Secretary John Gummer in 1995, HMIP asserted that it had only been able to make 60 per cent of the checks on regulated processes that it should have made in the preceding year. Relating this situation to its supposed preventative role, HMIP linked this lack of checks to a doubling of pollution incidents over this period (Ghazzi and Grant, 1995). At a similar time HMIP asked its Advisory Committee, established in mid-1994, to review its efficiency and effectiveness, to support a request for an increase of one-third in its staff resources, to enable it to carry out what it regarded as the necessary level of regulatory effort. For a variety of reasons, not necessarily linked to a rejection of HMIP's arguments, the committee refused to do this (ENDS, 1996b). The following quote from a HMIP Inspector is representative of the wider view within the agency:

> *We are understaffed, the resources aren't available... I think everyone pulls together to try and achieve a standard of professionalism but the staffing is not adequate.*

Beyond simply reducing the number of site visits, interviews with HMIP Inspectors before they became part of the Environment Agency would suggest that this shortage of resources has affected the regulatory function in a variety of ways. In many instances a lack of time and resources makes meaningful coordination with interested parties, other than statutory consultees, difficult if not impossible. Even in the case of statutory consultees only minimal coordination is possible. In such instances it becomes easier for regulated companies to try and play one regulator off against another, knowing that consultation between agencies is limited. Such shortages also have significant implications for the regulatory style adopted as discussed below.

The pressure on the resources allocated to the regulatory function is particularly acute given the nature of the staff that have been employed to implement

IPC. Typically, regulatory inspectors involved in the day-to-day delivery of IPC have ten years' or more prior experience working in the types of industries that they regulate. Recruiting inspectors with industrial experience of this nature comes at a price for the regulator and contributes to the widely held belief that IPC is expensive legislation to implement.

Aside from concerns related to the cost of implementation, the background of many inspectors has also led to the fear that, intentionally or otherwise, inspectors will be overly sympathetic to industry in the application of IPC. The inspectors within the regulatory agency and the managers that they interact with in regulated companies tend to be drawn from the same professional comunity. It is common for the regulatory inspectors to have worked in the industries that they regulate. In some instances regulatory inspectors have left to become environmental managers in regulated companies (Fineman, 1997). The common professional background and in some instances the shared aspirations of the individuals within the regulatory agency and within regulated companies has the potential to influence the implementation phase significantly. As an integral part of the implementation phase, regulators are commonly drawn into a process of negotiation with regulated companies to reach an agreement on the exact interpretation of the qualitative principles and therefore on the specific requirements of IPC (Smith, 1997). Because of the discretionary nature of the central elements of IPC, it is possible that the demands of the regulator will be made less stringent through this process of negotation. The flexibility associated with the exercize of discretion during the implementation phase may therefore lead to a dilution of the demands of regulation and to a reduction in the imperative that is presented to regulated companies to explore new options for improving their environmental performance. In the absence of a clear and comprehensive framework of standards and targets for environmental improvement and measures of environmental performance, the transparency and accountability of the regulatory function therefore assume a particular significance.

The costs of implementation and the potential for a dilution of the stated goals of IPC are of critical importance. However, the background and experience of the inspectors, allied with the delivery style outlined below, can also have a number of benefits. The expertise of inspectors allows them to bring not only formal knowledge to their interactions with regulated companies but also a tacit understanding of the processes that they are regulating and of the technologies and techniques that they are prescribing. As one inspector said:

> *I understand the processes I regulate. I can see how BATNEEC and BPEO apply in those situations because I've worked in the area for years, although not on this side of the fence. These terms are so flexible, it is down to us to apply them. We have to understand our areas in sufficient depth to do that.*

The impact of this experience and understanding is also highlighted in the following description of the role of an inspector as described by the environmental manager of a large industrial installation:

They are professional and meticulous. You have knowledgeable inspectors, techni-
cally very competent, who may not know the last thing about the specific
manufacture of (x) but who know enough to understand in general what they're
seeing, and to ask some very pertinent questions.

Because of their experience and understanding, inspectors are more able to
recognize and assess the causes and effects of an emissions stream, to identify
the possible responses to a problem and to understand the costs and benefits
of the various options. Thus, where there is appropriate expertise and understanding, the regulator is less dependent on the information supplied by
regulated companies when it is interpreting and applying the qualitative principles (BPEO, BATNEEC) that are at the heart of IPC. Furthermore, given their
industrial backgrounds, the inspectors tend to be accepted in industry and the
tendency for industrialists to adopt a defensive position when faced with an
environmentalist is reduced. The potential for proactive or innovative responses
to regulation is thereby enhanced.

Implementation Styles

At its core IPC is concerned with the implementation of two qualitative principles, BPEO and BATNEEC. The regulatory agency is charged with the
interpretation and application of these terms in order to prevent, minimize and
as a last option render harmless emissions of prescribed substances.
Consequently, IPC legislation is essentially process focused and anticipatory in
its emphasis.

Difficulties with interpreting and applying BPEO have dogged the IPC
regime throughout its history. Seemingly, despite BPEO being a central element
of IPC, it has been almost impossible to operationalize in a methodical way.
Various working documents have been produced by the regulator in an attempt
to do this but all have been unsuccessful in convincing inspectors and industry
about the most appropriate way to interpret the term (ENDS, 1995c). At one
point an attempt was made effectively to change BPEO into a standard based
on the calculation of an Integrated Environmental Index. This index sought to
give a value to indicate the most appropriate destination (air, water, land) for a
given waste stream to allow comparison of incommensurate variables.
However, in the absence of a comprehensive network of statutory environmental quality standards to guide such a calculation the regulator itself sought
to establish various environmental quality objectives. Unfortunately, even in
these instances the calculation of the index was complicated and produced
erratic results.

These problems appear to have produced a consensus between inspectors
and industry concerning BPEO. They accept that if a BPEO assessment is
done then, at least at present, it can only be done qualitatively in a relatively
pragmatic way with little day-to-day reference being paid to formal policy
documents. The following quote from an inspector explains how this works:

*Well, for example, where we have cadmium and mercury, we don't want those in
the aquatic environment, we certainly don't want them in the air so the best thing
is to fix them and put them to land, if they are there anyway.*

Thus, in practice the BPEO requirement has been operationalized in an informal and relatively intuitive way. Although such an approach, which in many
ways defines the nature of IPC in practice, may appear haphazard, it is usually
based on some degree of accumulated experience and expertize. More recent
guidance has simply sought to make this process more transparent and
auditable (HMIP, 1996).

Due to the problems associated with the interpretation of BPEO, the application of BATNEEC has attained the highest profile in the IPC process.
Attempts have been made to direct the interpretation of BATNEEC through a
series of guidance notes issued to inspectors and industry. These guidance
notes outline the release levels that are currently attainable by applying
BATNEEC to regulated processes. In these notes BATNEEC is often
expressed as a performance standard to avoid the risk of constraining innovation or of restricting an operator's choice of approach to achieving the
standard. However, these notes are flexible and remain only guidance and are
not commonly referred to by inspectors in their day-to-day activities.

Although guidance is provided nationally, in practice BATNEEC is determined locally on a site specific basis. Formally, regulated companies are required
to investigate and define BATNEEC for themselves, with the inspector there to
confirm the choice or to suggest alternatives. However, as discussed above, the
practical interpretation of BATNEEC is influenced by the informal interactions
that take place between the regulator and the regulated company. This process is
in turn influenced by the background, experience and values of the individuals
involved. Smith (1997) argues that although the regulator has the legal authority
to apply and enforce BATNEEC, it is dependent on regulated companies both
for information and for the financial and organizational resources that are
needed to secure improvements in the environmental performance of regulated
companies. Consequently, despite its authority, the regulator is drawn into a
process of negotiation with regulated companies. Because of the resource
dependencies within this process of negotiation, Smith (1997) suggests that in
practice the interpretation of BATNEEC can be altered, potentially significantly,
so that it better reflects the objectives of regulated companies. Clearly such a
process has the potential to reduce the imperative for innovation in regulated
companies if the demands of regulation are made less stringent. Additionally,
because the outcomes of such a process of negotiation are inherently unpredictable, it may also reduce the propensity for innovation by introducing
uncertanties and inconsistencies into the implementation process.

On the issue of what constitutes excessive economic cost, inspectors
suggest that they rarely get involved in detailed economic arguments. There are
two possible explanations for this. Firstly, the interpretation of BATNEEC may
be accepted by both parties in the absence of a detailed assessment of the costs
and benefits of any measures that are prescribed by the regulator. This is partic-

ularly the case where environmental improvement can be secured at low or no cost through the adoption of relatively simple organizational and technical change. Secondly, whilst inspectors have extensive process specific experience, they may not have the economic expertise or the access to information necessary to judge what level of investment can be reasonably expected from an industrial installation. The interpretation of excessive cost therefore remains problematic. It is likely that the regulator's interpretation of excessive cost will be more actively contested by regulated companies as the easily exploitable opportunities for environmental improvement become less apparent.

In relation to the style of implementation associated with IPC, the regulator initially adopted a rigid and arm's-length approach which did not encourage consultation or interaction between inspectors and regulated companies. The application of such an arm's-length regulatory style contrasted with the relationship that had generally existed between the regulator and industry under the previous regulatory regime related to air pollution control. This relationship had been viewed with suspicion by many because of the perception that a cosy relationship dominated the relationship between the regulator and regulated companies. In relation to IPC, despite the fact that a purposeful decision was made by the regulator to adopt an arm's-length approach, it soon became apparent that the application of such a style was untenable. Almost immediately HMIP was drawn into consultation with industry about the requirements of IPC because the first round of applications for authorization under IPC were of such poor quality that the majority had to be rejected (Jordan, 1993).

Although the decision to adopt a more hands-on, interactive delivery style was the result of pragmatism rather than strategy, such an approach does have a number of functional merits. The anticipatory, process focused nature of IPC requires an inspector to have a detailed knowledge of the regulated process and not simply its emissions. The more interactive delivery style that emerged in the early stages of IPC allowed regulators to understand the specificities of the processes that they regulated. The following quote from one inspector highlights some of the benefits that are associated with this interactive approach:

> *With me going out doing tests I used to find that we would come along to a particular process and find that release levels were very high and at that particular time there was no control on it at all. That immediately set alarm bells ringing, saying these are very high and we must do something about it. That involved continuous dialogue with that company and a manufacturer of technology and various trials and tests till eventually what I could only describe as BAT [best available technique] coming out for that particular process...*

This specific understanding, coupled with their willingness to apply their experience in a relatively hands-on way, has allowed the regulator to encourage regulated companies to shift from a reactive to an anticipatory response to regulation. It has also allowed the regulator to transfer information and understanding to regulated companies. This in turn has increased their capacity to search for and to apply more effective and more efficient responses to regulation.

Thus it is apparent that in some respects the interactive approach adopted by the regulator is a more effective way of delivering IPC legislation as it encourages companies to extend their search for a response to regulation beyond the most expedient short term option. Although it may lack transparency, this approach at least provides for the possibility of interactive learning between the regulator and industry so that the capacity of regulators to deliver and of companies to respond to regulations effectively accumulates over time. However, it can be argued that because of the ability of industry to influence the requirements of legislation through negotiation with the regulator, the imperative to innovate is reduced.

Very much linked to the hands-on and interactive delivery style that is associated with IPC is a conciliative and consensus based enforcement style. To some extent, this could be contrasted with the approach of the National Rivers Authority (NRA) between 1990 and 1996 which delivered emissions focused legislation and had a media specific remit to safeguard the water environment. The NRA had a much more litigious and adversarial approach to regulation but in the words of one IPC inspector this was not very useful for process oriented legislation:

> We are involved in a debate. We must establish what is possible between ourselves and then consider over what time frame improvements are to be made. Yes, we will prosecute, but it isn't black and white when you're dealing with BATNEEC. It is better to develop a working relationship and encourage them to do their best. To exert continuous pressure by asking questions and being on site is a better approach.

Although it is possible to argue about the strengths and weaknesses of a conciliative or litigious enforcement style, it is likely that the choice will be made to a large extent as a result of the delivery style that is adopted. Although IPC has resulted in some significant prosecutions, on the whole it has been characterized by an intensive hands-on delivery style in association with a consensual relationship between regulator and regulated company and a reluctance to adopt a sanction based strategy to compliance. However, this does not mean, as is now occurring, that it is necessarily possible or advisable for a regulator such as the Environment Agency to establish one code of practice on enforcement or an overall prosecution policy regardless of the nature of the legislation that is being delivered (see ENDS, 1996d).

Therefore, it is apparent that the flexibility that surrounds the implementation and enforcement of IPC has a variable impact on the level of innovation for environmental improvement that is likely to take place in regulated companies. If the demands of regulation are watered down through a process of negotiation, then the imperative for innovation is reduced. If the demands of regulation are uncertain or inconsistent because of the unpredictability of this process of negotiation, then the propensity of regulated companies to innovate is reduced. However, if a flexible and interactive approach to implementation that transfers information and understanding to regulated companies is adopted, then the capacity of regulated companies to innovate is increased.

THE IMPACT OF MANDATORY ENVIRONMENTAL REGULATION IN THE UK: THE CASE OF INTEGRATED POLLUTION CONTROL

This section, which draws extensively on interviews with regulators and regulated companies, assesses the impact of the IPC regime on industrial behaviour. The discussion is structured to examine the technological, the organizational and the strategic dimensions outlined in Chapter 2. Where appropriate, the economic and environmental implications of each form of response to IPC are highlighted.

The Technological Dimension

At present both inspectors and industry perceive the impact of IPC to be evenly divided between changes that are primarily technological in nature and those that are primarily organizational. However, the balance between technological and organizational change demanded by the regulator is heavily influenced by the nature of the regulated plant in question. Broadly, emphasis is commonly placed on the introduction of new technologies for new plant and for plant approaching a major upgrade, whilst during normal operations emphasis is placed on developing organizational improvements.

Where IPC conditions require technological solutions, inspectors suggest that end-of-pipe control options, as opposed to cleaner and more integrated solutions, are still the first to be proposed by industry. The explanation for this centres largely on the short-term expedience of end-of-pipe control technologies, which may be the result of a variety of pressures as described by the environmental manager of a large chemical plant:

> Yes, end-of-pipe solutions still creep in. They are easy to plan for and produce quick solutions. It shows that you're doing something and you can cost for it. Of course, in the longer term they may not be desirable.

However, the position of the regulator on this issue is clear, as one IPC inspector explained:

> We would always encourage companies to improve the way they are carrying on the process to meet whatever emission standards we require. But if they can't do that, then they may have to fit abatement technologies. But the preferred way is to have them minimize at source and have the minimum of abatement equipment necessary.

Although in the early stages of IPC the preferred short term response of industry to regulation was the installation of end-of-pipe technologies, industry increasingly accepts that the application of integrated cleaner technologies may be preferable, both economically and environmentally, at least in the medium to long term. An example of this increasing realization is provided by the following quote from the site environmental manager of a multinational chemical company:

Well, we have deliberately moved away from end-of-pipe whenever we can. Even as recently as 1992 we were moving quite swiftly toward an end-of-pipe effluent treatment plant, but it is not an environmental solution, particularly for our type of effluent and our location. It would just turn organic waste into sewage sludge and make it an environmental problem in some other media. We very deliberately and very publicly decided that wasn't the solution and instead would try waste minimization. We got full backing from the HMIP Inspector. Unfortunately it means we don't have an overnight success, and now we will have to manage maybe 30 or 40 small projects with all their problems. But in the long run it is a better option.

This example begins to illustrate the economic and environmental implications associated with the selection of different forms of technological innovation, namely that although integrated clean technology responses may be less expedient in the short term, in the medium to long term they commonly offer a range of economic and environmental benefits relative to responses based on the application of end-of-pipe technologies. Economically, the range of relative and in some cases absolute benefits associated with investments in clean technology can be impressive. The benefits can either relate to tangible reductions in cost or to less tangible improvements in product quality as illustrated by the following extract from an interview with the group environmental manager of a multinational company:

We were producing one product, and not much of it, but we had to do a recrystallization from methanol. This was not very good, there were significant wastes associated, the yields were low and there were significant losses to atmosphere. We have been looking around for ways to obviate the use of methanol and in the last two or three years we have found a way. We have now gone on to a new process using water based technology. The yield is significantly higher, there is virtually zero waste coming out of the process, we are not using methanol at all so we don't have the same emissions to air. Also, it has enabled us to instead of having an oven dry product to go for a spray dry product which our customers love.

IPC has clearly played a role in encouraging firms to examine the potential for the application of integrated clean technologies before automatically accepting the need for an end-of-pipe response to environmental problems. Those firms that have developed and applied clean technologies as a response to IPC regulations have commonly achieved the necessary improvements in environmental performance at a lower cost than those which would be incurred through investments in end-of-pipe technologies. In some cases the improvements in process efficiency or product quality that have been realized as a consequence of the investment in clean technologies have secured economic benefits which have been in excess of associated costs. As a result many of the companies regulated by IPC are satisfied with the overall costs of compliance as they are recovering costs or securing benefits as a result of the changes made.

The Organizational Dimension

Organizational innovation, involving changes in management or working practices, should not be seen in isolation from technological innovation. Technological and organizational changes are commonly required in combination if technological responses to regulation are to be successfully adopted. This is particularly the case for integrated clean technologies which commonly require accommodating changes to be made throughout the production system. However, despite their combined importance, it is still possible to identify explicitly organizational innovations which occur as a result of the IPC regime. These are equally important, and in some cases more important, than the technological solutions upon which attention commonly focuses.

In general IPC has improved awareness of environmental issues in regulated companies, largely as a result of the interaction between the company and the regulator. As stated above, a critical issue in this respect is the experience of the inspector, including not only their formal knowledge and expertise but also their tacit understanding of the issues affecting the environmental performance of an industrial facility. For regulated companies, this interactive learning has been accelerated by an increase in their knowledge about the performance of the processes which has been facilitated by the increased investment in monitoring technology. One of the most significant outcomes of all these impacts is that regulated companies have been increasingly able to respond to IPC by changing the organization and management of operations rather than by developing or installing new technologies. This change in emphasis from the technological to the organizational has been encouraged by the regulator. In the words of one inspector:

> I think we have been getting the operators to improve their techniques in the soft sense rather than in a technological sense. Also to look at minimization and look at prevention, look back through their data on how the process builds up, improve their training and management structures, improve their software techniques.

From the industry perspective, placing the emphasis as much on the techniques of environmental management as on the technologies has had a considerable impact. In most cases regulated companies, with the help of the regulator, have identified areas for environmental improvement which entail almost no investment and improve both environmental and economic performance. The environmental manager of one large manufacturing facility stated that:

> We've had success in terms of environmental improvements from sitting down and thinking and improving existing processes, by reducing the amount of product changes... People are prepared to sit and think about what they do and there has been success because of it.

Another environmental manager explained the impact of IPC as follows:

> *To be fair, when we started off the whole object was to comply with the legislation. As it turned out that has almost become secondary because we gained so much from it... We have saved a lot of money from environmental measures. In fact very few of the environmental measures we have put in, apart from one, have cost us money. The pay back period has been remarkable, some have cost us nothing and we have saved thousands of pounds. The staff have got little projects going all over the site now. Most of them are very simple operating conditions. Instead of putting that drainage down there, if it goes down there we can use it again. If we turn that pipe around it won't go into the river and we can reuse it. Regulation was the kick start for it really.*

This experience is confirmed in detailed work undertaken by HMIP with the chemicals company Allied Colloids. In a detailed study of the impact of IPC if it is applied with the aim of minimizing waste, it was shown that considerable economic and environmental gains could be made by a range of relatively inexpensive organizational changes to industrial processes (see HMIP, 1995; HMIP and Allied Colloids, 1996; HMIP and Business in the Environment, 1996).

Thus, in many instances regulated companies have not had to invest in relatively expensive technologies in order to improve their environmental performance and comply with IPC. Many improvements have been derived from managerial and organizational changes, for instance from changes to operating instructions, instrumentation, maintenance and general working practices. However, in many cases regulated companies acknowledge that, despite their economic and environmental benefits, relatively simple organizational changes would not have taken place without the initial stimulus of IPC and the regular presence of an inspector on site. If a weakness is apparent in this search for organizational and managerial change it is that the changes adopted to date have not always been pursued as part of a longer term strategic process. Consequently, the changes implemented have generally focused on operational and incremental changes to existing systems rather than on the selection and development of new approaches.

The Strategic Dimension

Having discussed the technological and organizational impacts of IPC, the final issue to consider is the impact of IPC on the strategic decision making processes of regulated companies. This section will necessarily be briefer than the previous sections because research would suggest that a significant weakness of the IPC regime has been its inability, as yet, to place the environment fully on the strategic agenda of industry.

Managers of regulated companies freely acknowledge that IPC has had an impact on their operational activities. In this respect it is accepted that IPC has accelerated the development of new technologies and techniques which can be added to or integrated into existing production processes. However, overall they did not feel that IPC had yet encouraged the integration of environmental considerations into the strategic decision making processes of regulated companies. Broadly, therefore, IPC has yet to encourage a fundamental reappraisal of the design or objectives of regulated processes.

In a dynamic setting the fact that the influence of IPC is constrained to operational rather than strategic change is important for both economic and environmental reasons. A continued focus on operational change and incremental improvement must eventually encounter diminishing marginal returns. Without a strategic as well as an operational focus, opportunities for more radical change will either be overlooked or rejected. Consequently, further phases of operational change and incremental improvement will be impossible. Under circumstances such as these, demands for further environmental improvement are likely to encounter spiralling economic costs.

The short term focus of IPC has been associated by inspectors with a lack of clear targets which can be used to guide the implementation of the legislation. Without a comprehensive framework of targets, inspectors regularly identify that they have encountered difficulties in promoting the environment onto the strategic agenda of industry. This was explained by one inspector as follows:

> Our focus is operational as it should be. But it should also be strategic, shouldn't it. But for that to happen we need a strategy to work within and I'm not sure we are getting that from government. It certainly isn't clear to me what role IPC plays within a wider approach to managing the environment. It isn't clear what IPC is ultimately aiming at.

This lack of strategic guidance reflects the relative lack of targets in the broader UK policy framework. To a degree this lack of targets has been reduced recently by the formulation of national strategies in areas such as air and waste.

SUMMARY: THE IMPLEMENTATION AND IMPACT OF IPC IN THE UK

Integrated Pollution Control was introduced in England and Wales by the Environmental Protection Act of 1990 and has transformed industrial environmental regulation for the largest and most environmentally significant industrial installations. In the discussion above, the implementation and impact of this legislation has been outlined, considering first the regulatory framework within which it was introduced. This was followed by an analysis of the structures and styles associated with the implementation of IPC.

When considering the regulatory framework in the UK a number of important points were established. Firstly, at the national level it is possible to identify an approach to environmental regulation which has traditionally involved reliance on expert decision-making at the local level in preference to the imposition of inflexible regulatory frameworks. Secondly, there has also been a tendency for scientific proof to be required before action has been taken. Thirdly, in recent years the UK government has allied itself with a view of the relationship between regulation and the economy which sees regulation as tending to have a negative impact on industrial competitiveness.

To a large extent the components of this national regulatory climate are reflected in the two most important environmental policy documents to emerge from the government during the 1990s, *This Common Inheritance* and *Sustainable Development: The UK Strategy*. These policy documents, although they do have some positive aspects, are largely symbolic and rhetorical with a limited number of concrete proposals with respect to the environment. They are particularly remarkable for their lack of clear targets for environmental improvement, although, as noted above, recent initiatives have responded to this lack of guidance by formulating strategic goals for regulation in specific areas such as air quality or waste management. This is clearly linked to the scepticism of government when faced with evidence of an environmental crisis. It is also linked to the established reluctance to regulate industry, especially with rigid frameworks which define the degree and nature of any action to be taken.

The UK's policy style and the policy documents mentioned help to establish the policy framework within which IPC legislation has been applied. However, unlike the policy framework, the institutional structures associated with the implementation of IPC reveal a number of strengths. There has been an amalgamation of legal structures and an integration of institutional structures which in both cases has required the comprehensive restructuring of previous approaches. For example, in the case of the institutional structures there has been a progressive shift away from the traditionally fragmented nature of environmental regulation in the UK. In 1987 this resulted in the formation of Her Majesty's Inspectorate of Pollution and in 1996 this regulator itself became part of the larger Environment Agency.

The resource structures associated with the delivery of IPC from 1990 onwards have been of a variable nature. For example, the staff recruited to deliver IPC had a considerable amount of practical industrial experience before they became regulators and evidence indicates that this has some advantages. It allows the inspectors to interpret the requirements of legislation on a case-by-case basis in an informed way. It helps them to understand the processes that they regulate and therefore to deliver regulation in an anticipatory way. It also helps them to transfer information and a tacit understanding of the critical issues to regulated companies. However, because of the levels of expertise involved, IPC is often considered to be expensive legislation to implement.

The implementation styles which have accompanied IPC have a number of strengths and weaknesses. By design IPC is anticipatory and process focused as in the first instance it seeks to prevent the emission of pollutants. It has been delivered in a largely hands-on fashion by the regulator, who has adopted a relatively intense and interactive relationship with regulated companies. In combination with the expertise that is present in the regulatory agency this approach appears to place the inspector in a good position to transfer information and understanding on good practice to regulated companies. This in turn allows the inspector to increase the capacity of regulated companies to overcome the barriers they face in addressing environmental issues. Partly as a consequence of this interactive approach, a consensual and conciliative enforcement style also characterizes the implementation of IPC. The hands-on delivery style is consistent with a compliance based strategy to enforcement. However, in the absence of a broad framework of targets for performance, or of measures to facilitate public scrutiny and enhance the degree of accountability that surrounds the regulatory process, the close relationship with the regulator is viewed with suspicion by some parties. This is particularly the case given that the key requirements of IPC are interpreted and applied through a process of negotiation between the regulator and regulated companies. Within this process of negotiation, it is possible that the amount of discretion awarded to the regulatory agency and to the individuals within it can allow the demands of regulation to be made less stringent. In such instances, whatever the capacity of regulated companies to innovate in response to regulation, the imperative to do so is reduced.

The impact of IPC in practice can be clearly linked to the nature of the regulatory framework, structures and styles outlined above. Considering the technological dimension of innovation, the evidence suggests that IPC is having an impact by raising the awareness of regulated companies on the opportunities of clean rather than control technological solutions to environmental problems. It is also playing a role in encouraging companies to change working practices to comply with legislation rather than simply installing technology. In both cases these impacts may have positive economic as well as environmental benefits and the ability of IPC to have this impact is intrinsically related to the expertise of regulatory staff combined particularly with the design and delivery styles associated with IPC. However, IPC appears to have been less successful at encouraging industry to think strategically about environmental issues. This raises the fear that incremental improvements to existing production processes will eventually encounter diminishing marginal returns without the radical changes that are associated with strategic decision-making and industrial restructuring. The weakness of IPC in this respect can be associated with the UK's broader regulatory framework. The comparative lack of clear strategic vision at the broadest policy level does not provide a firm foundation for mandatory regulations like IPC and both industry and inspectors have identified that well designed legislation like IPC appears to be implemented without an overarching framework to guide it.

VOLUNTARY REGULATION IN THE UK: THE CASE OF THE EU'S ECO-MANAGEMENT AND AUDIT SCHEME

The discussion above has focused on the design, delivery and impact of mandatory environmental regulation in the UK. However, while this form of regulation is a critical factor driving the development and application of new technologies and techniques in industry, it is also apparent that companies are increasingly taking voluntary action to improve their environmental performance. The following section will focus on an example of such action, exploring the implementation and impact of voluntary regulation in the form of environmental management system (EMS) standards. Particular emphasis is placed on the EU's Eco-Management and Audit Scheme (EMAS) although the International Standards Organization's environmental management systems standard (ISO14001) is also considered. The work presented draws on interviews with the environmental managers of many of the first companies in the UK to be registered for EMAS and certified for ISO14001. It also makes use of interviews with representatives of the UK competent body for EMAS along with the accreditors and verifiers who assess the compliance of companies who wish to register under EMAS or become certified for ISO14001.

Implementation Structures and EMAS in the UK

The implementation of EMAS and other EMS standards in the UK is taking place in the same policy context that was outlined at the start of this chapter. While it is not necessary to discuss the policy context again, one dimension of it merits further investigation in relation to the role of voluntary regulation. Through the 1980s and 1990s the UK government has emphasized the importance of the market and its reluctance to impose mandatory regulations. This implicit support for voluntary action with a minimum of government intervention has encouraged the development and application of EMS standards. It has also encouraged mandatory regulators to examine the ways in which the links between mandatory and voluntary regulation might be developed so that the role of government can eventually be reduced. Although these links are currently embryonic, at the extreme this process might be associated with a privatization of regulation if government transfers regulatory responsibilities to the private sector.

In the UK there are both explicit and implicit links between voluntary EMS standards such as EMAS and mandatory regulations such as IPC. However, at least in an explicit sense, as yet there are only tenuous connections between IPC and EMS standards. From the perspective of IPC the only formal connection that has been made has been through the Operator Pollution Risk Appraisal (OPRA) initiative which was published by HMIP in 1995. OPRA proposes a way of ranking companies, on various criteria, to assess the risk they present to the environment. In this scheme companies that have an auditable EMS, such as EMAS, are likely to be placed in a lower category of risk than those that have not. However, the impact of these calculations on the operation of the Environment Agency has not been fully determined. It is assumed that this kind of assessment may be used to guide the day-to-day operations of the regulator and the allocation of their resources. By implication this may mean that companies that are registered under an acceptable EMS standard may be regulated less intensively and may pay lower fees for authorization under IPC than those which are not.

While mandatory regulations such as IPC are only beginning to explore their potential to interact with voluntary EMS standards, schemes such as EMAS are based on clearly established links with mandatory regulations such as IPC. A significant breach of an IPC authorization as determined by the Environment Agency must be communicated to the competent body for EMAS. If so informed, the competent body has no choice but to suspend the registration of that company under EMAS. However, the guidance issued by the EMAS competent body on the issue of compliance with the requirements of EMAS itself gives a considerable amount of discretion to verifiers. This makes it unlikely that the decision to inform the competent body of a breach of compliance will be applied consistently.

In practical terms there are other explicit links between IPC and EMS standards. For example, many IPC regulated companies have used parts of their IPC authorization to fulfil requirements of their EMS. In an interview one company claimed that 95 per cent of its effects register, required by the EMS standard, was taken from work done for its IPC application. Mandatory regulation can therefore make registration under a voluntary EMS standard easier. Also, in all cases where conditions of improvement have been given to companies under IPC those conditions have been stated as objectives and targets under the EMS. In reverse, one company believed that:

It might be possible for our EMS standard objectives and targets to be adopted by the regulator. They might agree that they become the conditions of the improvement programme. When you start thinking about it it all merges together...

In this case the company expresses the belief that because of the management system the initiative can be taken by the company and the mandatory regulator may accept this as compliance with certain aspects of IPC regulation.

Implicitly many more links exist between EMS standards and mandatory regulation. These links focus on the building of trust between the company and the mandatory regulator. This trust can develop as a result of regulators recognizing an effective EMS in regulated companies. The following quote illustrates how this operates in practice:

We had the Environment Agency down last week to see if they could improve things. One thing they came up with was that we should have a site drain map to identify where things are going in the event of a spillage. Because of the EMS we had one. He went away and said they've got their act together. It puts us in good stead really.

Consequently, although some explicit links between mandatory and voluntary regulation are in place, and despite rhetorical support for voluntary action, the UK situation is currently defined by a fairly limited and cautious view of how voluntary regulation could interact with mandatory regulation. This is the case despite the fact that mandatory regulation is commonly accepted as the most important driver encouraging the uptake of EMS standards (ENDS, 1996f; ENDS, 1996c). As a result there have been calls for more concrete ways of encouraging the uptake of EMS standards in industry, including altering the charging scheme associated with IPC authorization to reward proactive companies such as those that are registered with an EMS standard (ENDS, 1996b). However, a range of implicit links are developing in advance of formalized procedures, resulting overall in semi-coordinated legal structures.

Beyond the legal structures outlined above, EMS standards are associated with a range of institutional structures. In the UK, the Department of the Environment (DoE) was assigned the task of being the EMAS competent body and thus of establishing and holding the register of EMAS sites. The decision was also made to allocate the accreditation task to a separate organization, the National Accreditation Council for Certification Bodies (NACCB) which has now been renamed the United Kingdom Accreditation Service (UKAS). Essentially this utilized the existing institutional structure which surrounded other voluntary standards in the UK.

As the accreditation body, UKAS assumed much of the responsibility for operationalizing EMAS. The most important task was to develop criteria for the accreditation of EMAS verifiers. The existing Environmental Accreditation Criteria (NACCB, 1994), associated primarily with accrediting certification bodies under BS7750 and ISO14001, was therefore supplemented with The Accreditation of Environmental Verifiers for EMAS (UKAS, 1995). Together these documents outline what UKAS looks for when accrediting environmental verifiers.

The UKAS accreditation system introduces a number of central considerations associated with the delivery of EMAS. It outlines that before and whilst being accredited verifiers will be assessed on a range of issues including their capacity to select, provide and manage employees who have appropriate collective competencies to conduct EMAS verifications and validate EMAS statements. It also establishes measures to judge the performance of the verifier in practice, including post-verification audit assessments or direct witnessing of EMAS verification in operation. Thus, the competence of the verifier must be continually demonstrated. Beyond these competencies the verifier must ensure that they operate in an objective and independent way as required by the EMAS Regulation (Falk and Wilkinson, 1996). In this way the competent body and UKAS have attempted to ensure that robust institutional structures are established which clearly communicate to accredited verifiers what is expected of them and what must be demanded from companies seeking EMAS verification. In practice, however, it is not clear whether UKAS has the resources to ensure that these structures are effective in practice. The concern has been raised amongst some consultants that it does not (ENDS, 1996a).

A critical aspect of the implementation of EMS standards, including EMAS and ISO14001, are the resource structures associated with it. This includes the grants that may be provided to offset the cost of registration and the qualifications and areas of expertise of the staff recruited for the purpose. Both of these areas have raised concern in the UK. Some governmental assistance has been available to offset the costs associated with EMAS but the uptake of this assistance has been very limited. This support is particularly channelled toward small and medium sized enterprises that may otherwise be deterred from participation due to the cost of employing consultants and verifiers. However, the uptake of grants under the DoE's Small Company Energy and Environmental Management Assistance Scheme (SCEEMAS) has been limited (ENDS, 1996e). In a further attempt to encourage participation the DoE has also sought to promote the scheme during the first years of the scheme's operation, by waiving the costs of registration with the competent body once verification and validation have occurred.

The impact of resource structures is also heavily dependent on the people that deliver or enforce the standard through interaction with companies seeking verification. To a large extent the performance of EMS standards in practice depends on the nature of these human resources. Understanding the background and expertise of the organizations and individuals involved with the delivery of EMS standards is therefore critically important. In the case of EMAS verification this may involve either a team of people or an individual.

In the UK, the nature of the individuals and organizations employed for the verification of EMAS has been a source of concern for a number of reasons. If they are to be fully effective, EMS standards require an interdisciplinary approach to address the wide range of factors that collectively define the environmental performance of a company. This need for inter-disciplinarity demands a combination of scientific, technical, managerial and legal expertise within the organization responsible for verification. Given that these areas of expertise have tended to be polarized in discrete professions and organizations over time, demands for their integration are likely to meet resistance and inertia, particularly in the short to medium term. Related to this is the concern that, at least in the early stages of the development and application of EMS standards, there is likely to be a relative shortage of organizations and individuals with a significant amount of accumulated expertise which is specific to this area. Thus, the need to develop new combinations of skills and to accumulate specific experience in verification may in turn necessitate a degree of institutional reorganization and capacity building.

While institutional reorganization and capacity building is undoubtedly taking place to some extent, the concern remains that the verification role will not be fully interdisciplinary. Instead, it is possible that it will include organizations and individuals from particular professional backgrounds that, intentionally or unintentionally, shape the delivery of EMS standards to reflect their own background and values. In the UK, concern about this issue has focused on the prospect of organizations or individuals with a background in quality management systems moving into the environmental sphere to become verifiers and certifiers for EMS standards. This in turn will influence the regulatory styles associated with the verification of EMS standards.

IMPLEMENTATION STYLES AND EMAS IN THE UK

As Falk and Wilkinson (1996, p 4) state in relation to the EMAS Regulation:

> *...the Regulation provides the accredited environmental verifier with the competence – and, if necessary, requires him (sic) to do his own analysis at the site considered. Only in that way can EMAS ... promote continuous improvement in environmental performance. Any interpretation suggesting a merely system-orientated check by the verifier will endanger the achievement of this aim.*

With this in mind the involvement of quality systems auditors as verifiers under EMAS raises the concern that they may lack specific environmental knowledge and expertise and that they will be more concerned with systems auditing than environmental improvement. Clearly the risk is that where emphasis can be placed either on environmental improvement or systems improvement, the use of staff with a management systems background and culture will reduce the emphasis on environmental improvement. Also, potentially those with management systems experience will be less effective at disseminating technical information concerning environmental management options between different companies. At present the real impact of this trend is impossible to determine given the early stage of development of EMS standards; however, it is likely to be closely related to the interpretation given to key principles within the standard, particularly the interpretation of 'continuous improvement'.

At present representatives of the competent body, the accreditation body and registered companies in the UK indicate that because each registered site is unique no standard set of objectives and targets can be drawn up to operationalize continuous improvement consistently. However, in practice verifiers should expect to see that goals are linked to an environmental effects evaluation of the site that is determined in a methodologically transparent way. Following from this, auditors may expect to see some, but not necessarily all, of the most significant environmental effects of an organization being addressed as objectives and targets. As a result continuous improvement is taken to refer to general improvement in environmental performance over a number of years, but not necessarily in all areas all the time.

As yet, anything other than a short-term analysis of the interpretation of continuous improvement is difficult, but an environmentally significant interpretation in the UK is made less likely for a number of reasons. Firstly, UK industry has not had a comprehensive set of environmental targets communicated to it. If this were the case and these targets for performance and improvement were devolved down to company level from a broad strategy document this would help to inform the interpretation of continuous improvement. Without this, continuous improvement could evolve into simply improving in line with the requirements of mandatory regulation and doing very little extra. The extent to which EMS standards demand performance to extend beyond compliance is unclear. Secondly, the levels of discretion that verifiers are afforded may allow commercial or political objectives to determine the interpretation of continuous improvement rather than environmental objectives. The desire to register companies for EMAS and the reluctance to remove companies from the register are obviously potential issues in this respect.

The desire for the EMAS scheme to be successful and the desire for EMAS verifiers to receive work could be strong incentives for a less than rigorous interpretation of continuous improvement. However, as one verifier emphasized:

Continuous improvement must be on a case by case basis. It must be down to the means and measurements offered by the companies themselves… they need to demonstrate that they produced an objective and target, that has a measure and timescale. In the course of our assessment we look at the programme and when we get to the end of the timescale we look to see if there has been some improvement. Hopefully this is in line with the target. Improvement on a specific environmental effect, not the system. A management system is all about delivering targets, about environmental performance. OK there are those arguing that it is about system improvement, it is up to the accreditation authorities, it is up to the people who control how the standard is applied.

The delivery of EMAS in the UK involves a fairly hands-on and intensive relationship between the company and the verifier for a limited period. This issue is crucial with respect to the potential role played by verifiers in transferring good practice between companies. Although the EMAS regulation requires an independent and objective delivery style, this does not stop verifiers from being cooperative and from suggesting useful environmental management options and techniques to registered sites. In this sense verifiers could act as a conduit for the transfer of best practice between companies. However, this will be more apparent if a cooperative relationship is developed which still respects the need for independence and objectivity. A more arm's-length approach is unlikely to encourage the same useful exchange of information.

In practice the first EMAS companies in the UK all felt that the verifiers they had used had done a thorough job (ENDS, 1995b). The companies themselves did not expect verifiers to have a detailed knowledge of their operations but they valued intelligent auditors with a healthy amount of scepticism. During the verification process the verifiers have typically visited sites on a number of occasions to interview personnel and management to ensure that they understand the potential environmental impacts of their activities. Other checks have included the review of monitoring records, bills for water, oil and energy use and effluent discharge rates. On the positive side companies have been confident of the broad benefits of verification, with one environmental manager saying:

It's a good push towards a culture change within the company. There is nothing easier than to start not doing the odd thing when one is busy if nobody is checking… [This] is a very good way of keeping one on track.

The enforcement style associated with EMAS is complicated by the question not only of what to do in cases of non-compliance with the EMS standard but also in cases of non-compliance with the requirements of mandatory regulation. For EMAS, the minimum requirement is that sites comply with the legal

95

obligations established for instance by IPC. The competent body has to satisfy itself that this is the case. The DoE has issued guidance to mandatory regulators concerning this issue but in practice this gives a considerable amount of discretion to the mandatory regulator as to when or if they notify the competent body for voluntary regulation of breaches in compliance. The DoE suggests that 'proportionality' should be observed, ensuring that registered companies do not lose their registration as a result of trivial breaches of the law. In practice many of the first companies to achieve registration under EMAS have ongoing compliance problems. For example, one company achieved EMAS registration whilst acknowledging that it was not always complying with trade effluent consents as out of 1500 samples only 80 per cent were within consent. The majority of the 20 per cent of samples associated with non-compliance were deemed to be relatively minor problems relating for example to marginal breaches of pH limits. However, 3 per cent were related to more serious issues such as heavy metals. In this case the regulator was satisfied that the company had an investment programme which will address these issues and as a result EMAS registration was not affected (ENDS, 1995b).

Therefore the evidence indicates that the enforcement style being adopted by the competent body and others with respect to EMAS in the UK is relatively conciliatory and consensual. There is a reluctance to jeopardize the registration of EMAS sites in any but the most serious cases of non-compliance. However, such a compliance based strategy raises credibility problems for the standard. It may be difficult for the public at large to understand how a company that is officially operating illegally can achieve EMAS registration whilst the regulators are aware this is the case. It may limit the potential for EMAS to interact fully with mandatory regulation. If EMAS does not in practice mean that a company is complying with its legal obligations then it may be difficult for mandatory regulators to take account of EMAS registration as a sign that a company presents a lower environmental risk.

THE IMPACT OF VOLUNTARY REGULATION IN THE UK: THE CASE OF THE EU ECO-MANAGEMENT AND AUDIT SCHEME

In the discussion above, the implementation of EMS standards has been outlined with particular reference to EMAS. The central dimensions of the implementation of this form of voluntary regulation in the UK have been outlined. In the following section the technological, organizational and strategic impacts of these standards on business activity will be considered.

The Technological Dimension

At present EMS standards appear to be having a limited direct impact on technological innovation. Some investment in monitoring technology and other more process specific technological investment has been linked to EMS standards. However, investment in technologies is generally uncommon unless the demands of mandatory regulation have been included as a target for improvement under the EMS. There are two principal reasons why this may be the case. Firstly, given the relatively recent uptake of schemes like EMAS it is understandable that techniques of environmental management may be dominant at the outset as the requirements for continuous improvement can be achieved solely through such organizational change. It is therefore possible that investments in technology will be required at some point in the future if the requirements for continuous improvement are to be met. Secondly, it is possible that some dimensions of the framework, structures and styles of implementation associated with EMAS have not encouraged technological innovation. For example, verification teams with a systems background and a lack of detailed process specific knowledge and a flexible implementation style coupled with a conciliative enforcement style may restrict the ability of EMAS to drive technological innovation. This may be reinforced by the lack of explicit targets for environmental improvement within the wider policy framework. These problems are particularly important given the well established barriers to technological change which have been outlined in previous chapters.

The Organizational Dimension

The most tangible impact of EMS standards in the UK has been the increased levels of understanding that companies with an effective EMS have over their processes and operations. This increased understanding enhances the ability of companies with an EMS to control their environmental impacts. In interviews companies have regularly admitted that, prior to the development and application of an EMS, their ability to manage certain aspects of the environmental performance of their processes was limited. This position is illustrated by the following quote from an interview with one environmental manager:

> ...one of the significant environmental effects of this factory is the fact that in the recent past we have had a relatively large number of uncontrolled emissions. The fundamental cause has been neglect of the systems side of our process, whether you are talking about routine checks on instruments or whatever. The standard requires us to systematically investigate this. In fact we have identified it as a significant environmental effect. So we will address it as a formal objective.

In this respect, the EMS can be seen as a heuristic device that galvanizes commitment, focuses minds, motivates action and challenges preconceptions in order to explain the causes and effects of industrial environmental management.

The learning process which is associated with the application of an EMS has two identifiable impacts. Firstly, the increased levels of understanding have encouraged the search for and development of relatively inexpensive organizational responses to environmental impacts. Secondly, increased levels of understanding have allowed options for cost reduction from improved efficiency to be recognized and pursued. In many cases these two outcomes appear simultaneously so that environmental improvement has commonly been secured at lower costs than would have been the case in the absence of an EMS. In many cases the short term costs associated with developing an EMS have been more than offset by the medium to long term benefits that it allows. The following outline, provided by the representative of one company, gives an example of this:

> *We had two electric meters on site, one to monitor the workshops and one for the office block, but we couldn't work out the energy efficiency of the tank wash. How much electricity was it using? Because of the system we had another electric meter fitted and once we analysed that we put timers on to reduce the wash, and work out how much energy and money we have saved.*

Similar organizational impacts were apparent in another EMAS registered site as described by their environmental manager:

> *We are really just beginning to appreciate what the potential is for savings. There is an opportunity to save a tremendous amount of money by looking at waste minimization. Getting people to look at the wider picture... When you look at the targets and managers say they could save 2 per cent here, 5 per cent there, 1 per cent here. We have put a target date against them, some till the end of the century. Potentially when they start going and we start sharing the information we have the opportunity of saving a lot of money. For example, one of the things that we have done, and had great success with, is our compacted waste and segregated waste. We are now selling pallets, plastic, cardboard and paper, where previously it went to landfill. We had compactor units on site, big automatic machines filling 30 yard containers of compacted waste. We used to get rid of something like 50 of those units a month and now it is five, big saving.*

As a result it is clear that EMAS is having a significant impact on the techniques of environmental management that are applied in registered companies. Although explicit impacts on technology are not common as yet, the identified organizational impacts are serving to improve the levels of control achieved over processes in registered companies. This in turn serves to help in the identification of areas where relatively simple managerial options can improve environmental performance, resulting in economic savings (see ENDS, 1997).

The Strategic Dimension

As with mandatory regulation, it is important to assess both the operational and strategic impacts of EMS standards. It is not unusual for operational issues to be the focus of attention at the outset but in some cases EMS standards have shown evidence of extending their influence to the strategic timescale. The following quote shows the operational focus of an EMS:

> *I think the EMS standard's benefit and impact to us in the 12 months since we have had it has been very much on internal and local operations, engineering and*

negotiating. Understanding that this environmental impact has been brought through operational management and is worthy of consideration. I think it has been mainly in that line rather than at the big strategic level.

The following quote shows the movement of an EMS to impact on strategic decision-making:

...we now have a very active say in new equipment capitalization, looking at environmental impacts of new equipment into the future, so that has come out of it. We sit on the capital review body... there has been equipment specified in capital papers which we have asked them to go again to re-evaluate alternatives because of the environmental impacts of some of the processes inherent in the kit that was coming in. We have changed that around quite significantly. That is an output of the management system.

These quotes show how environmental management systems have the potential to impact not only on operational issues but also to change the context of strategic business decision-making and investment. This is the case whilst accepting the problems identified previously. It is also of critical importance because it is at this level that the potential for radical innovation must be recognized. When considered in this context, environmental management systems, if influencing both operational and strategic issues, can play a crucial role in establishing conditions which are conducive to both incremental and radical innovation however it may be stimulated.

SUMMARY: THE IMPLEMENTATION AND IMPACT OF EMAS IN THE UK

In the discussion above, the framework, structures and styles of implementation associated with EMS standards have been outlined with particular reference to UK experience related to EMAS. When considering the wider policy context it is important to recognize that in principle the UK has encouraged the application of voluntary action in recent policy documents. In practice this has been combined with a reluctance on the part of the UK government to provide strategic vision and targets for industry. As a result schemes like EMAS become particularly important because it is voluntary action of this type that is encouraged rather than mandatory regulation.

More specifically the implementation structures associated with the implementation of EMAS reveal a number of strengths and weaknesses. There has been an attempt to start to integrate EMAS into existing legal structures although overall it is not apparent that a clear vision of how this should happen has been established. Alongside this, more implicitly, EMS standards are being acknowledged by mandatory regulators as evidence of a responsible approach to environmental management by industries. In relation to the structures associated with the implementation of the scheme, it is apparent that there has been an attempt to establish a robust institutional underpinning for EMAS. Together the competent body and the accreditation authority have issued clear guidance about the implementation of EMAS in the UK. A number of verifiers have become accredited but concerns have been raised that, particularly as a result of management systems staff moving into the verification of EMS standards, the requirement for improvement in environmental performance may give way to a focus on systems improvement. While some steps have been taken to ensure that EMAS and ISO14001 focus on environmental performance and not systems performance, it is still possible that staff involved in verification may lack specific experience or insight and may not be able to offer detailed advice to companies on environmental management options.

The implementation styles which have accompanied EMAS also reveal a number of strengths and weaknesses. By design, EMAS is concerned with environmental impacts and emphasis is placed on interpreting continuous improvement with the aim of realizing direct improvement in environmental performance. Improvement in the performance of management systems alone is not seen to be consistent with the requirements of EMAS. The delivery style adopted is reasonably intensive, although with a relatively short audit period it is difficult for a truly hands-on approach to develop. With respect to enforcement, a conciliative and consensual approach has been established. This is allowing companies which periodically fail to comply with the requirements of mandatory regulation to achieve or retain registration under EMAS. Under such circumstances it is difficult to see how EMAS can have the credibility it requires to be accepted by regulators and by the public. It also raises the prospect that companies who show only very limited improvements in environmental performance over time will be able to retain EMAS registration.

The impact of EMAS in practice can be linked to the nature of the regulatory framework, structures and styles outlined above. Considering the technological dimension of innovation, the evidence suggests that EMAS is not yet having a very noticeable impact. This may be due to the relatively recent uptake of EMS standards or because of a range of factors which characterize the implementation of EMAS. A combination of the two is most likely. However, evidence suggests that EMAS is having a significant impact on the organizational structures and behaviour of registered firms. It is increasing the knowledge of industrial processes present within regulated companies and is revealing opportunities for relatively inexpensive changes which improve both the environmental and economic performance of industrial processes. Furthermore, it is apparent that the presence of an effective EMS helps to establish conditions within companies that are conducive to innovation. Thus EMS standards such as EMAS are likely to increase the responsiveness of industry to the variety of regulator and market pressures for environmental improvement that it faces.

With respect to the strategic dimension, the evidence suggests that over time environmental management systems raise awareness of environmental issues and may therefore lead to a change in the cultures of registered companies. Thus it is likely that the presence of an EMS helps to promote the environment onto the strategic agenda of industry. This in turn will help to promote more the integration of environmental considerations into mainstream business decision-making. If as a consequence industry begins to consider what it does as well as the way that it does it this will enhance the prospects for radical as well as incremental change. However, as mentioned before, this whole process in hampered by a lack of strategic planning and target setting on the part of government.

CONCLUSIONS

This chapter has reviewed the implementation of mandatory regulation and voluntary regulation in the UK. The examples chosen were Integrated Pollution Control, as introduced in England and Wales by the 1990 Environmental Protection Act, and the EU's Eco-Management and Audit Scheme. In each case the regulatory framework and the implementation structures and styles associated with these instruments have been described. Following this the impact of these instruments on industrial behaviour was considered. In each case it has been shown that specific dimensions of implementation determine the nature of the impacts that these instruments have in practice.

IPC legislation has had a notable impact on industrial behaviour. Generally however this impact has been of an operational rather than a strategic nature. This primarily operational impact is particularly related to the process focused nature of IPC which emphasizes the prevention of pollution. It is also aided by the integrated nature of the legislation and the institutions involved in its implementation, together with the presence of inspectors with a considerable amount of expertise who deliver the legislation in a hands-on and intensive way. Consequently, although IPC legislation has been accused of being expensive legislation to implement, it is having an important impact on industrial operations and regulated companies have commonly identified a range of beneficial impacts that have followed from its implementation. These are often associated with the development and application of clean technologies and techniques which in many instances have improved the economic and environmental performance of regulated companies simultaneously. However, despite these apparent benefits, the implementation process that surrounds the IPC framework is viewed with suspicion by some parties. This is particularly the case as a consequence of the close relationship that exists between the regulator and regulated companies and because the key requirements of IPC can be interpreted and applied on a case-by-case basis through a process of negotiation which has the potential to make the requirements of legislation more lenient. The lack of the transparency and accountability that could be provided by a clear and comprehensive framework of standards, targets and performance measures tends to reinforce these suspicions.

Overall this discussion indicates that EMS standards have the potential to establish conditions in companies which are conducive to innovation. They can raise awareness about environmental issues and at the same time highlight potential areas for improvement in environmental performance. Many of these improvements may require little or no initial capital investment. EMSs have a broad focus and can encourage a systematic approach to environmental management, but it is unlikely that they can be left to deliver environmental protection in isolation without some baseline of mandatory regulation. Consequently the nature of the interaction between voluntary and mandatory regulation is critical. Some tentative steps have been taken to encourage such interaction in the UK.

However, one of the most significant weaknesses in UK environmental policy relating to the implementation of both IPC and EMAS relates to the wider policy framework. *This Common Inheritance* and *Sustainable Development: The UK Strategy* establish only a very weak policy framework within which these forms of regulation must be applied. In the case of mandatory regulation the lack of clear targets for industrial environmental performance makes it difficult for IPC to promote strategic change in industry. It also restricts the accountability of the regulatory process. To a degree however, these weaknesses have been reduced recently by the formulation of national strategies for areas such as air quality and waste management. In the case of EMAS, although there is general support for voluntary action, it does not clearly establish what role EMS standards can or should play within a complementary mix of policy instruments.

Chapter 6

THE IMPLEMENTATION AND IMPACT OF INDUSTRIAL ENVIRONMENTAL REGULATION IN THE NETHERLANDS

INTRODUCTION

It has been argued in previous chapters that the nature of industrial environmental regulation can be examined through an analysis of the frameworks, structures and styles that are associated with its implementation. Similarly, it has been argued that the impact of industrial environmental regulation can be assessed by considering the influence that regulation has on the technological, organizational and strategic behaviour of regulated companies. As in the previous chapter, which focused on the nature of industrial environmental regulation in the UK, this chapter will draw on these categories and variables to analyse the implementation and impact of mandatory and voluntary environmental regulation in the Netherlands. This chapter presents the results of fieldwork conducted in the Netherlands during 1995 and 1996. This work consisted largely of semi-structured interviews with policy-makers, regulators and representatives of industrial installations associated with the mandatory and voluntary regulations in question.

The discussion that follows is broadly divided into three sections. Firstly, the context for environmental policy in the Netherlands is outlined to establish the general nature of the policy framework within which the other more specific instruments operate. This discussion focuses on some of the innovative features of Dutch environmental policy by examining the nature of the various National Environmental Policy Plans (NEPPs) and of the covenanting process that is associated with the implementation of the NEPPs. Secondly, the implementation and impact of mandatory environmental regulation in the Netherlands is examined. While the influence of the various NEPPs and of the covenanting process is considered, the discussion focuses primarily on the Environmental Management Act (EMA) of 1993 and the Pollution of Surface Waters Act (PSWA) of 1969. These acts establish the legal basis for mandatory environmental regulation in the Netherlands and together represent the closest approximation that the Netherlands currently has to the EU's Integrated Pollution Prevention and Control (IPPC) directive. Thirdly, the implementation and impact of voluntary environmental regulation is assessed with particular reference to the European Union's Eco-Management and Audit Scheme (EMAS) regulation and the International Standards Organization's environmental management systems standard (ISO14001).

THE DUTCH CONTEXT FOR ENVIRONMENTAL POLICY

The context for environmental policy and regulation in The Netherlands is characterized by two principal features, namely the consensus-based political system and the government-led approach to national planning. In the following section each of these features will be examined to provide the background for the subsequent discussion of the Dutch approach to environmental policy in the 1990s.

The Netherlands is generally accepted as having a cooperative and consensus-based political system. Lijphart (1975) describes the 'consociational democracy' in The Netherlands which is built on well defined social groups that rarely mix but which are directed by elites involved in constant discussion and negotiation. The evidence for this pillared society is declining, but consensus and cooperation continue to characterize the Dutch political system. Reflecting this, Lijphart has more recently chosen to use the more general term 'consensual democracy' to describe the Dutch political system (Dogan and Pelassy, 1990). This predisposition for consensus impacts on all forms of policy making to produce a neo-corporatist approach to government (Andeweg and Irwin, 1993). Essentially it is accepted that all interested parties, including industry and pressure groups, should have an input into the policy process. In many cases government will sponsor these groups to ensure that this is the case.

The cooperative and consensus-based climate that characterizes the political system in The Netherlands has emerged from a much older trend toward cooperation which was initially associated with efforts to prevent flooding and to reclaim land from the sea. The Netherlands is a relatively small country with a unique physical environment. Although the altitude reaches 321 metres in the east, 30 per cent of its land area is below sea level. The majority of The Netherlands is composed of the Rhine delta and land that has been reclaimed from the North Sea. Inundation is prevented principally by a system of natural dunes and man made dykes. The associated flood protection and land reclamation began in the Netherlands in the 13th century and continues today (OECD, 1995). For example, in February 1953 a flood in the delta region resulted in 1,825 deaths in the south of the country. The response was the *Deltaplan*, an incredible engineering project which resulted in the closure of a number of estuaries and the heightening of dykes to ensure such a catastrophe never happened again. According to Hajer (1995, p 178–9):

> ... *[the* Deltaplan*] became the central historical example of a successful national approach to national crises... [and it] is the story-line that embodies the ultimate evidence of regulatory capability of Dutch government.*

The cooperative approaches taken to land reclamation and flood protection have had a broader impact on policy and planning in The Netherlands. For example, largely as a consequence of flood protection and land reclamation, the Dutch public has traditionally accepted the need for government intervention and has placed faith in the ability of government to plan and manage development. In response, the capacity of government to develop and apply strategic plans at the national level has evolved over a considerable period of time. The impacts of the consensus-based political system, of the widespread public acceptance of government intervention and of the highly developed planning and regulatory function within government are far reaching. In the following section the impact of these themes on Dutch environmental policy in the 1990s is apparent.

THE DUTCH ENVIRONMENTAL POLICY FRAMEWORK IN THE 1990S

Concern about the state of the environment in the Netherlands has grown steadily in recent decades. With the help of *The Limits to Growth* (Meadows, 1972) and *Blueprint for Survival* (Goldsmith et al, 1972), environmental issues were placed on the political agenda as a distinct policy issue in The Netherlands in the early 1970s. More recently, the environmental problems facing The Netherlands were highlighted in 1988 with the publication of *National Environmental Outlook 1: Concern for Tomorrow* (RIVM, 1989; see also RIVM, 1991; RIVM 1994). This national environmental survey suggested that the environmental performance of The Netherlands was declining rapidly. Amongst other things it argued that emissions of the most important polluting substances would have to be reduced by 80–90 per cent if development in The Netherlands was to become sustainable.

The *National Environmental Outlook 1* report generated a considerable amount of discussion and political debate which helped to establish a cross party consensus that environmental issues should be addressed with immediate and severe measures. This consensus helped to establish the basis for the first National Environmental Policy Plan (NEPP 1) entitled *To Choose or to Lose* which was published in 1989 (VROM, 1989). This established the form that Dutch environmental policy would take through the 1990s and for the first time introduced a strategic dimension into environmental policy planning. At the broadest level, the Ministry of Housing, Spatial Planning and Environment (VROM) states that: 'Dutch environmental policy aims to solve environmental problems within one generation and to achieve sustainable development.' (VROM, 1994a, p 12)

In recent years the most important initiatives driving The Netherlands toward this goal have been the NEPPs that have revised and updated those targets and measures originally introduced by NEPP 1 in 1989, namely NEPP Plus (VROM, 1990) and NEPP 2 (VROM, 1994b).

NEPP 1 has been reviewed extensively as a case study of national strategic planning for the environment. Carley and Christie (1992) consider that it has five key elements (see also Weale, 1992; Wintle and Reeve, 1994; van der Straaten and Ugelow, 1994; Wallace, 1995). Firstly, it established multiple timescales for action with short term policy proposals, medium term strategic goals and long term aspirations to 2010. Secondly, drawing on *National Environmental Outlook 1* it established five scales at which ecological problems must be tackled: local, regional, fluvial, continental, global. Thirdly, emphasis was placed on the integration of environmental concerns into all policy areas and into planning by principal societal actors. Fourthly, specific policy developments were based on environmental themes such as acidification and climate change. Fifthly, an extensive process of consultation and cooperation was initiated so that various target groups in Dutch society such as agriculture and manufacturing industry became involved in policy discussions.

One of the most important aspects of NEPP 1 was its emphasis on cooperation with target groups. This cooperation and the associated process of negotiation established a clear and demanding framework of quantified targets for reductions in the emissions of almost all major pollutants and waste streams. These reductions were in line with those suggested by The National Institute of Public Health and Environmental Protection (RIVM) in *National Environmental Outlook 1*. As a result the document supported RIVM's view that if The Netherlands was to reach the goal of sustainability by 2010 the volume of almost all wastes and emissions would have to be reduced significantly.

NEPP 1 was replaced by NEPP Plus in 1990 (VROM, 1990). This document retained all of the principle features of NEPP 1 but strengthened its proposals for action. The updating of the original NEPP so soon after its publication was the result of a change of government. However, the fact that NEPP Plus was in many ways an even more demanding document than NEPP 1 lends support to Carley and Christie's (1992, p 257–8) conclusion that:

> ... *the political developments in question demonstrate the remarkable level of consensus across party lines achieved in the evolution of the Plan... [and this] ensured continuity of policy on sustainable development.*

NEPP 1 and NEPP Plus were replaced by NEPP 2, at the end of 1993 (VROM, 1994b). NEPP 2 relates to the planning period up to 1998 and is built on an analysis of the progress made toward the goals of NEPP and NEPP Plus. This analysis concluded that advances had been made toward the strategic goals that had been established previously but that further action would be required if the Dutch environment was to become sustainable by the target date. Consequently, although the targets of NEPP 2 remain largely the same as those established by NEPP 1, emphasis was placed on three major issues, a strengthening of policy implementation, the introduction of additional measures where targets will not be met by existing approaches and further encouragement of sustainable production and consumption (VROM, 1994c; see also VROM, 1994d).

The philosophy underlying these three policy initiatives is that the government should create the appropriate conditions for target groups to fulfil their responsibilities. This shift, from the top-down imposition of regulations on industry to self-regulation within a framework, is explained by the Environment Minister Margaretha de Boer (1995, p 21) as follows:

> *The NEPP 2 argued that the time was ripe to transfer responsibilities to the implementers; self-regulation within a framework. The authorities set the standards and the objectives, but the manner of implementation and the timetable are where possible left to those implementing the measures. External monitoring and enforcement become more important.*

Thus it is apparent that the NEPP documents represent the corner stone of strategic planning for the environment in the Netherlands. Although the various NEPPs helped to prioritize environmental improvement as a major policy theme, it has been recognized that potentially significant changes will be needed if the goals of the NEPP documents are to be realized. Again according to the Dutch Environment Minister Margaretha de Boer (1995, p 17):

> *The National Environmental Policy Plan (NEPP 1) broke new ground. It set out to define how environmental policy could be placed permanently on the agenda and how environmental management could be securely anchored in society. The NEPP 1 presented society with a challenge...*

This claim about the impact of the various NEPPs is based on the fact that they set explicit targets for environmental improvement with definite timetables for action. These targets relate to the environmental performance of various groups in Dutch society. The plans as a whole have gained broad support in The Netherlands although, as will be discussed, there are some specific concerns regarding the nature of the plans in practice. However, in terms of the wider environmental policy context, the NEPP documents clearly establish an overall strategy within which specific regulations must operate.

IMPLEMENTING THE NEPPs: COVENANTS AND COMPANY ENVIRONMENTAL PLANS

Although the various NEPPs are significant policy documents in their own right, they are also part of a wider policy framework. Within this framework, progress toward the goals established by the NEPPs depends upon the application of a number of instruments by different institutions. One innovative instrument that has been developed to communicate the goals of the NEPPs and to foster commitment to environmental improvement is the covenant. In essence covenants are voluntary agreements that are concluded between interested parties, although in practice they frequently operate in areas where the government already has regulatory powers. Therefore, rather than viewing covenants as an example of voluntary regulation, it is better to consider them as a management tool and a communication instrument through which government attempts to disseminate information and mobilize support for its environmental targets.

In the case of environmental policy in The Netherlands, covenants are negotiated between government, trade associations, industry and other interest groups. In this context, covenants demonstrate the commitment of a sector or target group to work towards the objectives outlined in the NEPPs (VROM, 1994e). The covenant with the chemicals industry provides a good example of the system generally. Following the determination of objectives and targets at the national level within the NEPPs, the chemicals industry was identified as a target sector and a covenant was negotiated with its representatives. The parties involved in the negotiations with VROM (the lead agency) included the economic ministry, representatives of provincial government, the water boards, the Association of the Dutch Chemical Industry and individual companies. Following these discussions the covenant between the Dutch government and the Dutch chemicals industry was signed in 1993 (OECD, 1995; Consultative Group for the Chemical Industry, 1994).

Included within the covenant is an Integrated Environmental Target Plan (IETP) which is based on an emissions profile of the chemicals sector as a whole. The covenant represents an acceptance of the legitimacy of the IETP by government and by the industrial sector. Individual companies can then choose to commit themselves to a process of improvement that would realize a proportion of the targets for environmental improvement established for the sector as a whole by the IETP. To do this, each participating company must draw up a company environmental plan (CEP) which commits the company to a range of specific targets for environmental improvement. The CEP must take as its starting point the performance that would follow the application of the best available technologies whilst acknowledging economic limiting factors (VROM, 1993). It is accepted that technological limits or economic conditions may prevent the targets outlined in the IETP from being realized in the first round of covenanting. Nonetheless, the targets have been negotiated to include the potential improvements that would follow the development of new technologies and techniques over time, indeed it is anticipated that the presence of a clear framework of demanding targets may encourage such innovation.

Overall, within the NEPP framework considerable significance has been attached to the role of covenants as an instrument of environmental policy. This new approach is based on the recognition that government alone cannot bring about the necessary changes in the behaviour of target groups. The covenanting process was designed to increase awareness in target sectors and to mobilize action in participating companies by establishing clear targets for environmental improvement. However, despite these positive intentions, some concerns have been raised about the covenanting process (see Bierkart, 1995). For example, it has been argued that the covenanting process has resulted in a watering down of policy targets through negotiation. Similarly, it has been suggested that the covenanting process has delayed the development and application of other potentially complementary environmental policy initiatives. Further, it has been recognized that for some years government, regulatory agencies and industry have channelled their efforts toward the covenanting process itself rather than toward environmental improvement. More specifically, it is acknowledged that some of the earliest negotiated covenants were poorly designed as they allowed free riding by non-participating companies. Finally, despite the broad support for cooperation and consensus-building, it has been suggested that some covenants have been developed without any input from third parties and with limited access to information or third parties.

In summary, this section has discussed a number of the central dimensions of the environmental policy framework in The Netherlands. It has highlighted the general view in The Netherlands that government should assume responsibility for national strategic planning. It has argued that the relatively participative and cooperative style of government in The Netherlands is commonly associated with a degree of consensus about the forms of intervention that are adopted and applied. In relation to the environment, it has suggested that the programme of policy reform that the Dutch government instigated in the late 1980s has had a considerable impact on both policy and practice. It has recognized that the various NEPPs clearly establish the Dutch government's strategy on the environment and set out clear targets for improvement at different levels and for various timescales. However, despite the apparent strengths of Dutch environmental policy, it has acknowledged that there are concerns regarding the way that the policy framework in general and the covenanting process in particular have been applied in practice. Therefore, it is necessary to examine the frameworks, structures and styles that characterize the implementation of environmental policy in The Netherlands. As a result of the links between the covenanting process and the wider regulatory system it is not always possible to draw a clear distinction between mandatory and voluntary regulation. The following discussion will focus on the implementation of mandatory regulation in The Netherlands whilst acknowledging the influence of the covenanting process where appropriate.

MANDATORY ENVIRONMENTAL REGULATION IN THE NETHERLANDS: THE CASE OF INDUSTRIAL POLLUTION CONTROL

The NEPP framework and the associated covenanting process are fairly unique to The Netherlands although similar approaches have been initiated in other countries and interest in the wider potential of such an approach has been expressed by the European Union (see CEC, 1996). However, as well as the NEPP framework and the covenanting process, a more traditional framework of mandatory regulation exists and operates in The Netherlands. This framework of mandatory regulation operates alongside and in some instances interacts with the more innovative approaches that have been developed and applied in recent years. Having considered the NEPP framework in some detail, the following section will outline the nature of mandatory regulation in The Netherlands as it relates to the environmental performance of industry. Following the discussion in the previous chapters, this examination of the nature of mandatory regulation will focus on the structures and styles that are associated with its implementation.

Implementation Structures

While the framework of mandatory environmental regulation in The Netherlands is based on a number of different pieces of legislation, two acts of Parliament are of particular importance, namely the Environmental Management Act (EMA) of 1993 and the Pollution of Surface Waters Act (PSWA) of 1969. These establish the legal structures associated with mandatory environmental regulation for industry in The Netherlands. The EMA sought to promote the integration of environmental legislation by combining various pre-existing environmental laws. In practice this has led to the integration of five permitting systems associated with the Nuisance Act, Air Pollution Act, Noise Pollution Act, Waste Products Act and the Chemical Waste Act. As a result, following the legislative integration instigated by the EMA, most large industrial sites apply for an integrated environmental licence for almost all of the aspects of their operation that are covered by environmental regulation other than their discharges to water (VROM, 1994f; OECD, 1995).

Although a number of previously established environmental acts have been subsumed within the EMA, the PSWA has been retained and continues to operate as a separate piece of legislation. The PSWA is designed to protect the quality of surface waters in The Netherlands and it contains provisions for permits to be issued to industrial plants to regulate their emissions to the water environment. These permits contain emissions limits and may prohibit waste and polluting or harmful substances from being discharged into surface waters (VROM, 1994a; VROM, 1995). However, the EMA demands that coordination between the different regulators associated with the EMA and the PSWA does take place. Nonetheless, as a result of the continuing independence of the PSWA, it is apparent that legislative restructuring in The Netherlands has led to the creation of a coordinated but not fully integrated system of pollution control.

The institutional structures associated with the implementation of mandatory environmental regulation have also been partially but not fully integrated. The implementation of mandatory environmental regulation in The Netherlands is undertaken by two groups of institutions. Firstly, 12 provincial licensing organizations (the provincial regulators) issue licences for solid and gaseous waste and assess the environmental impacts of industrial processes generally under powers established by the EMA. Secondly, various water regulators are responsible for regulating liquid industrial emissions under the PSWA including the Rijkswaterstaat, who oversee state waters. The Rijkswaterstaat is part of the national government and is a department within the Ministry of Transport, Public Works and Water Management (OECD, 1995).

The lack of a fully integrated institutional structure to implement industrial environmental regulation has influenced the nature of regulation in a number of ways. The representative of an industrial trade association outlined one of the problems associated with this lack of integration as follows:

> ... you have the problem where you have the water quality regulator looking after water quality and air quality is dealt with by a separate authority...
> Unfortunately the water people are used to getting a lot done on the water side and the companies spend all their money there, nothing is left to improve things on the air side. Prioritizing is difficult because one says I want the water cleaned and the other the air.

The impact of this regulatory division is more apparent in regulated companies. The following statement by the environmental manager of a large manufacturing facility reflects a commonly held view:

> At times it appears that the [water regulator] isn't concerned about environmental problems in any other media. We have good arguments for spending money elsewhere but they demand more and more on the water side. Often the investment just doesn't make sense, the priorities are all wrong. There is no attempt to optimize investment.

Thus it is evident that regulated companies are not necessarily encouraged to consider emissions to air, water and land simultaneously. Consequently, scarce investment resources need not be channelled toward reductions in the most significant emissions stream. Instead, companies tend to respond to the various demands of the different regulators in an ad-hoc way. These ad-hoc responses are made more likely by the practical limits to discussion, coordination and transfer of information between the relevant regulators. While the partially fragmented legal and institutional structures associated with mandatory environmental regulation may have been to the detriment of the environment as a whole, companies have tended to prioritize the demands of the most vociferous regulator. Consequently, since the water regulator has historically been perceived as the most demanding and coercive regulator, there have been significant improvements in the quality of the water environment (see Andersen, 1994). It is important to note however that in recent years the different approaches to environmental regulation applied in The Netherlands have converged so that the practical discrepancies between acts such as the EMA and the PSWA have been reduced.

Given the complex, dynamic and site specific nature of the interactions between the regulator and regulated companies, the process of negotiation that characterizes the licensing function is not generally amenable to external scrutiny. Consequently, there is a degree of suspicion that regulations are enacted on the basis of too cooperative a relationship between the regulator and regulated companies. However, while the process of negotiation between the regulator and regulated companies itself is not monitored, the impacts of this process of negotiation are revealed through the publication of data on the environmental performance of regulated companies. Furthermore, an independent Inspectorate for the Environment monitors and publishes data on the performance of the regulatory agencies themselves and on their ability to achieve environmental standards and to work towards environmental targets. In essence, therefore, the collective impacts of the numerous processes of negotiation between the regulator and regulated companies are opened up for external scrutiny. In this way the accountability of the regulatory framework is maintained without sacrificing the ability of the regulator to fine-tune the implementation of regulation to reflect the specific circumstances in regulated firms.

Aside from the impact that the associated legislative and institutional structures have on the nature of mandatory regulation in practice, the resource structures associated with implementation are also of great significance. Within the implementing agency, the background and experience of regulatory staff and the behaviour of individual regulators are of particular importance. The analysis below focuses on the case of one of the provincial regulators that is associated with the delivery of the EMA in The Netherlands. In the region considered, the staff of the provincial regulator with licensing and authorization responsibilities are from two distinct backgrounds: approximately half have extensive industrial experience and half are science and engineering graduates with little or no prior industrial experience. Generally the graduates are trained and gain experience regulating the less complicated industrial processes before assuming responsibility for the larger industrial sites. The more experienced staff are responsible for implementing the regulations in the larger and more complicated plants.

The staff profile outlined above has a number of implications for the day-to-day delivery of environmental regulation. On the whole, the provincial regulator is considered by regulated companies to be staffed by knowledgeable and competent staff. This has helped to produce an open and cooperative relationship between the regulator and regulated companies. This was identified by the environmental manager of a small manufacturing company as follows:

> *I think that it benefits discussion of what is reasonable and not reasonable. You have to get people understanding what you are talking about, if you have an inspector who has experience sitting opposite to you, talking is much easier.*

Thus, the experience and background of the individual regulator has an important impact on the level and the nature of the dialogue with regulated companies that takes place during implementation. Where levels of expertise on both sides allow mutual understanding there is greater potential for an open and cooperative relationship. The potential for the transfer of information and understanding between these actors is also improved.

The importance of the level of expertise of regulatory staff can be confirmed by considering a countervailing example. In some cases, where communication between the regulator and the regulated company has broken down, the problem is perceived to be the result of a lack of mutual understanding. The following quote from the environmental manager of a large processing installation illustrates this point:

> ... *our contact person at [the provincial regulator] is a very experienced man, that's why the relationship is very good. But I know there are companies who are having much trouble, where communication with the regulator is about zero. That's because the understanding is not good and everyone is going their own way, instead of going together to some kind of point you want both to reach.*

Beyond simply enabling the development of an open working relationship between the regulator and the regulated company, the expertise of the regulator also impacts on the potential for interactive learning in the implementation phase. This is explained by an environmental manager as follows:

> *The problem is if they are not process engineers and technical engineers they may not be much good and the knowledge we have is much better here. If they are well trained and have experience then they understand what others are doing and can guide us. They can point out areas of improvement. But it depends on who you get.*

Thus, it is evident that less experienced and less knowledgeable staff are less able to provide useful information to regulated companies. Regulated companies prefer regulatory staff with recent industrial experience as they understand the processes that they regulate. This helps them to suggest management options and to disseminate information and understanding, particularly of a tacit nature, whilst at the same time promoting a positive working relationship with the regulated company.

Therefore, it can be seen that there are variable resource structures associated with the implementation of mandatory environmental regulation in The Netherlands, at least in relation to the implementation of the EMA. In some instances knowledgeable and experienced staff are able to explore a process of interactive learning with regulated companies. Through this process they are able to transfer information on best practice to the companies that they regulate. However, the experience and understanding of regulatory staff varies. Restrictions in the experience and understanding of the regulator limit the ability of the regulator to assimilate and to transfer information on best practice to regulated companies. At the extreme, restricted experience and understanding can result in a complete breakdown in communication between the regulator and the regulated company. Thus, the potential for the regulator to enhance the capacity of regulated companies to respond to regulation in an effective and efficient way is not consistently exploited. However, the existence of a framework of standards and targets and the presence of an independent organization to monitor the performance of regulatory agencies help to ensure that the imperative for environmental improvement is maintained.

Implementation Styles

As a consequence of their design, the EMA and the PSWA differ in some important respects. The EMA has tended to be anticipatory and process focused as it is concerned with the operation of industrial processes as well as with the significance of their emissions (OECD, 1995). In contrast the PSWA has tended to be more reactive and emissions oriented as it is primarily concerned with the quality of the water environment. However, some convergence of the different aproaches to regulation has been apparent in recent years. The requirements of these acts are interpreted and operationalized by the regulators, who establish emissions limits for individual companies which are underpinned by national environmental quality standards which deal with specific pollutants and are established for air and water by VROM (OECD, 1995).

The impact of the differing design styles of the EMA and the PSWA is particularly apparent when considering the delivery and enforcement styles associated with each act. In relation to the delivery of regulation, regulators can tend toward either a hands-on, intensive relationship with regulated companies or they can favour an arm's-length, extensive relationship. Significantly different regulatory styles have been associated with the EMA and the PSWA. Generally, provincial regulators have worked in a more hands-on way than the water regulator although the approach of the latter has changed in recent years. Within the region studied, the provincial regulator has also been seen to be more open and cooperative than the water regulator. These differences in style are exemplified by the following quote from the environmental manager of a company that is regulated by both regulators:

> With [the provincial regulator] our contact is very good. We have many discussions about the limits, if we can reach them or not, what our problem is and how we will solve them. When we have problems we discuss that with them. They may have some solution which we both look at and in that way you can do a lot more than if you don't have that kind of relationship. On the water side we don't.

In a number of instances, regulated companies noted that there had been a complete breakdown in communication with the water regulator. In these instances, a situation of mutual suspicion and mistrust had developed which, from the perspective of the regulated companies, was as a result of an unwillingness on the part of the water regulator to be involved in discussions and negotiations. The general feeling was that they preferred simply to establish and enforce emissions limits in a rigid way with a limited amount of interaction with regulated companies.

It is clear that the delivery style has related closely to the enforcement style associated with each regulator. In the case of the provincial regulator a conciliative and consensual approach to enforcement has been dominant while the water regulator has tended to adopt a more litigious and adversarial approach to enforcement. As the environmental manager of a manufacturing plant describes:

> *It depends on who you get but on the whole they [the water regulator] like to send letters rather than discuss things. They tell you what you have to do rather than consider possible options. They are also much quicker to prosecute. The two go hand in hand.*

The implications of the different delivery and enforcement styles can be illustrated by considering the role of the provincial regulator. In the case of a company that will not cooperate, or that cannot be trusted, they have the option of imposing detailed formal prescriptions and legal sanctions. Thus, although the provincial regulator generally perceives a cooperative and conciliative approach to be more effective, they can resort to a litigious and adversarial delivery and enforcement style if necessary. One of the inspectors outlined the implications of each approach:

> *Formal regulation means you do each step slowly, it's very bureaucratic… We are not as cooperative as we could be, it is not a real negotiated process any more. Unfortunately we write down rules that are not true in practice. We think that the company is working in such a way and we make rules on it. But in practice the rules do not fit with the way the company works because we haven't been able to get to know and understand the company. So in the end the company has a set of rules that don't really fit and the government has a set of rules that don't really fit. But if they had been more open the rules would have been able to match to their situation.*

This illustrates the problems of regulating in the absence of open discussion and trust between parties and of not being able to fine-tune the requirements of regulation to fit the specific circumstances found within regulated companies. This highlights a tension between the need for formal measures which limit the extent to which the exercize of discretion during implementation can lead to a weakening of the goals of regulation and the requirement to fine-tune the demands of regulation so that it fits the specific circumstances of its application.

This discussion has focused on the significance of the styles that characterize the design, delivery and enforcement of mandatory regulation. In The Netherlands it is apparent that anticipatory and process focused legislation has been combined with a hands-on and intensive delivery style and with a conciliative and consensual enforcement style. Such a combination of design, delivery and enforcement styles characterizes the implementation of the EMA in The Netherlands. Conversely, it is evident that reactive and emissions focused legislation has been combined with an arm's-length and extensive delivery style and a litigious and adversarial approach to enforcement. This combination of regulatory styles has tended to characterize the implementation of the PSWA in The Netherlands although a shift toward a more interactive and flexible approach has been apparent in recent years.

THE IMPACT OF ENVIRONMENTAL REGULATION IN THE NETHERLANDS: THE CASE OF THE NEPP FRAMEWORK AND MANDATORY REGULATION

In the discussion so far, two different approaches to environmental regulation in The Netherlands have been outlined, namely the innovative NEPP framework and the associated covenanting process and the more traditional framework of mandatory regulation. The following section, which draws extensively on interviews with regulators and regulated companies, assesses the impact of these approaches on industrial behaviour. Due to the interaction of the two approaches in practice, the following discussion considers their impact simultaneously. The discussion considers the impacts of these complementary forms of government intervention on the technological, organizational and strategic behaviour of regulated companies.

The Technological Dimension

The NEPP framework exerts an influence on the technological behaviour of companies in a number of ways. In line with the consensus-based approach to policy that is generally applied in The Netherlands, the negotiations which establish and operationalize the NEPP targets seek to produce a mutually satisfactory outcome for both government and industry. Although this process of negotiation can mean that targets are weakened or are not met in the first instance, one of the primary goals of this process of negotiation is to mobilize support and establish commitment to environmental improvement.

This process of target-setting and awareness raising has an impact on the innovative behaviour of firms. As the representative of an industrial trade organization explained:

> When people look at the covenant and see targets for 2010, that will trigger innovation… They think we have to do quite a lot, we had better think about new developments. When you see you have to climb very high you will start to think is there sufficient food? Can I survive? And that is better than just walking off and not knowing where you are going.

Therefore, it is likely that the various NEPPs and their targets will have an impact on the level of technological innovation that takes place within companies in the various target sectors. While the impact of targets will not become fully apparent for some time, it is evident that mandatory regulation in The Netherlands has stimulated the development and application of both control and clean technologies. It is already apparent that the presence of the longer term targets for improvement established by the various NEPPs will help to shift the emphasis of the industrial response to regulation away from control and toward clean technologies. This shift is described by the representative of an industrial trade association:

There have been a lot of end-of-pipe solutions and that is worrying because it is very expensive. You can be lucky and be building a brand new plant, use modern technology, and so reduce significantly your emissions. But that is not true for all the cases and sometimes you have to do something like end-of-pipe, but that can be very costly. We are trying to motivate companies to try and think a bit more about the prospects for clean technologies.

It is apparent that clean technologies are more readily adopted during periods of process re-engineering, major upgrading and rebuilding. This is described by the environmental manager of a large manufacturing plant:

Mostly we have end-of-pipe, but we try as much as possible to get integrated solutions. But this is an old process and that is not easy. When you build a new plant then you can concentrate on the integrated solution.

Given that clean technologies can be more readily adopted during periods of major process change, it is apparent that the ability of regulation to promote the development and application of clean technologies is a strategic as well as an operational concern. As stated by a representative of VROM:

In the past, in the 1980s and 1990s, it has been mainly end-of-pipe technology. Now we have realized that we should go a step further into the process integrated technologies. So we have to look at a more strategic time-frame for technology than we did five to ten years ago.

However, as the following example demonstrates, the shift in emphasis toward the development and application of clean technologies is not always straightforward. One regulated company interviewed had recently completely redesigned its production process as a response to the concerns of the water regulator about liquid emissions from the old process and become aware of a newer process which they perceived to be both environmentally and economically advantageous. The new process was more efficient and used a very pure feedstock which generated significantly lower emissions levels. However, in the opinion of the company this meant that any further environmental improvements would demand the application of expensive control technologies as it was impossible to alter the process further to achieve higher environmental objectives. Thus, once the process had been redesigned and new process technology had been installed, the costs of further environmental improvement would escalate. Following the initial investment in the new process technology, the water regulator returned to request a further reduction in the levels of one substance in the liquid effluent. The only way that this could be achieved was through the application of an expensive piece of control technology. Thus, the company embarked on a second round of investment in control technology as all of the opportunities for improvement through the application of clean technologies had been exploited.

117

In relation to the impact of the different regulatory styles, it is apparent that the hands-on and conciliative approach to implementation that is associated with the EMA has had a number of advantages when compared with the arm's-length and litigious style that has been associated with the delivery and enforcement of the PSWA. Generally companies welcome the interaction with the provincial regulator, although the impact of this interaction depends upon the expertise and insight of the individual inspectors. Furthermore, companies perceive that the conciliative enforcement style adopted by the provincial regulator allows them to explore the longer term potential of new technologies and techniques as in the short to medium term the risks associated with non-compliance should these technologies and techniques fail are reduced. However, the imperative to innovate remains as companies recognize the willingness of the provincial regulator to adopt a rigid and litigious enforcement style if over time companies do not demonstrate their commitment to environmental improvement.

Although there is some evidence to suggest that the arm's-length style of implementation and the litigious style of enforcement associated with the PSWA are changing, it is also important to acknowledge the perceptions that regulated companies have of such an approach. The arm's-length approach was generally resented by regulated companies who tended to respond to regulation defensively by resisting change. The application of an arm's-length and at times adversarial regulatory style reduced the commitment of regulated companies to search for innovative responses to regulation or to move beyond compliance. It also prevented the transfer of information and understanding from the regulator to regulated companies. Consequently, it missed an opportunity to enhance the capacity of regulated companies to respond to regulation in a positive way. Finally, because of the perceived readiness of the water regulator to resort to legal action in the short term, companies felt that the risks associated with the development and application of innovative technologies and techniques which were untried and untested were too great. Established responses with predictable impacts were therefore favoured. Perhaps as a consequence of these perceptions and reactions, the implementation and enforcement of the PSWA has more recently been characterized by a more interactive and flexible regulatory style.

The discussion above illustrates the many dimensions of the impact that government intervention has had on the technological behaviour of regulated companies in The Netherlands. It is apparent that the process of setting and communicating targets encourages strategic thinking in regulated companies. The presence of these targets increases the ability of companies to plan ahead and to integrate environmental considerations into their production processes at the design stage. Thus, a framework of targets tends to support the development and application of clean technologies. However, the impact of the NEPP framework and of the covenanting process ultimately depends upon the nature of mandatory regulation, or more particularly the behaviour of the mandatory regulator, as this may reinforce or undermine the influence of the targets that are established both for industrial sectors and for individual companies. In this respect the importance of the appropriate capacities for environmental improvement in regulated companies is particularly apparent as these capacities allow an effective and efficient response to the imperatives established by the various standards and targets.

The Organizational Dimension

The technological changes that are promoted by regulation can be complemented by a range of organizational or managerial changes. While organizational change commonly creates the conditions for technological innovation, in many cases technological changes are optimized by subsequent organizational adaptation. This is described by one environmental manager:

As a company we have an at source policy but sometimes you must use end-of-pipe. At one of our plants we used a particular catalyst system and got a tremendous amount of waste, several thousand tonnes per year. By changing the catalyst system we were able to halve that. But changing the catalyst system also allowed other optimization and we halved that again. So the technology changed and that allowed us to change our work practices.

Organizational changes may take place between as well as within organizations. As an example of inter-organizational change, the environmental manager of a medium sized industrial plant explained:

One of our key streams of waste is a product we call black-cake. Due to whatever circumstances in the production process we might have a product which is not useable, we used to bring it to a place where you could put it into the ground. It was legal and there was no problem. But through regulatory pressure and a local industrial ecosystem we've just found out that the power plant who supply our company can use it. It is still minimum 95 per cent pure carbon and in almost every case it is more. They can use this for their fuel. But, once again, the next step should be to try not to produce the so-called black-cake. Because, if tomorrow this company calls us and says they don't need our product it becomes waste again.

Organizational innovations such as this appear to be an increasingly common response to regulation in the Netherlands. In part at least this reflects the flexibility that surrounds the way that mandatory regulations are interpreted and applied by some regulatory agencies.

The organizational impacts of the NEPP framework, of the associated covenanting process and of mandatory environmental regulation are most significant where government intervention has stimulated the application of environmental management systems. Various steps have been taken by the Dutch government and the regulatory agencies to encourage the adoption of EMSs. For example, in 1989 VROM began a specific programme to stimulate the uptake of EMSs in industry with the objective of encouraging the adoption of EMSs in 10 thousand large companies and 250 thousand smaller companies by 1995. More specifically, the covenanting process demands that participating companies install an EMS, which in the Dutch context is termed an environmental care system. Regulatory agencies may also issue simplified permits to those companies who have recognized and externally audited environmental management systems in place. In such instances it is assumed by the regulator that if objectives and targets have been established for a regulated company, and if progress toward these targets can be monitored, then as long as they are of a suitable quality EMSs can be relied upon to establish the conditions that are necessary if the required improvements in environmental performance are to be realized. Companies that have an accredited EMS are thus subjected to less intensive scrutiny than those that do not. Mandatory regulation thereby establishes an implicit incentive for companies to participate in the covenanting process and to register for schemes such as EMAS and ISO14001.

The Strategic Dimension

One of the most significant impacts of the framework of targets established by the various NEPPs is that companies have responded in a strategic as well as an operational way. The influence of the targets for various timescales is explained by a representative of a large manufacturing plant:

> It gives some clarity to what is expected from industry and in what time. It sets requirements for management at the highest level. It impacts on innovation and you respond in a different way. Engineers look from the beginning at environmental issues, not half way through development. The targets are set for the future and get considered all the time, particularly when we upgrade the plant.

Because of this strategic impact it is apparent that target-setting is encouraging companies to adopt anticipatory rather than reactive responses to regulation. The presence of a clear and credible system of targets allows companies to plan ahead in order to satisfy their regulatory obligations in the most efficient way. Commonly, the presence of targets allows companies to integrate environmental considerations into their strategic decision-making practices. More particularly it encourages companies to reorientate their research and development activities and to redefine their product and process design initiatives. Thus, rather than having to respond to regulatory demands at short notice by disrupting existing activities, because of the framework of targets that exists in The Netherlands regulated companies are able to synchronize their responses to regulation with their natural investment schedules and thus with their product and process life-cycles. Given the greater flexibility and freedom that anticipatory planning affords, it is apparent that strategic responses to environmental regulation allow more radical changes to be pursued. The performance of these radical responses to regulation, which can fundamentally change what companies do as well as the way that they do it, can then be further improved over time through subsequent phases of incremental innovation. Consequently, the escalating costs associated with a reliance on incremental change alone are avoided and the efficacy and efficiency of environmental regulation is enhanced.

Summary: The Implementation and Impact of Industrial Environmental Regulation in the Netherlands

The preceding discussion has outlined the context within which Dutch environmental policy operates. It has examined the nature of the NEPP framework and of the covenanting process. Against this background it has examined the implementation and impact of two of the central pieces of industrial environmental regulation in The Netherlands, namely the 1969 Pollution of Surface Waters Act and the 1993 Environmental Management Act. The implementation of these forms of mandatory regulation has been analysed with reference to the frameworks, structures and styles of regulation. The impact of these regulations has been analysed with reference to the technological, organizational and strategic dimensions of the responses that have been developed and applied in regulated companies. A number of observations can be made following this analysis.

The NEPP documents have established a clear framework of targets for environmental improvement for different levels and for various timescales. The analysis put forward above suggests that a comprehensive framework of targets such as that developed by the various NEPPs has had a beneficial impact on the level and on the nature of the technologies and techniques that are developed by companies as a response to regulation. The impact of the framework of environmental targets depends upon the extent to which the negotiated targets are communicated to target groups. It also depends upon the perceived legitimacy, credibility and clarity of the targets in regulated companies. In The Netherlands it is apparent that the targets established for industrial environmental performance, which are embodied in the covenants that have been agreed between government and industrial sectors, are perceived to be challenging but achievable in the medium to long term.

Aside from the wider policy framework, the impact of mandatory environmental regulation depends upon the structures and styles associated with its implementation. In relation to the regulatory structures that are associated with the implementation of environmental regulation in The Netherlands, it is apparent that both the legislative and the institutional structures have yet to be fully integrated so that they simultaneously address emissions to air, water and land. This coordinated but partially fragmented regulatory structure restricts the ability of the various regulators and of regulated companies to focus their attention and resources on emissions to the most sensitive or saturated receptor environment. However, the presence of an external organization that monitors the performance of regulatory agencies increases the accountability of the regulatory framework, particularly as performance can be judged against a clearly established and fully transparent set of targets and performance measures. Because it increases the accountability of the regulatory function, such a structure helps to protect the ability of the regulator to exercize a degree of discretion in the way that regulations are interpreted and applied. Thus, while it may not be possible to scrutinise the process of negotiation between regulators and regulated companies, it is possible to analyse the outputs of this process.

In relation to the resource structures associated with mandatory regulation, it is apparent that the different staff involved in the implementation of the EMA in particular bring differing levels of expertise and understanding to the task. This influences the extent to which regulators are able to transfer information and insight to regulated companies and therefore the extent to which regulators are able to enhance the capacity of regulated companies to respond to the demands of regulation in an effective and efficient manner. In relation to the regulatory styles that are applied, in the past there has been a contrast between those that relate to the EMA and those that have related to the PSWA. This includes differences in the design, delivery and enforcement styles of regulation. In The Netherlands it is apparent that a hands-on, intensive delivery style combined with a conciliative and consensual enforcement style has been associated with anticipatory and process focused legislation in the case of the EMA. Conversely, although some convergence with the approach to the implementation of the EMA is apparent, a more arm's-length delivery style and a more litigious and adversarial enforcement style has been associated with reactive, emissions-focused legislation in the case of the PSWA. However, coordination between the agencies responsible for implementing these regulations does take place and there is some evidence that the regulatory style associated with the PSWA is moving toward the approach that has more commonly been associated with the EMA.

In relation to the impact of industrial environmental regulation in The Netherlands, it is apparent that the framework of targets established by the various NEPPs is facilitating forward planning in regulated companies. In turn this forward planning increases the prospects for clean technologies to be developed and applied and for radical rather than incremental changes to be made to production processes. The technological impacts of industrial environmental regulation have been complemented by a range of organizational changes, particularly those related to the wider development and application of EMSs. In some instances it is apparent that companies have realized the required improvements in their environmental performance through organizational change alone. It is also apparent that the presence of an EMS helps to establish conditions within regulated companies that are conducive to the development of new technologies and techniques. Similarly, the presence of an EMS allows companies to integrate environmental considerations into their strategic decision-making processes so that environmental concerns can be effectively and efficiently incorporated into the design and application of new processes and products. The strategic impact of industrial environmental regulation is enhanced by the presence of a clear framework of company specific targets for environmental improvement for the short, medium and long terms.

VOLUNTARY REGULATION IN THE NETHERLANDS: THE CASE OF THE EU'S ECO-MANAGEMENT AND AUDIT SCHEME

Aside from those environmental initiatives that are developed and applied by industry as a response to mandatory regulation, it is apparent that companies are increasingly taking voluntary action to improve their environmental performance. The following section focuses on one example of such action. Following a brief assessment of the links between mandatory and voluntary regulation, the discussion explores the implementation and impact of voluntary regulation in the form of EMS standards. Particular emphasis is placed on the EU Eco-Management and Audit Scheme (EMAS) although the International Standards Organization's environmental management systems standard (ISO14001) is also considered. The work presented draws on interviews with the environmental managers of many of the first companies in The Netherlands to be registered for EMAS and certified for ISO14001. It also makes use of interviews with representatives of the Dutch competent body for EMAS along with the accreditors and verifiers who assess the compliance of companies who wish to register under EMAS or become certified for ISO14001.

Implementation Structures and EMAS in The Netherlands

As discussed above, one of the defining features of the Dutch approach to environmental policy and regulation in recent years has been its willingness to explore the application of innovative policy instruments. This policy context has served to support the development and application of voluntary approaches to regulation. The various NEPPs and the associated covenanting process have introduced a voluntary dimension into the regulatory framework of The Netherlands. Although companies can choose whether to contribute toward the targets for environmental improvement established by the covenant for an industrial sector, various links have been established between mandatory and voluntary regulation to encourage participation in the covenanting process.

From the voluntary perspective, the competent body and the accreditation body for EMAS have stressed the importance of developing a standard which will win the confidence of government and of the public. If confidence in the efficacy of voluntary regulation can be enhanced, voluntary schemes such as EMAS will be more able to influence the formulation and implementation of mandatory regulation. Generally, this demands that EMAS and other EMS standards are applied in a way that will convince government, the regulatory agencies and the public of the commitment and capacity of EMAS registered sites to work toward the pre-established targets for environmental improvement without a significant amount of external supervision or intervention. In such circumstances, although government and the regulatory agencies will continue to set standards, to establish targets and to monitor compliance with the requirements of mandatory regulation, where possible responsibility for realizing environmental improvement will be transferred to industry itself. Consequently, it is proposed that once company specific targets have been established and an effective EMS has been developed as part of the CEP, the company will be left to work towards these targets without interference from mandatory environmental regulators. It is felt that the efficacy of an EMS can more readily be secured and demonstrated through verification and registration with schemes such as EMAS. Therefore, government may adopt a more arm's-length approach to regulation as long as it is convinced that standards such as EMAS establish the necessary conditions for improvement in regulated companies. In instances where a regulated company is registered for an EMS standard, rather than issuing a detailed permit which explicitly sets out the measures that a company must adopt to ensure compliance, the mandatory regulator will consider issuing a simpler licence or permit which obliges the company to work toward the targets negotiated and adopted under the covenanting process or by mandatory regulation.

The boundaries between mandatory and voluntary regulation in The Netherlands are therefore far from distinct. There are numerous links between the covenanting process, the framework of mandatory regulation and the voluntary regulations such as EMAS or ISO14001. Because of the intertwined nature of mandatory and voluntary regulation within the broader policy framework, it is impossible to analyse the impacts of EMAS in isolation in The Netherlands. However, EMAS is implemented by a distinct group of organizations who interpret and apply the requirements of the Regulation in a particular way.

As a scheme established by an EU Regulation, the Dutch government was obliged to establish institutional structures to oversee the delivery of EMAS in The Netherlands. This has required the establishment of a competent body to hold the register of EMAS companies and an accreditation body to accredit consultants who wish to become verifiers under the scheme. The function of the competent body has been allocated to The Association for Coordination of Certification of Environmental Management Systems (SCCM). This is a private organization which, although operating with a remit from government, is independent and must become self financing. SCCM was established specifically to manage the development and application of EMS standards and to hold the register of EMAS companies. It has also played a central role in establishing the accreditation system. However, the most important contribution to the operationalization of EMAS made by SCCM has been the development of a verification system (SCCM, 1995). This system establishes the organization of the verification structure and the procedure to be followed by the verifier during verification. This essentially defines the requirements associated with the scheme.

Beyond the role played by SCCM, in practice the delivery of EMAS begins with the accreditation procedure. Accreditation of EMAS verifiers is undertaken by the Dutch Council for Accreditation (Raad voor de Certificatie (RvA)). The role of RvA is to ensure that consultants (individuals or companies) who wish to act as EMAS verifiers and validate EMAS statements have the required skills to undertake the task. Consequently they assess potential verification bodies before they are awarded EMAS verifier status. Related to this, RvA have issued a set of guidelines for the accreditation of certification bodies for EMSs which outline what is expected from potential verifiers (Raad voor de Certificatie, 1995; Falk and Wilkinson, 1996).

Therefore two of the most important EMAS organizations in The Netherlands are SCCM and RvA. However, they are supported by a Central

Committee of Experts (CCvD) which has 15 members including representatives of government, industry, NGOs and unions. The CCvD has the power to change the nature of the structures that operationalize EMAS in The Netherlands. They play a key role in determining the nature of the verification system and are responsible for changing the system to take account of new developments and recent experience. Beyond SCCM, RvA and the CCvD are the verifiers themselves who have direct involvement with companies who wish to register for EMAS. The staff involved in this role have a major impact on the practical character of EMAS. It is these resource structures that will now be assessed.

The process of operationalizing EMAS demands that verifiers audit companies who wish to register with the scheme to ensure that they comply with its requirements. This is followed by the validation of their environmental statement. The Dutch system, particularly as outlined by SCCM (1995, p 13), clearly outlines the nature of the staff that are allowed to fulfil this verification role:

> *Audit teams acting as verifiers under EMAS in The Netherlands should include knowledge of the best available control techniques for reducing the environmental effects of those operations they are auditing. They should also be able to undergo an environmental effect analysis. More specifically verifiers are expected to be highly skilled and knowledgeable and this has to be demonstrated on the basis of education and/or work experience but there must be a minimum of four years' relevant practical work experience. Particularly with respect to the Lead Verifier of the verification team they should have all the above and ability to lead the verification team.*

Interestingly, due to the relatively recent development of EMS standards in The Netherlands it is anticipated that initially there may be some problems finding Lead Verifiers who fulfil the criteria. This is likely to be the case until EMAS has been running for a reasonable length of time. It is proposed that as an interim and transitional measure experienced auditors of ISO 9000 quality management systems, with appropriate training, can be used as lead verifiers under EMAS (SCCM, 1995).

Implementation Styles and EMAS in the Netherlands

With regard to its implementation, the design of EMAS in The Netherlands has been influenced by a committee installed to advise VROM, which is the agency responsible for establishing the competent body and the verification structures. This committee focused on three particular aspects of EMAS, namely its compatibility with other EMS standards such as ISO14001, the relative emphasis that it placed on management systems and environmental improvement and the standards applied by different verifiers.

Firstly, concerning compatibility the committee decided that competition between the different EMS standards would be counter productive. Consequently, it suggested that steps should be taken to build on the commonality of the different EMS standards. Therefore, as a representative of the

EMAS Competent Body in the Netherlands (SCCM) stated: 'The basic assumption was that it must be possible to use an EMS certificate [issued under another EMS standard] as the basis for EMAS registration.' Thus, the implementation structures for EMAS were designed in a way that would allow companies that were certified under an EMS standard such as ISO14001 to bypass certain aspects of the EMAS verification process. In this way it was predicted that more companies would eventually register for EMAS, particularly if over time EMAS was recognized as the more demanding and therefore more prestigious EMS standard.

Secondly, building on the experience that had accumulated in The Netherlands relating to quality management systems standards, it was suggested that the emphasis of EMAS in general and of the verification structures in particular should not be placed on the performance of the management system *per se* but on its ability to influence the environmental performance of registered companies. Again according to a representative of SCCM:

> *We have learned from the quality management systems that too much emphasis was placed on internal procedures. An EMS must be operational and must be capable of realizing environmental objectives.*

In SCCM's view this emphasis on environmental performance is particularly important because EMAS demands the publication of a verified environmental statement. It is suggested that the perceived integrity of the EMAS scheme will be undermined unless registered companies demonstrate that they have delivered real improvements in their environmental performance. Furthermore, it is recognized that it is critically important to establish, maintain and demonstrate the environmental credentials of EMAS if it is to be accepted by government and the regulatory agencies and therefore if the links between mandatory and voluntary regulation are to be fully explored. Thus, the verification requirements for EMAS in The Netherlands are designed to emphasise the impact that the management system has on the environmental performance of registered companies.

Finally, it was considered important that the requirements of EMAS should be consistently interpreted and applied by the different organizations and individuals involved in verification. Consequently, the requirements for verification were set out in detail to minimize the extent to which discretion could be applied in the verification process. Again this concern related to the actual and perceived integrity of the EMAS scheme as this was seen to be a prerequisite for the scheme's success not only in isolation but also in combination with mandatory regulation.

In relation to the delivery and enforcement styles associated with the implementation of EMAS in The Netherlands, it is apparent that an issue of critical importance is the way that the qualitative principles that define the scheme are interpreted and applied in practice. The question of what constitutes continuous improvement is of particular significance. A representative of SCCM gave the following definition of continuous improvement, revealing how it could potentially impact on the development and application of new technologies and techniques under the Dutch system:

> *A company must have a system for inventorizing all the technological possibilities that there are. Then it has to make a plan for how it will implement these state of the art approaches and must have a good story where this does not happen. The certification body checks this plan.*

The implementation of EMAS in The Netherlands demands that an intensive relationship between the verifier and the company operates only during the verification phase. Although verifiers can generally be employed as environmental consultants at other times, this is at the discretion of the company seeking verification. During the verification phase, which typically lasts for two to three days in every audit cycle, the verification agency has the potential to transfer an amount of information and understanding on the various environmental management options to the company or site seeking verification. However, the verification requirements establish the role that the verifier should play and the functions that they should fulfil in detail. While the requirements for independence and objectivity are seen to be of paramount importance, the precisely defined verification procedures encourage or perhaps even demand that an arm's-length approach to implementation is adopted by verifiers. Even during the limited interaction between the verifier and the site seeking verification, such an approach to implementation does not lend itself to any significant degree of interaction or to the transfer of information on best practice.

The enforcement style adopted in relation to EMAS is complicated not only by the question of what to do in the case of non-compliance with the requirements of EMAS but also of what to do in the case of non-compliance with the requirements of mandatory regulation. In The Netherlands this is further complicated by the different enforcement styles that are adopted in relation to mandatory regulation and by the intertwined nature of the relationship between mandatory and voluntary regulation. As discussed above, the targets for environmental improvement established by the covenanting process can be adopted as the requirements of mandatory regulation and as the goals for continuous improvement under EMAS. A failure to realize a target in one area of regulation could therefore have a direct impact on compliance in another. Furthermore, as a result of the different styles that are applied by the various agencies associated with the enforcement of mandatory regulation, a breach of consent in one area of mandatory regulation may not be comparable to a breach of consent in another. As a consequence of these complications the enforcement style for EMAS has yet to be clearly established.

Thus, the structures that surround the implementation of EMAS in The Netherlands are designed to ensure that the scheme functions effectively and efficiently. A number of steps have been taken to establish, maintain and demonstrate the integrity of the EMAS scheme so that its perceived integrity is protected and so that its potential to interact with mandatory regulation is realized. The styles of implementation associated with EMAS reflect this concern with the integrity of the scheme.

THE IMPACT OF VOLUNTARY REGULATION IN THE NETHERLANDS: THE CASE OF EMAS

In the discussion above, the frameworks, structures and styles associated with the implementation of EMS standards in The Netherlands have been outlined with particular reference to EMAS. In the following section the technological, organizational and strategic impacts of these standards on business activity will be considered.

The Technological Dimension

Other than stimulating investment in monitoring technologies, EMS standards appear to have had a limited direct impact on the development and application of new technologies in The Netherlands. However, it is apparent that the presence of an EMS helps to establish conditions within industry that are conducive to technological innovation. For instance, it is evident that the presence of an EMS increases awareness of environmental issues throughout the company. It also enhances ability of managers to assimilate information on the need for environmental improvement and on the availability and applicability of new technologies and techniques. These impacts were explained by the representative of a large processing plant:

> *A company has the EMS to inform itself about what is possible... I think this will have a positive effect on innovation. When you have a problem, whatever it is, there is an endless source of information to deal with concerning solutions. That must be managed in a way that results in helpful suggestions and lines of enquiry. The management system can do this if you document approaches. It can help to identify technologies and techniques.*

Beyond highlighting the need for innovation and the potential of different approaches, the presence of an EMS helps to establish a climate within the firm that is receptive to the introduction of new technologies and techniques. This is particularly the case with respect to clean technological options which, as identified above, often require organizational changes throughout the company if they are to be implemented successfully. In the following quote an environmental manager outlines how this can happen in practice:

> *People must understand change. Changing technologies impact on people. Yes, you need their help because new technology and old working practices are not good. No, it will not work. An environmental care system should explain change to people and prepare the way. If technology is changed it should automatically set a procedure in motion which ensures that education accompanies it.*

Thus, the presence of an EMS can help to raise awareness of the need for innovation and of the availability and applicability of new technologies and techniques. It can also help to establish conditions within companies that are conducive to the development and application of new technologies, particularly by facilitating the change throughout the organization that is commonly needed if a technological innovation is to be successfully accommodated within existing structures and systems.

The Organizational Dimension

Environmental management systems are an organizational innovation in themselves. However, evidence from The Netherlands suggests that the range of organizational impacts associated with the adoption of an effective EMS is potentially very large indeed. The following outline of some of these impacts was provided by the manager of small manufacturing plant:

> If you define a management system as a set of procedures where you have written down all the agreements between the functions in your organization and it's filled with some instructions about checklists and so on, then yes, it helps. If you look at a specific procedure to cope with the management of change, it triggers all kinds of checks and you are forced to do some studies before you start rebuilding or modifying your plant. You need specific meetings, you need specific reporting channels, you need to skill people, you need to train them, you need to tell them, you need to manage the process of communication between people so that they can work together.

Therefore it is possible to view the EMS as a mechanism for managing change and for dealing with often unpredictable events and pressures within the firm.

One of the most important aspects of the organizational impact of an EMS is the integration of environmental concerns into other areas of business operation and decision-making. An effective EMS can allow environmental issues to be approached in a cohesive and integrated way that spans the functional boundaries of the individuals and departments within the firm. Evidence from The Netherlands indicates that an EMS can assist in this through education and awareness raising as described by one environmental manager:

> Are people alert enough, careful enough, this is the role of an environmental care system. We must make people aware every moment what is their contribution, through lectures, training, policy... [companies] have a better insight into their processes and their products, what's going in and coming out. It is a good basis to think further. But all new ideas have to come from a sound basis and these systems provide that.

Therefore, it is evident that EMSs have generated a range of organizational benefits for industry in The Netherlands. They have encouraged and facilitated the application of new technologies and techniques by increasing awareness, by enhancing managerial capacities and by helping to reduce the significance of the functional boundaries within firms that can restrict a company-wide response to an environmental issue. In some instances they have helped to shift environmental concerns from the periphery to the core of business decision making. As they have been used to manage change throughout organizations, they have also facilitated a shift from reactive or end-of-pipe approaches to anticipatory or integrated approaches to environmental improvement.

The Strategic Dimension

In the medium to long term the presence of an effective EMS can help to change the culture of an organization. When accompanied by the appropriate capacities, levels of commitment and incentives or imperatives, it is apparent that the increases in awareness that have tended to follow the development and application of EMSs in The Netherlands have allowed environmental concerns to permeate the operations and strategies of industry. As a mechanism for change, an EMS can help a company to overcome the inertia that commonly restricts change. According to one environmental manager from a medium-sized processing facility:

> *The EMS helped to identify areas where performance was improving and those where it was not. For the, let's say, laggards, it was an embarrassment really for them that they were seen to be preventing progress toward something that everybody was committed to. And over time the EMS helped us to go for change throughout the company, it became a systems thing and that allowed us to go for more significant changes in the longer term.*

It is also apparent that because of the impact that EMSs have had on the level of environmental awareness in those companies that have adopted them, they have begun to catalyse a change in the nature of strategic decision making in some companies. Although these changes have been reasonably subtle to date, decision-makers in Dutch industry have begun to anticipate the need for continuous environmental improvement. Thus, EMSs have extended the time horizons of those companies that are planning environmental improvement. Because of their impact on managerial awareness, they have also altered the selection environment which channels and screens the search process for new technologies and techniques. This combination of longer term planning and a more sympathetic selection environment has shifted the emphasis of industrial environmental management from control technologies to clean technologies and techniques and from incremental to more radical change. However, it is important to note that while EMS standards have clearly encouraged a change in the nature of strategic decision-making in Dutch industry, this change has also been the consequence of the framework of targets for environmental improvement established under the various NEPPs and by the covenanting process.

SUMMARY: THE IMPLEMENTATION AND IMPACT OF EMAS IN THE NETHERLANDS

The discussion above has analysed the implementation and impact of EMS standards in The Netherlands with particular reference to EMAS. It has highlighted the fact that a clear distinction does not exist between mandatory and voluntary regulation and that in many ways The Netherlands is attempting to apply a complementary mix of policy instruments that builds on the combined strengths of mandatory and voluntary approaches to regulation. Thus, it is apparent that government and the regulatory agencies will continue to establish targets and to monitor compliance with the requirements of mandatory regulation but that responsibility for delivering environmental improvement will be transferred to industry. This policy context favours the development and wider application of EMS standards such as EMAS in a number of ways. If the increased emphasis on self-regulation within a frame-work of targets and monitoring is to be environmentally effective, companies must be able to demonstrate that they are able to work toward the pre-established targets for environmental improvement without a significant amount of external supervision or intervention. If developed, applied and verified appropriately, EMS schemes such as EMAS can demonstrate that verified or certified companies have the commitment and capacity to realize environmental improvement on a voluntary basis. The requirement for continuous improvement under EMAS should lead companies beyond the baseline of compliance with mandatory regulation which will continue to be monitored and enforced by government and by the regulatory agencies.

In relation to the implementation structures that surround EMAS in The Netherlands, it is apparent that the primary goal of the competent body and of the accreditation body has been to establish mechanisms which assure the integrity of the scheme. Therefore, a significant amount of effort has been channelled toward the development of effective accreditation and verification structures. These structures attempt to ensure that verifiers have the appropriate capacities to interpret and apply the requirements of the scheme and that they implement EMAS in a rigorous and consistent way. Measures have also been adopted to ensure that in practice verifiers emphasize the importance of environmental improvement rather than the performance of management systems in companies that choose to participate in the scheme. The prescriptions that have followed this focus on the integrity of EMAS as a mechanism for environmental improvement have had a significant influence on the implementation of the scheme in practice as the requirements for verification have been established in detail. However, while the requirement for continuous environmental improvement is clear, the enforcement of EMAS is complicated by the nature of the links between mandatory and voluntary regulation that characterize the regulatory framework in the Netherlands.

It is apparent that EMS standards such as EMAS are having an increasing impact on the behaviour of companies in The Netherlands. The development and application of EMSs has helped to raise the general level of environmental awareness in adopting companies. The information that EMSs have helped to collect and analyse has increased the capacity of managers to respond to environmental issues in an effective and efficient way. The responses to environmental issues in companies with an EMS have tended to be more systematic as the EMS has helped companies to break down the functional boundaries that may in the past have led to fragmented or departmentalized responses. At an operational level this has favoured the application of clean technologies and techniques as these often require accommodating changes throughout the company. At the strategic level EMSs have encouraged antici-patory planning and the integration of environmental concerns into mainstream business decision-making. This has allowed companies to search for and apply more radical responses to the various demands for environmen-tal improvement. Thus, it appears that the presence of an EMS helps to establish conditions within the companies that adopt them that are conducive to the development and application of new technologies and techniques. However, it should be noted that the relatively widespread adoption of EMSs within Dutch industry is largely the consequence of the broader regulatory framework which establishes various incentives or inducements that encourage companies to overcome the short term barriers which commonly restrict the diffusion of EMSs and therefore the development of EMS standards.

CONCLUSIONS

This chapter has reviewed the implementation and impact of industrial environmental regulation in The Netherlands. Initially, the analysis focused on the broad policy framework established by the various NEPPs and by the associated covenanting process. It then moved on to consider the nature of mandatory and voluntary regulation. In relation to mandatory regulation, the chapter examined the nature of the 1969 Protection of Surface Waters Act and the 1993 Environmental Management Act. In relation to voluntary regulation, the nature of the Eco-Management and Audit Scheme was assessed as an example of a broader range of EMS standards. In each case the regulatory framework and the implementation structures and styles associated with these instruments were assessed. The impact of these instruments on the behaviour of Dutch industry was also considered.

The NEPP documents have established a clear framework of targets for environmental improvement for different levels and for various timescales. The impact of these targets on industrial behaviour is evident throughout the analy-sis of the regulatory framework in The Netherlands. For example, it is apparent that the framework of targets has facilitated forward planning in regulated companies. This forward planning has increased the potential for clean technolo-gies and techniques to be developed and adopted. It has also enhanced the ability of regulated companies to explore radical as well as incremental change.

The impact of the various NEPPs has been reinforced to some extent by the framework of mandatory regulation. While the framework of mandatory regulation has a number of clear strengths, related particularly to its links with the targets established by the NEPPs and its interaction with voluntary regulation, it also has a number of weaknesses. For example, it is apparent that both the legislative and the institutional structures associated with mandatory environmental regulation in The Netherlands are increasingly coordinated but have yet to be fully integrated. This continued fragmentation is significant for a number of reasons. Because of the differing demands of the different regulators, regulated companies cannot always channel scarce resources toward the most environmentally significant emissions stream. Instead it is apparent that, as a consequence of the different regulatory styles that have tended to be associated with the PSWA and the EMA, investment in environmental improvement has tended to follow the demands of the more vociferous regulator. Thus, although the water regulator has successfully achieved its goal of protecting the water environment, this may have been achieved at the expense of the quality of the other environmental media.

Aside from this lack of a fully integrated approach, the contrasting regulatory styles associated with the PSWA and the EMA have had differing impacts on industrial behaviour. The arm's-length style of implementation and the litigious style of enforcement that have more commonly been associated with the PSWA have on occasion led to a more adversarial relationship between the regulator and regulated companies. In such instances where this is apparent, this has encouraged companies to respond to regulation defensively by resisting change. Conversely, the hands-on approach to implementation and the conciliative approach to enforcement that have generally been associated with the EMA have been received positively by regulated companies. Consequently, it has engendered a degree of commitment to environmental improvement in regulated companies. It has also allowed the regulator to transfer information and understanding to regulated companies which has increased their capacity to respond effectively and efficiently to regulation. However, it is apparent that this transfer of information and understanding depends not only on the regulatory style but also on the expertise of the individual regulator. The variable level of expertise within some regulatory agencies has meant that the potential to transfer information and understanding to regulated companies has not been consistently exploited. The readiness of the provincial regulator to adopt a more arm's-length and litigious approach to implementation for recalcitrant companies, coupled with the existence of a framework of standards and targets and the presence of an external organization to monitor the performance of regulatory agencies, has to some extent protected the integrity of the EMA by maintaining the imperative for environmental improvement.

In relation to the implementation of EMAS in The Netherlands, it is apparent that a considerable amount of attention has been paid to measures which establish, protect and demonstrate the ability of schemes such as EMAS to deliver environmental improvement in the absence of external supervision or intervention. While these measures appear to have been effective as government is placing an increasing amount of faith in self-regulation, they have also led to a somewhat mechanistic approach to the interpretation, implementation and enforcement of the key principles and requirements of EMAS. In relation to the impact of schemes such as EMAS, it is apparent that the presence of an effective EMS helps to establish conditions within regulated companies that are conducive to the development and application of new technologies and techniques. Similarly, it appears that the presence of an EMS helps companies to integrate environmental considerations into their strategic decision-making processes so that environmental concerns can be effectively and efficiently incorporated into the design and application of new processes and products. The strategic impact of voluntary environmental regulation is enhanced by the presence of a clear framework of company specific targets for environmental improvement for the short, medium and long terms.

Consequently, it is evident that the Dutch approach to industrial environmental regulation has a number of clear strengths, particularly in relation to the impact of the targets established by the various NEPPs. These strengths have been widely acknowledged. For example, Weale (1992, p 125) states that the NEPPs:

> ... *[represent a legitimate] attempt to change the standard operating procedures of government ... [and are] perhaps the most serious attempt to integrate environmental concerns into the full range of public policy.*

While it is certainly important to acknowledge the positive aspects of the Dutch approach to environmental policy planning, it is also appropriate to point out that The Netherlands demonstrates many of the strengths and weaknesses that typically characterize the implementation of environmental regulation in other countries. As a result it is likely that The Netherlands can lead by example in some areas whilst learning from others elsewhere.

Chapter 7

SUMMARY AND SYNTHESIS: RESHAPING REGULATORY REALITIES

INTRODUCTION

The preceding chapters have analysed the implementation and impact of industrial environmental regulation in the UK and The Netherlands. In relation to the implementation of industrial environmental regulation, the analysis focused on the frameworks, structures and styles of regulation in each country. In relation to the impact of industrial environmental regulation, the analysis considered the influence of regulation on the technological, organizational and strategic behaviour of regulated companies.

This chapter draws together the various conceptual and empirical elements of the preceding discussion to present a detailed overview of the implementation and impact of both mandatory and voluntary forms of industrial environmental regulation in the two case study countries. Drawing on the variables for analysis discussed above, it suggests that a range of strengths and weaknesses are associated with the framework of industrial environmental regulation applied in each country. In order to combine the strengths of each national framework, a composite model of industrial environmental regulation is developed. It is proposed that this model would enhance the environmental efficacy and economic efficiency of regulation if adopted in both the UK and The Netherlands. Whilst acknowledging the importance of the various specificities and contingencies upon which the operation of any framework of regulation depends, it is also suggested that this composite model is generic enough to be adapted and applied in a wider variety of settings.

THE IMPLEMENTATION OF MANDATORY ENVIRONMENTAL REGULATION

Policy Frameworks

Government in the UK has traditionally been reluctant to take precautionary action to protect the environment in the absence of scientific certainty. This has reduced the prospect of a comprehensive framework of targets for environmental improvement being adopted. Thus, although there are various statutory standards that guide the regulatory process, until recently the wider policy framework has provided little strategic guidance either for regulators or for regulated companies at least in the form of quantified targets for the medium to long term. Because of this lack of goal orientation in the policy process, the UK's approach to environmental protection has generally been shaped more by the available means than by the desirable ends.

The environmental policy framework in the UK has also been influenced to a significant degree by the free market doctrine adopted by government between the early 1980s and the mid 1990s. Throughout this period, government sought to remove those bureaucratic hurdles that in its view restricted the efficient operation of the market. Thus, various steps were taken to minimize the overall level of government intervention. Consequently, voluntary rather than mandatory approaches to environmental regulation were generally preferred in principle and some measures were taken by government to support the development of a number of voluntary initiatives. In general, however, government did not accept that it could or should play a central role in catalysing voluntary action by creating the structures within which voluntary initiatives might successfully operate. One consequence of this is that opportunities to build complementarity between mandatory and voluntary modes of regulation have yet to be fully explored. In the field of industrial environmental regulation only limited and relatively informal links have been developed between mandatory regulations such as Integrated Pollution Control (IPC) and voluntary regulations such as the Eco-Management and Audit Scheme (EMAS).

The Dutch approach to environmental policy contrasts with that of the UK in a number of respects. A central feature of the Dutch approach to environmental policy has been its emphasis on cooperation and consensus-building. This emphasis both reflects and builds upon the faith that the Dutch public has traditionally placed in the ability of government to plan and manage the process of economic development. In relation to the formulation of the various National Environmental Policy Plans (NEPPs), it was acknowledged at an early stage that a process of consultation and dialogue with the various stakeholders in government, in industry and in society at large was necessary if widespread support for a framework of targets for environmental improvement was to be secured. This process of consensus-building also reduced the need for scientific certainty and therefore enhanced the prospect of precautionary action.

The framework of targets that arose from this process of consensus-building has had a defining influence on the nature of Dutch environmental policy and practice in recent years. For example, the presence of the targets that are embodied within the various NEPPs has allowed the government to move toward its objective of creating a system of self-regulation within a framework. Thus, government has been able to explore the potential of various innovative policy instruments, particularly in the form of voluntary agreements or covenants, as part of its goal oriented approach to environmental regulation. A number of measures to develop the links between mandatory and voluntary regulation have also been taken. The legitimacy of this shift toward self-regulation has been protected both by the presence of a framework of targets for environmental improvement and by the application of a system of monitoring which, as part of the broader regulatory system, assesses the environmental performance of regulated companies. The influence and credibility of the targets has been further strengthened by the provision of access to information on environmental performance and therefore on the progress that is being made toward the targets at different levels by the various actors.

From this discussion on environmental policy frameworks in the UK and The Netherlands, it is apparent that a clear and comprehensive framework of targets for environmental improvement can introduce a strategic dimension into the policy process. In such instances the regulatory system can become more goal oriented so that there is an increased prospect of new measures being adopted and of existing measures being refined if objectives are not realized. The regulatory system can also be made more accountable if external monitoring is maintained and if access to information on the performance of the various actors is secured. The presence of a comprehensive framework of targets, of a credible system of monitoring and of a transparent system of performance measures can enhance the ability of government and industry to explore innovative ways of securing environmental improvement as the various stakeholders can compare the results of such a process with the relevant targets. Under such circumstances complementarity between mandatory and voluntary regulation can be developed and the role of self-regulation within a broader regulatory framework can be enhanced. In the absence of such targets, monitoring and performance measures, a similar exploration of the potential for self-regulation may effectively be precluded because of actual or anticipated public suspicion that a shift to voluntary regulation may in fact mean a shift toward no regulation.

Implementation Structures

The UK has been at the forefront of attempts to introduce an integrated approach to industrial environmental regulation. The framework of IPC that was introduced in England and Wales in 1990 led to the integration of the previously fragmented legal framework so that the emissions to air, water and land from a range of industrial facilities were addressed by a single piece of legislation. The institutions associated with the implementation of industrial environmental regulation have also been reorganized so that, at least for the larger and more environmentally significant facilities, environmental regulation is now delivered, monitored and enforced by a unified environmental agency. To a degree this process of legislative and institutional integration has also been accompanied by a process of integration at the functional level although some significant differences in the cultures and working practices of the various departments within the unified agency remain. Nonetheless, the continuing process of integration has had more than merely a symbolic impact. Consequently, the framework of IPC has transformed the practical substance of industrial environmental regulation for many regulated companies. However, while the substance of environmental regulation may have changed for many companies, the style of regulation remains similar to that which was applied under previous legislative and institutional structures.

In relation to the resources structures associated with IPC, implementation has been undertaken by a regulatory agency which has been staffed by inspectors with a significant degree of experience and expertise in areas related to the processes that they regulate. These expert inspectors have delivered IPC within a relatively intensive relationship with regulated companies. Thus, implementation has been a relatively resource intensive, or more particularly a labour and skills intensive, process. This approach has had a number of implications. From the launch of IPC, the regulator was drawn into a process of negotiation with regulated companies. Because this process of negotiation between the regulator and regulated companies is not amenable to external scrutiny, and because of the lack of a clear and comprehensive framework of standards, targets and performance measures, the efficacy and accountability of the regulatory function have been questioned. However, this approach to implementation has also had some benefits. The flexibility that is built into the implementation phase has allowed the regulator to fine-tune the requirements of regulation to reflect the specific circumstances of its application. It has also encouraged a process of interactive learning which has allowed the transfer information and understanding from the expert regulator to regulated companies. These transfers of information and understanding have increased the ability of many regulated companies to comply with the minimum standards established by IPC and to explore the potential for further environmental improvement. The provision of this combination of resources has been maintained over time so that the capacity of regulated companies to respond to the evolving demands of regulation in a relatively effective and efficient way has continued to increase over time. Thus, the resources committed to the implementation process have increased the ability of regulated companies to work toward continuous environmental improvement without encountering escalating costs.

Aside from these issues related to the efficacy of the regulatory function, there are a number of issues related to the efficiency of the implementation phase. The intensity of the relationship between the regulator and regulated companies means that implementation is a relatively labour intensive process. The cost of this labour intensity is exaggerated because of the expense that is associated with the employment of expert inspectors. Consequently, it is generally acknowledged that IPC is expensive legislation to implement. This is particularly important as the regulatory agency, which bears the cost of such an approach, has been under constant pressure to cut its expenditure. However, as many of the benefits of this approach to implementation are realized by industry, particularly in terms of lower compliance costs, opportunities for cost recovery are increasingly being explored and applied.

In The Netherlands, the legislative and institutional structures associated with industrial environmental regulation are coordinated but have yet to be fully integrated to address emissions to air, water and land simultaneously. Although coordination between the various actors does take place, the partially fragmented regulatory structure that is maintained in The Netherlands restricts the ability of the various regulators and of regulated companies to assess their impacts holistically. Their ability to channel their resources toward the most environmentally significant emissions stream is therefore also restricted to some degree. Despite the coordination that takes place between the different regulators, investment in environmental improvement tends to follow the demands of the more stringent regulations and of the more vociferous and litigious regulator.

In relation to the resource structures associated with the implementation of the 1993 Environmental Management Act (EMA) which regulates emissions to air and land, it is apparent that the inspectors responsible for day-to-day interactions with regulated companies have varying levels of experience and expertise. Furthermore, the intensity of the relationship between the regulator and regulated companies is varied as some companies are subjected to less intensive scrutiny than others. This approach has a number of benefits, particularly related to the ability of the regulator to focus their attention and resources on those companies with the least developed capacities for environmental protection. However, it also increases the risk that regulated companies that do not have regular interaction with a regulator may adopt the most expedient short term response to regulation rather than the most efficient and effective medium to long term response. In such instances, although short term progress may be secured, the cost of continuous environmental improvement in the medium to long term will be more likely to escalate as the medium to long term limits of those responses that are expedient in the short term are realized. The sustained transfers of information that are associated with regular interaction between an expert regulator and the regulated company can help to prevent this from happening. Thus, because of the differing levels of expertise within the regulatory agency and of the variable intensity of the relationship between the regulator and regulated companies, the potential for the regulator to enhance the capacity of companies to respond to regulation in an effective and efficient way in the medium to long term has not been consistently exploited.

One benefit of the framework of environmental regulation in The Netherlands has been the presence of a distinct inspectorate that monitors and publishes data on the performance of the regulatory agencies in relation to their ability to achieve environmental standards and to work toward environmental targets. This process of monitoring the performance of the regulator has increased the accountability of the regulatory framework. Although the day-to-day nature of the interaction between the regulator and regulated companies is not open to public scrutiny, the collective outcomes from this process are monitored. Overall performance can be judged against a clearly established and fully transparent set of targets and performance measures. Thus, while the potential for the regulator to enhance the capacity of regulated companies to pursue environmental improvement is not consistently exploited, the imperative for environmental improvement is more effectively maintained because of the wider framework of targets and monitoring. Within the process of negotiation between the regulator and regulated companies, the potential for industry to reduce the stringency of the requirements of regulation is reduced by the presence of clear, quantified standards, targets and performance measures that are externally monitored and scrutinized.

From this analysis of the structures associated with the implementation of industrial environmental regulation in the UK and The Netherlands, it is apparent that the adoption of an integrated approach to regulation can generate a number of benefits. The legislative restructuring that accompanies the adoption of an integrated regulatory framework helps to establish a simplified administrative and regulatory system which can send clear and consistent signals to regulated companies. The associated institutional restructuring allows the benefits of administrative rationalization to be secured. Integrated approaches to pollution control reduce the prospect of emissions being diverted from one medium to another rather than being reduced as they allow companies to channel their scarce investment resources toward the most environmentally significant emissions stream. They also encourage companies to pursue environmental improvement rather than bureaucratic compliance.

Where the capacity of regulated companies to pursue environmental improvement is underdeveloped, the performance of industrial environmental regulation can be enhanced if an intensive, interactive relationship exists between an expert regulator and a regulated company. This demands the application of a particularly skills- and labour-intensive approach to implementation. Where such an approach to implementation is maintained over time, the capacities of regulated companies are likely to evolve to allow companies to overcome the various barriers to innovation that can prevent them from realizing continuous environmental improvement without encountering escalating costs. As the costs of such a resource-intensive approach to implementation are concentrated on the regulatory agency and the benefits are diffused throughout regulated companies, opportunities for cost recovery can readily be explored.

While it may not be possible to monitor the nature of the day-to-day relationship between the regulator and the regulated company, it is possible to monitor the impact of that relationship on the environmental performance of the firm. The presence of a distinct inspectorate to monitor the performance of regulatory agencies increases the accountability and protects the integrity of the regulatory framework. This is particularly the case if the environmental performance of both regulated companies and regulatory agencies can be judged against a clearly established and fully transparent set of targets for environmental improvement.

Implementation Styles

By design, the framework of IPC that operates in England and Wales is anticipatory as it emphasizes the importance of pollution prevention before pollution control. This anticipatory focus demands that the regulatory agency assess the nature of the production process as well as the nature of its emissions. Thus, the regulatory agency has been drawn into a closer working relationship with regulated companies because of the anticipatory and process focused nature of the legislation that it must implement. The rationale for a close working relationship between the regulator and regulated companies is further strengthened by the fact that IPC is based on the application of a number of qualitative principles which must be interpreted and applied on a case-by-case basis by individual inspectors from the regulatory agency. Therefore, at the discretion of the individual inspector, IPC regulations can be fine-tuned to reflect the specific circumstances in regulated companies.

In response to criticisms that too cosy a relationship existed between the regulator and regulated companies under the previous regulatory regime, the regulatory agency responsible for delivering IPC initially adopted a rigid, arm's-length approach to implementation. More recently, however, the regulator has been drawn into a process of interaction and negotiation with regulated companies. Consequently, IPC has been delivered in a flexible, hands-on way by individual inspectors who have adopted an intensive relationship with regulated companies. As discussed above, as individual inspectors within the regulatory agency have extensive industrial experience and expertise, the relatively hands-on and intensive approach to implementation facilitates the transfer of information and understanding from the regulator to regulated companies. Through such transfers, the capacity of regulated companies to respond to the requirements of regulation in an effective and efficient way is increased and the anticipatory remit of the regulator is at least partially fulfilled. However, one of the dangers of such a flexible approach to implementation is that the demands of regulation will be reduced through negotiation. Thus, while the capacity of regulated companies to respond to the requirements of regulation in an effective and efficient way appears to have been increased, the stringency of these requirements and therefore the imperative to respond appears to have been reduced in some instances.

The ability of the regulatory agency to assess and influence the nature of the production process and to enhance the environmental management capacity of a regulated company commonly depends upon the presence of a positive working relationship between the two parties. Because of the importance of this positive working relationship, a consensual and conciliative enforcement style has been associated with the implementation of IPC. Consequently, the regulatory agency only resorts to an arm's-length and litigious approach in cases of sustained non-compliance. However, it is apparent that the interactive, hands-on delivery style and the consensual and conciliative enforcement style that are normally associated with the implementation of IPC are viewed with suspicion by some parties as the imperative for environmental improvement can be reduced through negotiation and the sanctions for non-compliance with these lower standards are rarely applied. These suspicions are sustained in many instances because, in the absence of a clear and transparent framework of performance targets and measures, the accountability of the regulatory process is restricted.

By design, the two pieces of legislation that are at the heart of the framework of mandatory environmental regulation in The Netherlands differ in a variety of ways. The Environmental Management Act (EMA) which regulates emissions to air and land is essentially anticipatory and process-focused. Typically, it is associated with a flexible, hands-on approach to implementation and with a conciliative and consensual enforcement style. The Protection of Surface Waters Act (PSWA) which regulates emissions to water is perceived to be more reactive and emissions-focused. It has been associated with a rigid, arm's-length approach to implementation and with a litigious and adversarial approach to enforcement although a gradual shift to a more flexible and proactive approach is apparent in some instances.

It is evident that the regulatory style that is associated with the EMA has had a number of advantages when compared with that which has been associated with the PSWA. Although its impact depends upon the expertise of the individual inspector, a hands-on approach to implementation can increase the capacity of regulated companies to respond to regulation in an effective and efficient way. Similarly, a conciliative enforcement style allows regulated companies to search for innovative responses to regulation as, in the short to medium term at least, the risks associated with non-compliance are reduced should an innovative response to regulation fail. However, the imperative to innovate is retained as a consequence of the broader framework of targets and monitoring and because of the willingness of the regulator to adopt a rigid and litigious enforcement style if non-compliance is sustained. Conversely, as a rigid, arm's-length regulatory style and a litigious and adversarial approach to enforcement are generally resented, companies tend to respond to regulation that is delivered in this way by resisting change. This defensive reaction is reinforced by a reluctance in regulated companies to pursue innovative responses to regulation as, because of the readiness of the regulator to resort to legal action in the short term, the risks associated with the adoption of technologies and techniques which are untried and untested are seen to be too great. As a rigid, arm's-length regulatory style also prevents the transfer of information and understanding from the regulator to the regulated company, it also misses an opportunity to enhance the capacity of regulated companies to respond to regulation in a positive way. Where different regulatory styles are applied, as has been and to some extent continues to be the case in The Netherlands, investment in environmental improvement tends to follow the demands of the more vociferous regulator as well the more demanding legislation.

From this analysis of the styles of implementation in the UK and The Netherlands, it is apparent that under certain conditions hands-on and flexible approaches to implementation can have a number of benefits. These benefits are particularly apparent where regulation seeks to promote pollution prevention as well as pollution control. This is the case because pollution prevention commonly requires the regulator to assess and influence the conditions within a company that give rise to emissions as well as the emissions themselves. When adopted by regulatory inspectors with appropriate levels of expertise, flexible, hands-on approaches to implementation can encourage the transfer of information and understanding from the regulator to regulated companies. In this way, regulators can enhance the capacity of regulated companies to respond to the requirements of regulation in an effective and efficient way. The application of a consensual and conciliative approach to enforcement can allow companies to draw on this capacity by developing and adopting new technologies and techniques for environmental improvement. The imperative to innovate can be maintained if the regulator itself is obliged to realize certain standards and targets and if it readily adopts a rigid and litigious enforcement style when faced with continued non-compliance. The accountability of a regulatory framework that relies on the discretion of individual inspectors can be maintained by the presence of an independent environmental inspectorate and a clear framework of targets for environmental improvement to be secured by the regulatory agency. In such instances the ability of regulated companies to reduce the demands of regulation through negotiation with the regulator can be restricted.

THE IMPLEMENTATION OF VOLUNTARY ENVIRONMENTAL REGULATION

Policy Frameworks

Throughout the 1980s and early 1990s, government in the UK emphasized the importance of the market and stressed its reluctance to introduce and in some instances to retain various mandatory regulations. This desire to reduce the overall level of regulation was motivated both by the perceived need to limit the extent of public expenditure on regulatory agencies and by the belief that regulation imposed extra costs on industry. Consequently, within its wider policy strategy, the government of this period tended to support the development and application of voluntary or self-regulatory initiatives wherever possible. However, the practical impact of this support has been limited, as throughout this period government was reluctant to establish or administer frameworks for voluntary regulation and to provide the strategic vision that would encourage the wider adoption of voluntary regulation. Such strategic vision could have been established, for example, through the introduction of a clear and comprehensive framework of targets for environmental improvement.

Despite this lack of strategic guidance, government in the UK did encourage the various regulatory agencies to examine the ways in which the links between mandatory and voluntary regulation might be developed so that the level of government intervention could be reduced. However, the links between mandatory regulation and voluntary schemes such as the EU's Eco-Management and Audit Scheme (EMAS) have either remained under-developed or have been of an informal nature. In relation to IPC, the mandatory regulator has suggested that companies that have an effective environmental management system might eventually be regulated less intensively than those that do not, particularly if the management system has been externally verified under a scheme such as EMAS. However, despite the growing recognition of their potential, measures to link mandatory and voluntary regulations are only beginning to be formally adopted. Nonetheless, the regulator has acknowledged less formally that the presence of an effective environmental management system demonstrates some degree of capacity for environmental management in a regulated company. In such instances the regulator may, at its discretion, adopt a more arm's-length approach to implementation so that the regulated company is given more freedom to select, develop and apply its own response to regulation.

One of the defining features of the Dutch approach to environmental policy in the 1980s and early 1990s has been its willingness to explore the application of innovative policy instruments. In recent years it has been particularly evident that this has favoured the development and application of voluntary approaches to regulation. The various NEPPs and the associated covenanting process have introduced a significant voluntary dimension into the environmental policy framework in The Netherlands to the extent that the boundaries between mandatory and voluntary regulation are now far from distinct.

It has been recognized by the Dutch government and by the various industrial bodies in The Netherlands that voluntary regulations such as EMAS must establish, maintain and demonstrate their environmental integrity if they are to realize their full potential as a complement to mandatory regulation. Consequently, it is generally acknowledged that schemes such as EMAS should be applied in a way that will convince the various stakeholders of the commitment and capacity of EMAS registered sites to work toward the pre-established targets for environmental improvement without a significant amount of external supervision or intervention. Thus, great emphasis has been placed on the environmental performance of the framework of self-regulation. Where the integrity of the self-regulatory mechanism can be demonstrated, responsibility for realising environmental improvement has been transferred to industry itself. However, it has been stated that such transfers of responsibility will only take place under certain conditions. Broadly, government and the regulatory agencies will continue to set standards, to establish targets and to monitor compliance with the requirements of mandatory regulation. Thus, a system of self-regulation within a framework of targets and monitoring is envisaged. This establishes a clear basis for the wider development and application of voluntary regulations such as EMAS in The Netherlands.

It is apparent from the preceding analysis of the approaches to voluntary regulation that have been applied in the UK and The Netherlands that particular policy frameworks can support the wider application of voluntary regulation as one of a number of policy instruments. Where voluntary regulation is seen as an effective complement to mandatory regulation, suspicions that a shift toward voluntary regulation may in fact mean a shift toward no regulation can be reduced. Complementarity between mandatory and voluntary regulation can be enhanced where minimum standards and continuous improvement are secured through voluntary action within a framework established by government. Thus, government and the regulatory agencies can facilitate the wider uptake of voluntary initiatives by setting standards, establishing targets and monitoring baseline compliance and progress towards targets for environmental improvement.

Where voluntary regulation is effectively applied it can have a number of advantages for both government and industry. For government, effective voluntary action can reduce the need for mandatory regulation and therefore the requirement for costly regulatory agencies. For industry, reductions in the level of government intervention can allow scarce resources to be channelled toward environmental improvement rather than bureaucratic compliance. However, the benefits of a shift to voluntary regulation must be compared with the risk that in the absence of regular interaction with a mandatory regulator, companies will not search for, develop and apply those technologies and techniques that will allow them to improve their environmental performance most efficiently and effectively in the medium to long term.

Implementation Structures

As the institutional structures required to administer EMAS were prescribed in detail by the EU, technically there should be little variation in the nature of the structures for implementation that have been established in each member state. Both the UK and The Netherlands have introduced the various structures required to administer the scheme. They have also developed clear criteria to control and guide the implementation process. In both countries measures have been taken to promote the consistent application of the scheme by limiting the extent to which discretion can be applied throughout the implementation process. However, as the requirements of EMAS have to be interpreted and applied in each country on a case-by-case basis, the scope for the inconsistent implementation remains. This has been a source of concern for two main reasons.

The first relates to the background and capacities of the organizations and individuals associated with verification. The effective implementation of EMAS demands a combination of skills and experience drawn from a range of disciplines and professions. In both the UK and The Netherlands it was apparent that, particularly in the early stages of EMAS, few organizations and individuals had such a combination of skills and fewer still had a significant amount of appropriate experience. At the launch of EMAS, therefore, the capacities for effective implementation were underdeveloped in both countries. Many of the organizations and individuals who subsequently sought to become accredited environmental verifiers had a background in the application or accreditation of management systems, particularly those related to quality management.

145

Consequently, it was feared that because of their professional background many of the staff involved in the verification of EMAS would focus on the intermediate mechanism rather than on the ultimate objective, that is on the management system rather than on the environmental performance of the site seeking registration. In response, steps have been taken in both the UK and The Netherlands to ensure that verifiers are suitably qualified and that they focus on the environmental performance of the site rather than on the functionality of the management system. Over time, the organizations involved in the verification process have developed a more appropriate combination of skills and experience so that the capacity for effective implementation has increased in both countries.

A second area of concern relates to the commercial nature of the relationship between verifiers and companies seeking verification. Environmental verifiers essentially act as regulators by checking that those sites that wish to register under the scheme comply with its requirements. Environmental verifiers are employed on a commercial basis by companies that wish to join the scheme. To a large degree the EMAS scheme has been resourced in this way as the costs of implementation can be automatically recovered by the verifier through charges for verification. However, as there is competition between different verifiers, it is possible that some verifiers will interpret and apply the requirements of the scheme more leniently to encourage the wider adoption of the scheme and to increase their prospect of further work. Various measures have been put in place in each country to reduce the prospect of such regulatory capture, particularly through direct witnessing of the verification process and through post-verification audits by the accreditation body. As well as assessing the nature of the verification process, the performance of EMAS registered sites can also be readily assessed through the data that must be published at regular intervals in the environmental statement. Technically therefore, although the implementation or verification process itself is not open to external examination, the impact of the measures adopted on the environmental performance of registered sites is amenable to public scrutiny. To an extent, therefore, EMAS can be judged by its results although this depends upon the quality of the environmental statements that are published.

From the preceding discussion, it is apparent that the credibility of voluntary regulation rests to a significant degree on the nature of the structures that are associated with its implementation and enforcement. Because of their voluntary and sometimes commercial nature, the integrity of these structures can readily be called into question. In response, it is possible for government and for private sector bodies to enhance the credibility of voluntary regulations by demanding that appropriate institutional structures and capacities are established. Where the capacities of the various institutions involved in the implementation phase are under-developed, the imposition of particular standards and requirements can stimulate the development of new skills and areas of expertise. Institutional capacities can therefore develop over time as expertise is developed and experience is accumulated. However, such a process of capacity building demands that the performance of the various institutions associated with implementation and enforcement is monitored and that these institutions respond to the feedback from such monitoring.

Implementation Styles

As well as establishing the structures required to implement EMAS, the institutions associated with EMAS in both the UK and The Netherlands have attempted to introduce clear criteria to guide the implementation process. Thus, attempts have been made to build confidence in the scheme by limiting the ability of the various organizations and actors involved in the implementation phase to influence the way that the requirements of the scheme are interpreted, applied and enforced. However, given the qualitative nature of some of the central requirements of the scheme, and the variety of companies and sites seeking verification, it has been impossible to impose uniform conditions for perfect implementation in each member state. Consequently, the styles of implementation that are adopted in each member state still have the potential to influence the practical nature of the scheme.

In the UK, it has been generally acknowledged that because each site is unique, no standard set of objectives and targets can be drawn up to ensure that the requirements of the scheme are interpreted and applied consistently. In seeking to address this potential for inconsistency, particular emphasis has been placed on the interpretation of the central requirement for continuous environmental improvement as this is perceived to be the most important component of the scheme. In this respect, it has been specified that verifiers should expect to see a comprehensive evaluation of the environmental effects of the site that has been determined in a methodologically transparent way. Following from this, verifiers may expect to see some but not necessarily all of the most significant environmental effects of the site being adopted as targets for environmental improvement. As a result, continuous improvement has been taken to refer to general improvement in environmental performance over a number of years, but not necessarily in all areas at all times.

In relation to the nature of the interaction between the verifier and companies seeking verification, it is apparent that a relatively arm's-length approach to implementation has been adopted. Verifiers are employed for a relatively short period, for example for one or two days in a yearly cycle, to ensure that sites seeking verification comply with the requirements of the scheme. Consequently, opportunities for any significant degree of interaction between verifiers and companies or sites seeking verification are restricted. These opportunities are further restricted if different verifiers are used in each cycle. Nonetheless, the expertise and experience that has developed over time in many of the organizations associated with verification ensure that some limited transfers of information and understanding can take place.

With regard to enforcement in the UK, it has been argued that proportionality should be observed so that registered companies do not lose their registration for EMAS as a result of trivial breaches of the law. Therefore, at the discretion of the various agencies and individuals involved in implementation, the enforcement style being adopted is relatively conciliative. There has been a reluctance to jeopardize the registration of EMAS sites in any but the most serious cases of non-compliance either with the requirements of mandatory regulation or with the requirements of EMAS itself. Aside from these formal enforcement measures, verified sites are obliged to publish detailed information on their environmental performance and therefore on the extent to which they have been able to realize continuous environmental improvement.

In The Netherlands, the procedures to be followed by the verifier have also been established in some detail to ensure that the qualitative principles that define the scheme are interpreted and applied in a consistent and rigorous way. Again the interpretation of continuous environmental improvement has been seen to be of particular significance. While it has been accepted that the precise requirements of the scheme cannot be defined generically because of the variability of the sites that may seek registration, criteria have been established to guide verifiers as they interpret the requirements of the scheme in practice. These criteria and the procedures and practices associated with implementation are very similar to those that are in place in the UK.

The style of enforcement adopted in The Netherlands is also similar to that of the UK in that a relatively conciliative approach has been adopted. However, as well as complying with minimum standards, companies in The Netherlands must also demonstrate their progress toward the targets for environmental improvement that have been adopted as part of the wider regulatory framework. Consequently, it is apparent that because of the degree of interaction between mandatory and voluntary regulation in The Netherlands, EMAS implementation and enforcement is inextricably linked with the implementation and enforcement of mandatory regulations which are more goal oriented than in the UK. Finally, companies are required to publish details of their environmental performance so that, in theory at least, the EMAS scheme can be judged by its results.

From this discussion it is evident that while the required institutional structures and capacities associated with the implementation of voluntary regulation can be specified in detail from the top down, it is less feasible to control the behaviour of the individuals who must interpret and apply the requirements of voluntary regulation on a case-by-case basis. Although basic guidelines and procedures can be prescribed to limit the extent to which discretion can be applied in the implementation phase, perfect control is impossible given the variety of companies and sites seeking registration. While the inappropriate exercize of discretion can allow inconsistencies which can erode the perceived integrity of the implementation process, if the implementation process can be judged by its results the impact of these inconsistencies on the credibility of the scheme as a whole can be reduced. Once more, therefore, the publication of externally verified data on environmental performance, for example in the form of corporate environmental reports, can raise the degree of accountability and therefore enhance the credibility of voluntary regulations.

THE IMPACT OF INDUSTRIAL ENVIRONMENTAL REGULATION

The Technological Dimension

The framework of IPC introduced in England and Wales in 1990 has had a range of impacts on the technologies that have been developed and applied by regulated companies. Possibly the most tangible impact, particularly in the early stages of IPC, was on the technologies applied by regulated companies to monitor their environmental performance. While this requirement for new monitoring technologies affected many regulated companies in a similar way, the wider technological impacts of IPC have varied according to the nature of the plant in question. Generally, IPC has had a greater technological impact when regulated companies have been redesigning or upgrading their basic process technologies. At such times of major process change, the regulator delivering IPC has ensured that opportunities for environmental protection are examined and where possible integrated into the design of the production process. In such instances the regulator has synchronized the technological demands of IPC so that they coincide with the natural investment schedules of regulated companies. As this has allowed the integration of environmental concerns into the design of the production process, it is a particularly effective way to stimulate the development and application of anticipatory clean technologies. However, in the absence of such opportunities for process redesign, companies were initially reluctant to explore the potential of clean technologies, preferring instead to draw on the expedience of control technologies. Over time, however, largely as a consequence of sustained interaction with the regulator, regulated companies have become more aware of the economic and environmental potential of clean technologies, not only in general but also in relation to the specific potential within the regulated company. Consequently, responses to regulation based on the application of control technologies alone have become much less frequent. Nonetheless, IPC has continued to demand the application of control technologies once the potential for environmental improvement through the application of anticipatory clean technologies and the associated organizational measures has been exhausted.

In The Netherlands it is apparent that the framework of targets established by the various NEPPs and the associated covenanting process has had a significant impact on the technological behaviour of regulated companies. The presence of the various targets, particularly those for the medium to long term, has raised the level of environmental awareness in regulated companies. To some extent the consensus that surrounds the framework of targets has also galvanized the commitment of regulated companies to work toward these targets. While their longer term impact has yet to be established, it is apparent that targets have begun to trigger the development and application of new technologies as companies integrate environmental considerations into their process design activities. Regulated companies have therefore been able to synchronise their investments in environmental protection with their natural investment schedules. Largely as a consequence of the framework of targets for environmental improvement, environmental considerations have therefore begun to permeate the strategic as well as the operational decision-making practices of regulated firms. In some instances the impact of the targets has been reinforced by the flexibility and medium to long term focus of the regulators. This has allowed companies to respond to regulation by developing and applying integrated and anticipatory clean technologies. In other instances, however, the relatively rigid stance of the regulator has led only to the development of defensive responses to regulation. These defensive responses have tended to take the form of investments in reactive control technologies. Increased investment in control technologies has also been apparent where the opportunities for incremental change through the integration of clean technologies into existing processes have been exhausted and where the scope for significant process redesign is limited. At this stage the costs of further environmental improvement begin to escalate.

In both the UK and The Netherlands the wider uptake of EMAS and other EMS standards has had a relatively limited impact on the technologies developed and applied by participating companies. In parallel with the initial response to mandatory regulation, EMAS and other EMS standards have stimulated the wider installation of monitoring technologies. Partly because of the information that these monitoring technologies have collected, analysed and presented, EMAS and other EMS standards have played a major role in raising the specific environmental awareness of decision-makers in verified and registered companies. Consequently, they have enhanced the capacity of firms to respond to particular issues in an effective and efficient way. In the absence of an effective EMS, departmental or functional boundaries can preclude change throughout the firm. In such instances reactive control technologies are preferred as they can be adopted as a stand alone measure without having to tackle the inertia that may exist in other departments or throughout the system. Where an effective EMS is in place, it can help to instigate the changes that are needed throughout the production process to accommodate integrated clean technologies. An effective EMS can also help companies to secure the benefits of the learning effect as they incrementally improve the performance of their existing technologies over time. EMAS and other EMS standards have therefore helped to establish conditions in participating companies that are conducive to the development and application of new technologies and techniques in general but of anticipatory clean technologies and techniques in particular.

Thus, it is apparent that there has been a gradual shift in the nature of the technologies that have been developed and applied by companies seeking to improve their environmental performance. Over time, companies have begun to recognize the economic and environmental potential of integrated, anticipatory clean technologies. Consequently, many companies have extended their search for a response to regulation beyond those reactive end-of-pipe technologies that have commonly been perceived as the most expedient option in the short term. Although the general level of environmental awareness in industry has increased in recent years, regulators can play a particularly important role in this process by transferring specific information on the various options for environmental improvement to regulated companies. The potential for the wider development and application of clean technologies can be maximized where the technological demands of regulation are synchronized with the natural investment schedules of regulated companies. The presence of a clear and comprehensive framework of targets for environmental improvement can encourage companies to reorientate their research and development activities and to integrate environmental considerations into business decision-making practices. The presence of an effective EMS can increase the capacity of a regulated company to develop and apply new technologies and techniques both by raising awareness and by facilitating the integration of new approaches into existing structures and systems. An effective EMS can also help a company to secure the economic and environmental benefits of incremental innovation once a new technology has been introduced.

The Organizational Dimension

By obliging companies to apply the best available techniques not entailing excessive cost (BATNEEC), the framework of IPC introduced in England and Wales in 1990 explicitly recognized the potential for organizational as well as technological change. In practice, it has been recognized that technological change must commonly be accompanied by organizational change if it is to be successfully adopted. However, in many instances regulated companies have responded to the demands of IPC through organizational change alone. Through a sustained process of interactive learning with the regulator, and as a consequence of the increased application of monitoring technologies, many regulated companies have gained a much more detailed understanding of the nature of their production processes and of the factors that define their environmental performance. This increased understanding, coupled with a realization that significant improvements in environmental performance could often be realized with little investment, has encouraged companies to re-evaluate the organization and operation of their production processes. Initially, organizational change commonly secured positive economic returns in the short to medium term. The combined realization of economic and environmental benefits has subsequently encouraged companies, with the help of the regulator, to extend their search for opportunities for organizational change. Such an extended search became necessary as the readily exploitable opportunities for environmental improvement became less apparent. Sustained interaction with the regulator has helped to raise the capacity and the commitment of companies to instigate such a search.

The framework of environmental regulation in place in The Netherlands has also emphasized organizational as well as technological change. As in the UK, it has been recognized by both the regulatory agency and by regulated companies that a series of organizational changes are often needed to accommodate and optimize the performance of technological change. Responding to the stimulus of regulation, many companies have also explored and exploited the potential for environmental improvement through organizational changes alone. While the process of organizational change commonly realized economic benefits in its early stages, regulated companies generally believed that most of the readily exploitable opportunities had now been exhausted and that more significant technological changes were required if performance was to be further enhanced. Some companies had extended the potential for organizational change by expanding their search for new opportunities beyond the boundaries of the firm itself. For example, the wastes or by-products of some regulated companies had been transferred to others for use as material inputs. However, in some instances the commitment and capacity of regulated companies to search for further opportunities for organizational change were reduced by the lack of sustained interaction with an expert regulator. As discussed above, this arm's-length regulatory style was justified on the basis that companies with an effective environmental management system could demonstrate their capacity to respond to regulation in an effective and efficient way without a significant amount of external supervision or intervention.

In both the UK and The Netherlands the wider uptake of EMAS and other EMS standards has had a significant impact on the organizational characteristics of participating firms. Clearly the development and application of an EMS is an organizational innovation in itself. However, it is apparent that in many companies the presence of an effective EMS has had a range of more specific impacts on organizational cultures, structures and procedures. One of the most tangible impacts associated with the installation of an effective EMS relates to the degree to which companies are aware of their environmental impacts, of the causes of these impacts and of the possible responses that they could apply. This increased understanding, coupled with the specific information that commonly flows from the management system, has challenged the preconceptions of managers and has increased their capacity for effective action. This fresh outlook and increased capacity has enhanced the ability of companies with an effective management system to recognize and exploit various organizational opportunities for environmental improvement. The exploitation of these opportunities has often yielded economic benefits, either absolutely or relatively when compared with alternative and more expensive technological responses to the demands of mandatory regulation. Thus, the short run costs of developing the management system have commonly been offset by a range of medium to long term benefits, although in many instances these benefits are less tangible than the associated costs. This balance of costs and benefits has tended to encourage a shift in the position of the environment from the periphery toward the core of business decision-making. In such instances environmental issues can be approached in a more holistic and integrated way so that the ability of managers to manage change throughout the company is increased.

From this discussion, it is evident that technological change is increasingly being combined with organizational change as companies seek to improve their environmental performance. In many instances, companies have been able to secure significant improvements in their environmental performance through organizational change alone. However, the readily exploitable opportunities for environmental improvement based on the exploitation of organizational change in isolation can rapidly diminish. In such instances the increased capacity of companies to extend their search for further opportunities for environmental improvement is of particular importance. Interaction with an expert regulator can positively influence the capacity of companies to search for and exploit these opportunities. An effective EMS can also facilitate this process because of the information that a management system can help to collect and analyse and because of its utility as a mechanism for managing change. Eventually, however, organizational change must be combined with technological change if diminishing marginal returns are to be avoided. Where diminishing marginal returns are encountered, the ability of the regulator to maintain the imperative and to enhance the capacities for further environmental improvement is of particular significance.

The Strategic Dimension

Over time, IPC in England and Wales has encouraged companies to explore the potential for anticipatory approaches to pollution prevention rather than reactive approaches to pollution control. Partly as a consequence of the emphasis placed on organizational as well as technological change, many companies have responded to regulation by changing the way that they operate. In many instances the large number of small changes that have typically been adopted have led to improvements in the environmental performance of regulated companies. In general however, other than for new or significantly altered processes, IPC has yet to influence the fundamental design of the production process in regulated companies. Where the basic process technologies of regulated companies are relatively stable, the incremental improvements that have been secured through the relatively simple forms of technological and organizational change have begun to encounter diminishing marginal returns both environmentally and economically. Consequently, as long as the capacities of companies to explore the potential for more fundamental change are not enhanced, the costs of further environmental improvement are likely to escalate. In such cases the ability of regulation to influence the strategies as well as the operations of regulated companies is of particular significance. In essence, if escalating costs are to be avoided, regulation must eventually influence what companies do as well as the way that they do it. In this respect the regulator has sought to ensure that environmental concerns are placed on the strategic agenda of regulated companies. However, the uncertainty that stems from the lack of clear, company specific targets for environmental improvement in the medium to long term restricts both the willingness and the ability of regulated companies to integrate the requirements of regulation into their strategic decision-making practices. Nonetheless, it is apparent that the sustained process of interactive learning that has taken place between the regulator and regulated companies has changed the climate for strategic decision-making. The increased levels of understanding in regulated companies, whether of their impacts, of the causes of these impacts, of the possible responses or of the likely costs and benefits of different responses, have increased the prospect that environmental issues will be at least considered in these processes.

In The Netherlands, companies have responded to the demands of regulation by adopting a combination of technological and organizational changes. However, while regulated companies in England and Wales generally perceive that the potential for environmental improvement through organizational change has not yet been exhausted, in The Netherlands regulated companies commonly suggest that they have been exploring this potential for some years and that the opportunities for further improvement through organizational change alone are increasingly limited. If this is the case, then more fundamental changes to the process technologies of regulated companies are required if further environmental improvements are to be secured in the absence of escalating costs. The framework of targets for environmental improvement that guides the regulatory process has encouraged companies to respond to regulation in a strategic as well as an operational way. The company specific targets that have been introduced have clarified the levels of environmental performance expected in the future. Thus, they have provided a degree of certainty that has allowed companies to plan ahead effectively. In many instances companies have responded to the future requirements of regulation by reorientating their research and development activities. Some companies have begun to explore the potential to reformulate their objectives and to redesign their production processes in a relatively fundamental way. To an extent, therefore, the framework of targets has begun to encourage companies to explore the potential for radical as well as incremental change. If and when such radical changes are adopted, a subsequent phase of incremental improvement will be possible.

In both the UK and The Netherlands, EMAS and other EMS standards have been adopted by some companies as a mechanism for managing their environmental performance. While management systems are essentially operational in their emphasis, depending on their quality they can have an indirect impact on the nature of strategic decision-making in companies that adopt them. EMAS and other EMS standards have obliged these companies to collect, analyse and present information on their environmental effects and performance. The general and specific levels of environmental awareness in companies have therefore been increased. These increased levels of awareness have enhanced the capacities of companies with an effective EMS to manage their environmental performance more effectively and efficiently. It has also increased their capacity to manage change and therefore to make the necessary adjustments if anticipatory approaches to environmental protection are to be effectively integrated into existing structures. Over time, as well as increasing environmental management capacities, EMSs have also had an impact on the cultures of participating companies. Where companies are aware of the opportunities for environmental improvement, and of the costs and benefits of the various options, the levels of uncertainty that may otherwise prevent environmental issues from influencing decision-making within the firm are reduced. In essence, therefore, the presence of an effective EMS can help to increase the awareness, capacities and commitment of companies to integrate environmental considerations into their decision-making practices. Any imperative to secure continuous environmental improvement in the medium to long term helps to ensure that environmental issues are included on the strategic as well as the operational decision-making agenda of companies.

From this discussion, it is apparent that the costs of continuous environmental improvement are likely to escalate as the limits of operational change are encountered. If these escalating costs are to be postponed or avoided, companies must integrate environmental considerations into their strategic as well as their operational decision-making practices. In essence, companies must begin to change what they do as well as the way that they do it. The presence of a clear framework of targets for environmental improvement for the medium to long term can allow companies to achieve this. The climate for strategic decision-making can also be altered through sustained interaction with an expert regulator. The commitment of companies to environmental improvement can increase as experience accumulates and as awareness of the various opportunities for change grows. The capacity of a company to manage the implications of strategic change can be enhanced where an effective EMS is applied.

POLICY PRESCRIPTIONS: TOWARDS A COMPOSITE MODEL OF INDUSTRIAL ENVIRONMENTAL REGULATION

The discussion above has suggested that a number of strengths and weaknesses are associated with the frameworks of industrial environmental regulation applied in the UK and The Netherlands. Consequently, it is possible to draw on the strengths of each national framework to build a composite model of industrial environmental regulation that, if adopted, could enhance the environmental efficacy and economic efficiency of regulation. It is important to acknowledge there are a wide range of cultural, political, institutional, economic, technological and environmental specificities and contingencies that can fundamentally influence the frameworks of regulation applied in different settings. However, the model that is advocated below is generic enough to be adapted and applied in a variety of settings. It is also important to acknowledge that the various components of the model advocated below are interdependent. The efficacy and efficiency of the framework as a whole could be compromised if the various components are not applied as a unified system. The components of the proposed system are as follows:

- A clear and comprehensive framework of minimum environmental standards and demanding targets for environmental improvement should be introduced for the international, national, regional and local scales. Regulatory agencies should ensure that minimum standards are realized in the short term and that progress toward the targets is secured in the medium to long term.

- A clear and comprehensive framework of minimum standards and demanding targets for improvement should be introduced for individual companies for the short, medium and long term. Regulated companies should be obliged to meet these minimum standards in the short term and to work toward these targets in the medium to long term.
- Anticipatory, process-focused regulation should be applied through an integrated legal and institutional framework.
- Within the broader framework of quantitative standards and targets, regulation should be based on the application of qualitative principles so that it can be fine-tuned by street-level bureaucrats to reflect the specific circumstances of regulated companies.
- Regulation should be delivered in an interactive and hands-on way by expert regulators through an intensive relationship with regulated companies.
- Regulators should seek to enhance the capacities of regulated companies to search for, develop and apply those technologies and techniques that can most effectively and efficiently improve their environmental performance in the medium to long term.
- Regulated companies should seek to move beyond the application of reactive control technologies to develop and apply integrated and anticipatory clean technologies and techniques. Short to medium term operational change should be combined with medium to long term strategic change.
- A shift to a less intensive approach to the implementation of mandatory regulation should only be adopted where regulated companies can continually demonstrate the appropriate capacities for effective environmental management.
- Mandatory regulators should only adopt a less intensive approach to implementation where companies have registered for a voluntary EMS standard if the efficacy and integrity of that standard, and therefore of the structures that administer, implement and enforce it, can be consistently demonstrated.
- Charges should be applied to recover the costs associated with an intensive and hands-on approach to implementation from regulated companies. Charges should be reduced where a less intensive regulatory style is applied to establish an incentive to develop appropriate capacities for environmental improvement.
- A flexible and conciliative approach to enforcement should only be adopted where companies meet minimum standards and where they can demonstrate progress toward medium to long term targets. A rigid and litigious approach to enforcement should be adopted where minimum standards are not met and where there is a sustained lack of progress toward targets for environmental improvement.
- The environmental performance of regulatory agencies should be monitored by an external body so that their ability to secure minimum environmental standards and progress toward environmental targets can be assessed. Related to a framework of standards and targets, a clear and

transparent set of performance measures should be published to increase the accountability of the regulatory process.

CONCLUSIONS

This book began by considering the nature of ecological modernization. It suggested that the relationship between economic development and environmental protection is not fixed and that policy has the potential to influence this relationship. However, rather than focusing on the prospects for a widespread programme of policy reform to promote an improved relationship between economic development and environmental protection, it focused on the contribution that may be made by the adoption of new approaches to the implementation of existing forms of policy.

The analysis of industrial environmental regulation highlighted the central role that mandatory regulation can play by establishing capacities and maintaining imperatives for effective action in regulated companies. It suggested that the efficacy and efficiency of environmental regulation will be optimized where these capacities and imperatives are found in combination. The analysis established the importance of a clear and comprehensive framework of standards, targets and performance measures to maintain the imperative for action. Where such a framework is in place, all stages of the policy process can be made more goal oriented so that they work towards the objectives of a strategic environmental policy plan. The analysis also recognized the significance of a hands-on approach to the implementation of regulation. Where imperatives for action are established and maintained by a broader framework of standards and targets, hands-on approaches to implementation that transfer the skills of expert regulators to regulated companies can increase their capacity for effective and efficient action. Such a hands-on approach is necessary because of the dynamic barriers to innovation that commonly preclude companies from exploring the medium to long term potential for continuous environmental improvement. The analysis also acknowledged the complementary role that voluntary regulations such as EMS standards can play. The presence of an effective EMS can establish conditions in regulated companies that are conducive to the development and application of new technologies and techniques.

Thus, it has been argued that the efficacy and efficiency of industrial environmental regulation could be improved if the various measures and approaches proposed above were adopted. These changes would be compatible with a wider programme of ecological modernization. In theory, such a programme could set clear limits for economic activity by establishing a comprehensive framework of environmental standards and targets. It could extend the scope of regulation beyond its traditional focus on large firms to address the cumulative impacts of smaller firms. It could widen the emphasis that regulation has tended to place on industry and the supply-side to address issues related to consumers and the demand-side. It could combine new forms of regulation to influence strategic decision-making processes at the micro-economic level. It could pursue a process of eco-tax reform to accelerate and reorientate structural change at the macro-economic level. Whether such a process of environmental policy reform is to be welcomed as a positive example of institutional learning or dismissed as an ultimately worthless technocratic project is debatable. This book has argued that, within the existing mode of capitalistic development, policy reforms could have a positive impact on the relationship between economic development and environmental protection.

References

Abernathy, B and Clarke, K (1985) 'Innovation: mapping the winds of creative destruction' *Research Policy*, 14, pp 3–22

Andersen, M (1994) *Governance by Green Taxes: Making Pollution Prevention Pay*, Manchester University Press, Manchester

Andweg, R and Irwin, G (1993) *Dutch Government and Politics*, Macmillan, London

Ashford, N (1993) 'Understanding the Technical Response of Industrial Firms to Environmental Problems: Implications for Government Policy' in Fischer, K and Schot, J (eds) *Environmental Strategies for Industry: International Perspectives on Research Needs and Policy Implications*, Island Press, Washington, pp 277–310

Bachrach, P and Baratz, M (1970) *Power and Poverty, Theory and Practice*, Oxford University Press, New York

Ball, S and Bell, S (1995) *Environmental Law*, Blackstone Press, London

Baram, M (1985) 'Implementation and Evaluation of Regulations' in Otway, H and Peltu, M (eds) *Regulating Industrial Risks: Science, hazards and public protection*, Butterworths, London, pp 57–75

Barnes, P (1994) 'The Environmental Audit Scheme', *EIU European Trends*, 3rd Quarter, The Economic Intelligence Unit, London, pp 80–86

Barrett, S and Fudge, C (eds) (1981) *Policy and Action: Essays on the Implementation of Public Policy*, Methuen, London

de Boer, M (1995) *The Environment, Space and Living Quality: Time for Sustainability*, Ministry of Housing, Spatial Planning and the Environment, The Hague

Bierkart, J (1995) 'Environmental Covenants Between Government and Industry: A Dutch NGO's Experience', *Reciel*, vol 4, no 2, pp 141–149

Blowers, A (1984) *Something in the Air: Corporate power and the environment*, Harper and Row, London

Boehmer-Christiansen, S and Skea, J (1993) *Acid Politics: Energy and Environmental Policies in Britain and Germany*, Belhaven, London

Boehmer-Christiansen, S and Weidner, H (1995) *The Regulation of Vehicle Emissions in Britain and Germany: The Catalytic Conversion*, Pinter, London

Burns, T and Stalker, G (1994) *The Management of Innovation*, Oxford University Press, Oxford

Cairncross, F (1995) *Green, Inc*, Earthscan, London

Carley, M and Christie, I (1992) *Managing Sustainable Development*, Earthscan, London

CEC (1993) *White Paper on Growth, Competitiveness and Employment*, COM (93) 700 Final, Commission of the European Communities, Brussels

CEC – Commission of the European Communities (1996) 'Council Directive Concerning Integrated Pollution Prevention and Control', 96/61/EC, *Official Journal of the European Communities*, 24th September

CEC – Commission of the European Communities (1996) 'Recommendation concerning Environmental Agreements implementing Community directives' *Official Journal of the European Communities*, 96/733/EC

CEST (1994) *Waste Minimisation: A Route to Profit and Cleaner Production*, Centre for the Exploitation of Science and Technology, London

Chemical Industries Association (1992) *Responsible Care*, Chemical Industries Association, London

Christoff, P (1996) 'Ecological Modernization, Ecological Modernities', *Environmental Politics*, Vol 5, No 3, pp 476–500

Collins, K and Earnshaw, D (1993) 'The Implementation and Enforcement of European Community Environmental Legislation' in Judge, D (ed) *A Green Dimension for the European Community*, Frank Cass, London, pp 213–249

Confederation of British Industry (1994) *Environment Costs: The Effects on Competitiveness of the Environment, Health and Safety*, CBI, London

Confederation of British Industry (1995) *Setting the Standard: Environmental Management Systems Guidelines for Business*, CBI, London

Consultative Group for the Chemical Industry (1994) *Annual Report of the Consultative Group for the Chemical Industry*, Consultative Group for the Chemical Industry, The Netherlands

Cridland, J (1994) 'Meeting the Cost of Environmental Regulation' in Boyle, A (ed) *Environmental Regulation and Economic Growth*, Clarendon Press, Oxford

Davis, K (1969) *Discretionary Justice: A Preliminary Inquiry*, University of Illinois Press, Chicago

Department of the Environment (1995) *The EC Eco-Management and Audit Scheme: A Participant's Guide*, Department of the Environment, London

Dieleman, H and de Hoo, S (1993) 'Toward a Tailor-made Process of Pollution Prevention and Cleaner Production: Results and Implications of the PRISMA Project' in Fischer, K and Schot, J (eds) *Environmental Strategies for Industry: International Perspectives on Research Needs and Policy Implications*, Island Press, Washington, pp 245–276

Dogan, M and Pelassy, D (1990) *How to Compare Nations* (2nd edition), Edward Artinian, New Jersey

Dosi, G (1988) 'The Nature of the Innovative Process' in Dosi, G, Freeman, C, Nelson, R, Silverberg, G and Soete, L (eds) (1988) *Technical Change and Economic Theory*, Pinter Publishers, London, pp 221–237

Downs, A (1967) *Inside Bureaucracy*, Little Brown, Boston

Dror, Y (1964) 'Muddling Through – "Science" or Inertia?' *Public Administration Review*, Vol 24, pp 153–157

DRI (1994) *Potential Benefits of Integration of Environmental and Economic Policies*, Graham and Trotman, London

DTI/DoE (1994) *The UK Environmental Industry: Succeeding in the Changing Global Market*, HMSO, London

Dunleavy, P (1980) *Urban Political Analysis: The Politics of Collective Consumption*, Macmillan, London

ECOTEC (1992) 'The Development of Cleaner Technologies: A Strategic Overview' *Business Strategy and the Environment*, 1, 2, pp 51–58

ENDS (1994) 'Advancing the Sustainable Development Agenda', *The ENDS Report*, No 228 (January), pp 18–21

ENDS (1995a) 'Treasury Told to Play its Part in Sustainable Development', *The ENDS Report*, No 246 (July), pp 26–27

ENDS (1995b) 'Benefits and Shortcomings of EMAS Revealed as First Five Sites Win Registration', *The ENDS Report*, No 247 (August), pp 18–24

ENDS (1995c) 'In Search of the Best Practicable BPEO', *The ENDS Report*, No 249 (October), pp 22–25

ENDS (1996a) 'Top Companies Play Waiting Game on Environmental Standards', *The ENDS Report*, No 252 (January), p 6

ENDS (1996b) 'HMIP Urged to Find Incentives for Industry to Improve', *The ENDS Report*, No 252 (January), p 34

ENDS (1996c) 'Chemicals Firms Use EMAS, ISO14001 in Push for Deregulation', *The ENDS Report*, No 254 (March), p 5

ENDS (1996d) 'Agency Enforcement Code Gives Business Right to Object', *The ENDS Report*, No 256 (May), p 34

ENDS (1996e) 'DoE Widens Small Firm Grants for EMAS Registration', *The ENDS Report*, No 260 (September), p 33

ENDS (1996f) 'ISO14001 Arrives – But EMAS Uptake Stays at Low Level', *The ENDS Report*, No 261 (October), p 7

ENDS (1997) 'Birdseye Wall's: Making Ice Cream with a New Environmental Flavour', *The ENDS Report*, No 264 (January), p 18–20

Etzioni, A (1967) 'Mixed Scanning: A "third" approach to decision making' *Public Administration Review*, Vol 27, pp 385–392

Falk, H and Wilkinson, D (1996) *The EU's Eco-Audit Regulation: The Role and Accreditation of Environmental Verifiers in Six Member States*, Institute for European Environmental Policy, London

Fineman, S (1997) 'When Regulator Meets Regulated: Contests for Sustainability', presentation to the *Workshop on Environmental Regulation and the Transformation of Government*, British Sociological Association/ERSC Global Environmental Change Programme, London, September 24th

Freeman, C (1992) *The Economics of Hope: Essays on Technical Change, Economic Growth and the Environment*, Pinter Publishers, London

Ghazi, P and Grant, I (1995) 'Polluters left to report their own spills' *Observer*, September 17th, p 8

Goldsmith, E, Allen, R, Michael, A, Davoll, J and Lawrence, S (1972) *Blueprint for Survival*, Houghton Mifflin, Boston

Gore, A (1992) *Earth in the Balance: Forging a New Common Purpose*, Earthscan, London

Gouldson, A and Murphy, J (1996) 'Ecological Modernization and the European Union' *Geoforum*, Vol 27, 1, pp 11–21

Gouldson, A and Murphy, J (1997) 'Ecological Modernization: Restructuring Industrial Economies' in Jacobs, M (ed) *Greening the Millennium? The New Politics of the Environment*, Blackwell, Oxford

Groenewegen, P and Vergragt, P (1991) 'Environmental Issues as Threats and Opportunities for Technological Innovation' *Technology Assessment and Strategic Management*, 3, 1, pp 43–55

Haigh, N and Irwin, F (eds) (1990) *Integrated Pollution Control in Europe and North America*, The Conservation Foundation and the Institute for European Environmental Policy, London

Hajer, M (1995) *The Politics of Environmental Discourse: Ecological Modernization and the Policy Process*, Clarendon Press, Oxford

Hajer, M (1996a) 'Ecological Modernization as Cultural Politics' in Lash, S, Szerszynski, B and Wynne, B (eds) *Risk, Environment and Modernity: Towards a New Ecology*, Sage, London, pp 246–268

Hajer, M (1996b) *The Politics of Environmental Discourse: Ecological Modernization and the Policy Process*, Clarendon Press, Oxford

Her Majesty's Inspectorate of Pollution (1995) *Operator and Pollution Risk Appraisal*, HMIP, London

Her Majesty's Inspectorate of Pollution (1996) *Best Practicable Environmental Option Assessments for IPC*, HMIP, London

Her Majesty's Inspectorate of Pollution and Allied Colloids (1995) *3Es Project Interim Report*, HMIP, London

Her Majesty's Inspectorate of Pollution and Allied Colloids (1996) *3Es Project Concluding Report*, HMIP, London

Her Majesty's Inspectorate of Pollution and Business in the Environment (1996) *Profiting From Pollution Prevention: the 3Es Methodology*, HMIP, London

Hill, M (ed) (1993) *The Policy Process: A Reader*, Harvester Wheatsheaf, London

HMSO (1990a) *This Common Inheritance*, HMSO, London

HMSO (1990b) *This Common Inheritance: A Summary of the White Paper on the Environment*, HMSO, London

HMSO (1994) *Sustainable Development: the UK Strategy*, HMSO, London

HMSO (1995) *Report From the Select Committee on Sustainable Development, Session 1994–1995*, HMSO, London

Hogwood, B and Gunn, L (1984) *Policy Analysis for the Real World*, Oxford University Press, Oxford

Hood, C (1976) *The Limits of Administration*, Wiley, London

Institute of Environmental Management (1995) 'Eco-Management and Audit Scheme: Enhancing the Impact of Environmental Management', *The Journal of the Institute of Environmental Management*, Vol 3, Issue 3

Irwin, A and Hooper, P (1992) 'Clean Technology, Successful Innovation and the Greening of Industry: A Case-Study Analysis' *Business Strategy and the Environment* 1, 2, pp 1–12

Jacobs, M (1991) *The Green Economy*, Pluto Press, London

Jänicke, M (1990) *State Failure: The Impotence of Politics in Industrial Society*, Polity Press, Cambridge (English translation)

Jänicke, M (1992) 'Conditions for environmental policy success: an international comparison' in Jachtenfuchs, M and Strubel, M (eds) *Environmental Policy in Europe: Assessment, Challenges and Perspectives*, Nomosvergsgessellschaft, Baden-Baden, pp 26–39

Jänicke, M, Monch, H, Ranneburg, T and Simonis, U (1989) 'Economic Structure and Environmental Impacts: East West Comparisons' *The Environmentalist*, Vol 9, Part 3

Jänicke, M and Weidner, H (eds) (1995) *Successful Environmental Policy: A Critical Evaluation of 24 Cases*, Sigma, Berlin, pp 351–363

Jänicke, M (1997) 'The Political System's Capacity for Environmental Policy' in Jänicke, M and Weidner, H (eds) *National Environmental Policies: A Comparative Study of Capacity-Building*, Springer Verlag, Berlin

Jenkins, T (1995) *A Superficial Attraction: The Voluntary Approach and Sustainable Development*, Friends of the Earth, London

Jordan, A (1993) 'Integrated Pollution Control and the Evolving Style and Structure of Environmental Regulation in the UK', *Environmental Politics*, Vol 2, No 3, pp 405–427

Kemp, R and Soete, L (1992) 'The Greening of Technological Progress' *Futures*, June, pp 437–457

Kemp, R (1993) 'An Economic Analysis of Cleaner Technology: Theory and Evidence' in Fischer, K and Schot, J (eds) *Environmental Strategies for Industry: International Perspectives on Research Needs and Policy Implications*, Island Press, Washington, pp 79–116

Levitt, R (1980) *Implementing Public Policy*, Croom Helm, London

Lindblom, C (1959) 'The Science of "Muddling Through"' *Public Administration Review*, Vol 19, pp 79–99

Lindblom, C (1979) 'Still Muddling, Not Yet Through' *Public Administration Review*, Vol 39, pp 517–526

Lijphart, A (1975) *The Politics of Accommodation: Pluralism and Democracy in The Netherlands* (2nd edition), University of California, Berkeley

Lipsky, M (1980) *Street Level Bureaucracy: Dilemmas of the Individual in Public Services*, Russell Sage Foundation, New York

Lovelock, M (1993) 'Landfill Auditing: Beyond Compliance', *Eco-Management and Auditing*, Vol 1, Part 1, pp 32–35

Lukes, S (1974) *Power: A Radical View*, Macmillan, London

Macrory, R (1990) 'The Legal Control of Pollution' in Harrison, R (ed) *Pollution: Causes, Effects and Control*, The Royal Society of Chemistry, Cambridge, pp 277–294

Majone, G (1976) 'Choice Among Policy Instruments for Pollution Control', *Policy Analysis*, Vol 2, pp 589–613

Mann, D (ed) (1982) *Environmental Policy Implementation*, Lexington Books, Lexington

Mazmanian, D and Sabatier, P (eds) (1981) *Effective Policy Implementation*, Lexington Books, Lexington

McCormick, J (1991) *British Politics and the Environment*, Earthscan, London

Meadows, D (1972) *The Limits to Growth*, Universe Books, New York

Mol, A (1995) *The Refinement of Production: Ecological Modernization Theory and the Chemical Industry*, Van Arkel, Utrecht

Mol, A and Spaargaren, G (1993) 'Environment, Modernity and the Risk Society: The Apocalyptic Horizon of Environmental Reform' *International Sociology*, Vol, 8, No 4, pp 431–459

Muijen, van M (1995) 'Implementing EU Environmental Policy through Fine-Tuning' *European Environment*, Vol 6, Part 6, pp 160–164

National Accreditation Council for Certification Bodies (1994) *Environmental Accreditation Criteria*, NACCB, London

Nelson, R and Winter, S (1977) 'In Search of Useful Theory of Innovation' *Research Policy*, pp 36–76

OECD (1987) *The Promotion and Diffusion of Clean Technologies*, OECD, Paris

OECD (1992) *Technology and the Economy: The Key Relationship*, OECD, Paris

Ogus, A (1994) *Regulation: Legal Form and Economic Theory*, Clarendon Press, Oxford

Organization for Economic Co-operation and Development (1994) *Environmental Performance Review of the UK*, OECD, Paris

Organization for Economic Co-operation and Development (1995) *Environmental Performance Review: The Netherlands*, OECD, Paris

O'Riordan, T (1985) 'Approaches to Regulation' in Otway, H and Peltu, M (eds) *Regulating Industrial Risks: Science, Hazards and Public Protection*, Butterworths, London, pp 20–39

Owens, S (1990) 'The Unified Inspectorate and BPEO in the United Kingdom' in Haigh, N and Irwin, F (eds) *Integrated Pollution Control in Europe and North America*, Institute for European Environmental Policy, London

Palmer, K, Oates, W and Portney, P (1995) 'Tightening Environmental Standards: The Benefit-Cost or the No-Cost Paradigm?' *Journal of Economic Perspectives*, Vol 9, No 4, pp119–132

Perlman, M (1976) 'The Economic Theory of Bureaucracy' in Tullock, G (ed) *The Vote Motive*, Institute of Economic Affairs, London, pp70–79

Porter, M (1991) 'America's Green Strategy' *Scientific American*, April, 264

Porter, M and van der Linde, C (1995) 'Green and Competitive: Ending the Stalemate' *Harvard Business Review*, Vol 73, No 5, pp 120–133

Pressman, J and Wildavsky, A (1973) *Implementation*, University of California Press, Berkeley

Raad voor de Certificatie (1995) *Guidelines for Accreditation of Certification Bodies for Environmental Management Systems*, Raad voor de Certificatie, Utrecht

Rees, J (1990) *Natural Resources: Allocation, Economics and Policy*, Routledge, London

Richardson, G, Ogus, A and Burrows, P (1982) *Policing Pollution: A Study of Regulation and Enforcement*, Clarendon Press, Oxford

RIVM – Rijksinstituut Voor Volksgezondheid en Milieuhygiene (1989) *National Environmental Outlook 1: Concern for Tomorrow*, RIVM, Bilthoven

RIVM – Rijksinstituut Voor Volksgezondheid en Milieuhygiene (1991) *National Environmental Outlook 2*, RIVM, Bilthoven

RIVM – Rijksinstituut Voor Volksgezondheid en Milieuhygiene (1994) *National Environmental Outlook 3*, RIVM, Bilthoven

Rothwell, R (1992) 'Developments Towards the Fifth Generation Model of Innovation' *Technology Analysis and Strategic Management*, 1, 4, pp 73–75

Royal Commission on Environmental Pollution (1976) *Air Pollution Control: An Integrated Approach*, HMSO, London

SCCM – The Association for Co-ordination of Certification of Environmental Management Systems (1995a) *Verification system regarding the EMAS Regulation (EC no 1836/93) in The Netherlands*, SCCM, The Hague

Schot, J and Fischer, K (1993) 'The Greening of Industrial Firm' in Fischer, K and Schot, J (eds) *Environmental Strategies for Industry: International Perspectives on Research Needs and Policy Implications*, Island Press, Washington, pp 3–36

Selznick, P (1985) 'Focusing Organizational Research on Regulation' in Noll, R (ed) *Regulatory Policy and the Social Sciences*

Sharp, M and Pavitt, K (1993) 'Technology Policy in the 1990s: Old Trends and New Realities' *Journal of Common Market Studies*, 31, 2

Simmons, P and Wynne, B (1993) 'Responsible Care: Trust, Credibility and Environmental Management' in Fischer, K and Schot, J (eds) *Environmental Strategies for Industry*, Island Press, Washington, pp 201–226

Simon, H (1957) *Administrative Behaviour*, Free Press, New York (2nd edition)

Simonis, U (1989) 'Ecological Modernization of Industrial Society: Three Strategic Elements' *International Social Science Journal*, 121, pp 347–361

Smith, A (1997) *Integrated Pollution Control*, Ashgate, Aldershot

Soete, L and Arundel, A (1995) 'European Innovation Policy for Environmentally Sustainable Development: Application of a Systems Model of Technical Change' *Journal of Public Policy*, 2, 2, pp 285–385

Spaargaren, G and Mol, A (1991) *Sociology, Environment and Modernity: Ecological Modernization as a Theory of Social Change*, LUW, Wageningen

Stern, A (1994) *Managing Europe's Environmental Challenge*, The Economist Intelligence Unit, London

van der Straaten, J and Ugelow, J (1994) 'Environmental Policy in the Netherlands: Change and Effectiveness', in Wintle, M and Reeve, R (eds) *Rhetoric and Reality in Environmental Policy*, Avebury, Aldershot, pp 118–144

United Kingdom Accreditation Service (1995) *The Accreditation of Environmental Verifiers for EMAS*, UKAS, London

Verbruggen, A (1995) 'Environmental Policy Planning in Flanders' *European Environment*, Vol 5, Part 3, pp 39–44

Vogel, D (1986) *National Styles of Regulation: Environmental Policy in Great Britain and the United States*, Ithaca, Cornell University Press

VROM – Ministry of Housing, Spatial Planning and the Environment (1989) *National Environmental Policy Plan: to Choose or to Lose*, VROM, The Hague

VROM – Ministry of Housing, Spatial Planning and the Environment (1990) *National Environmental Policy Plan Plus*, VROM, The Hague

VROM – Ministry of Housing, Spatial Planning and the Environment (1993) *Declaration of Intent on the Implementation of Environmental Policy for the Chemical Industry*, The Hague, 2 April

VROM – Ministry of Housing, Spatial Planning and the Environment (1994a) *Environmental Policy of the Netherlands*, VROM, The Hague

VROM – Ministry of Housing, Spatial Planning and the Environment (1994b) *National Environmental Policy Plan 2: The Environment: Today's Touchstone*, VROM, The Hague

VROM – Ministry of Housing, Spatial Planning and the Environment (1994c) *National Environmental Policy Plan 2 (Summary): The Environment: Today's Touchstone*, VROM, The Hague

VROM – Ministry of Housing, Spatial Planning and the Environment (1994d) *Towards a Sustainable Netherlands*, VROM, The Hague

VROM – Ministry of Housing, Spatial Planning and the Environment (1994e) *Environmental Policy in Action No 1: Working With Industry*, VROM, The Hague

VROM – Ministry of Housing, Spatial Planning and the Environment (1994f) *Drinking Water in the Netherlands*, VROM, The Hague

VROM – Ministry of Housing, Spatial Planning and the Environment (1995) *Sixth Progress Report on Environmental Law Enforcement (Summary)*, VROM, The Hague

Wallace, D (1995) *Environmental Policy and Industrial Innovation: Strategies in Europe, the US and Japan*, Earthscan, London

Walley, N and Whitehead, B (1994) 'It's Not Easy Being Green' *Harvard Business Review*, Vol 73, No 5

Weale, A (1992) *The New Politics of Pollution*, Manchester University Press, Manchester

Webber, G (1994) 'Environmental Management Systems: Benefit or Burden?', *Eco-Management and Auditing*, Vol 1, Part 3, pp 2–6

Welford, R and Gouldson, A (1993) *Environmental Management and Business Strategy*, Pitman, London

Wintle, M and Reeve, R (eds) (1994) *Rhetoric and Reality in Environmental Policy*, Aldershot, Avebury

Young, S (1993) *The Politics of the Environment*, Baseline Books, Manchester

INDEX

Page numbers in **bold** refer to figures, tables and boxes

OTHER RELEVANT PUBLICATIONS FROM EARTHSCAN

Factor Four

Doubling Wealth, Halving Resource Use
Ernst von Weizsäcker, Wuppertal Institute for Climate, Energy and Environment, Amory B Lovins and L Hunter Lovins, Rocky Mountain Institute, Colorado

'One of the 1990s, most important books, *Factor Four* opens up a new way of thinking about efficiency that will be crucial to our long term survival, Geoff Mulgan, Head of Social Policy, Prime Minister's Office

'*Factor Four* made my spine tingle. This is a book which captures the moment, which crystallizes a set of seemingly conflicting trends and issues around a simple idea – that by organising our economies around the principle of "resource productivity" as opposed to labour productivity, we can, in Lovins' words, "live twice as well – yet use half as much"' *Tomorrow*

'choc-a-bloc with practical examples of technologies that can use the world's resources more efficiently, Frances Cairncross, *The Economist*

'a persuasive case for governments to accelerate the pace of change... By focusing on solutions rather than problems, this book at least illustrates that the environment need not make either boring or depressing reading' *The Financial Times*

'the message of a radical, profitable and sustainable change comes through loud and clear' Robert Day, *Nature*

'by any criteria a key "text for the millenium" ... for anyone involved in business and the environment' *Greener Management International*

Factor Four describes a new form of progress, resource productivity, one which meets the overriding imperative for the future: sustainability. It shows how at least four times as much wealth can be extracted from the resources we use. As the authors put it, the book is about 'doing more with less', but this 'is not the same as doing worse or doing without'.

Paperback £9.99 1 85383 406 8 1998 352 pages

Clean and Competitive?

Motivating Environmental Performance in Industry
Rupert Howes, Forum for the Future, Jim Skea, ESRC-GEC Programme, and Bob Whelan, former CEO, CEST

'This fascinating and illuminating book is replete with sophisticated analysis of the business–environment interface. It is objective and pragmatic, but never takes its eye off the fundamental challenge to business and society posed by the imperative of sustainable development. A state-of-the-art account of this complex area' Paul Ekins, Director, Forum for the Future

Explores the challenge of motivating industry to address environmental issues. The authors explore in detail industrial responses to prominent environmental issues, including: climate change; air quality; water pollution; waste minimization; and product recycling. They assess various approaches to environmental problems, such as: traditional regulation; partnership; voluntary agreements; and market-based instruments. Finally, they recommend practical ways forward for addressing an ever more complex environmental agenda.

Paperback £14.95 1 85383 490 4 1998 208 pages

Policies for Cleaner Technology

A New Agenda for Government and Industry
Tony Clayton, University of West Indies, Graham Spinardi and Robin Williams, University of Edinburgh

A ground-breaking and authoritative study on how to clean up the industrial system as the next stage of industrial development. Consumer pressure, taxes, regulations and international commitments are combining to make waste-free and resource-efficient production imperative.

Using extensive empirical analysis of many of the largest industrial sectors, the authors show how clean technology can be implemented, primarily by the businesses themselves. They analyse corporate behaviour in each area, as well as the regulatory environment and the technical requirements, to show how the entire production cycle can be re-engineered to introduce the new technologies, systems and policies.

The result is a study which will be essential reading for industrial management, policy makers, financial stakeholders and business students.

Paperback £16.95 1 85383 519 6 October 1998 256 pages

Bugs in the System

Reinventing the Pesticide Industry for Sustainable Agriculture
edited by Bill Vorley, Institute for Agriculture and Trade Policy, Minneapolis, and Dennis Keeney, Iowa State University

'a superb, level-headed account of how designing a healthy agricultural system addresses the dysfunctionality of all industrial systems ... makes an impressive contribution to ecological literacy' Paul Hawken, author of *Growing a Business* and *The Ecology of Commerce*

'An indispensable book for those who want to appreciate the challenge that the move to sustainable development provokes in terms of change to human systems, agricultural and otherwise' Nigel Roome, Chair of Environmental Management, Tilburg University

'a brave attempt to map a way forward for the pesticide industry – and for the agricultural industry which has come to depend on it. This volume laces environmentalism with economics and a firm understanding of the challenges facing pesticide companies, making it an important contribution to the debate on business and sustainable development' Frances Cairncross, *The Economist*

'takes us through the complexities of our modern industrial society....and offers us analysis, approaches and vision for moving from greening towards an understanding of sustainability' Kurt Fischer, The Greening of Industry Network, Clark University

Paperback £14.95 1 85383 429 7 1998 256 pages
Not for sale in the USA or Canada

ISO 14001

A Missed Opportunity for Sustainable Global Industrial Development
Riva Krut, Benchmark Environmental Consulting, USA, and Harris Gleckman, UNCTAD

ISO 14001 is the new industrial standard for environmental management systems, recently introduced and being widely adopted by businesses worldwide. The authors present here a fundamental critique of it, showing how much it might have achieved and how little it is likely to deliver, and explaining how the process of establishing it restricted its effectiveness. They argue that ISO 14001 does little or nothing to measure or improve environmental performance, and that its effect may even be to undermine the limited progress to date in agreeing international standards of environmental impacts and performance.

Paperback £14.95 1 85383 507 2 June 1998 192 pages

Trade and Environment

Conflict or Compatibility?
edited by Duncan Brack, Royal Institute of International Affairs

Can trade liberalization and environmental protection be pursued together, or do the two objectives inevitably conflict? The question goes to the heart of the policies to be pursued by governments and international organizations, and a consensus on it does not exist.

This volume includes prominent contributors from many of the most important bodies involved: the World Trade Organization, UNCTAD, the OECD, UNEP as well as representatives from industry, the voluntary sector, and research. They examine the impacts of trade-related environmental measures, competitiveness and investment under different regulatory regimes, industry and developing country concerns and procedures for dispute settlement.

Contributors: Sir Leon Brittan, Frits Schlingemann, James Lee, Jonathan Barton, William Seddon-Brown, Reinhard Quick, Magda Shahin, Sabrina Shaw, Michael Reiterer, Hussein Abaza, James Cameron, Robert E Brunck

Paperback £16.95 1 85383 577 3 August 1998 224 pages
Not for sale in the USA or Canada

Sustainability Strategies for Industry

The Future of Corporate Practice
edited by Nigel J Roome, Tilburg University

Sustainability Strategies for Industry provides a multidisciplinary examination of the meaning of sustainability and its practical implications for industry. It defines sustainability in an industrial context, and addresses how the shift to sustainability will affect the role of industry in society and its relationships with consumerism, employees, and the community at large. Contributors examine new industrial approaches and consider the key elements needed to achieve sustainable practice. It will be essential reading for those interested in the future of industrial organisations and in the relationship between sustainability and environmental management and protection.

Paperback £24.95 1 55963 599 1 September 1998 352 pages
Not for sale in the USA or Canada

The Earthscan Reader in Business and the Environment

edited by Richard Welford and Richard Starkey, University of Huddersfield

'The combination of a publisher like Earthscan which has been producing some of the more innovative work in the business—environmental area and an editor like Welford who has been involved in producing some of the more advanced texts on environmental management promises – and delivers. Any collection which contains pieces from Paul Hawken, James Robertson, Michael Jacobs, and Michael Porter is bound to be lively, and this is well balanced, stimulating and very well edited. I recommend it very highly' *Social & Environmental Accounting*

'A fine assessment of a vital subject' *New Scientist*

Brings together in one volume, the most important and innovative articles written on the interaction of business and the environment, with contributions by many of the world's leading practitioners.

Paperback £19.95 1 85383 301 0 1996 288 pages
Not for sale in the USA or Canada

Building to Last

The Challenge for Business Leaders
Colin Hutchinson

'a practical guide for senior managers in both large businesses and SMEs' *Community Affairs Briefing*

'This book will be a valuable textbook, but it will be even more useful to businesses, to consultants advising businesses, to environmentalists working with businesses and, finally, to governments and their concerned, but often ill-informed, citizens. I commend it to the wide audience it deserves' John Speirs, Managing Director, Norsk Hydro, UK

Paperback £15.95 1 85383 478 5 1997

Earthscan Publications Ltd
www.earthscan.co.uk